Sherl
Digita

MW00619556

Sherlock a
Digital Fan

The Meeting of Cre
Community and Advocacy

Jennifer Wojton *and*
Lynnette Porter

McFarland & Company, Inc., Publishers
Jefferson, North Carolina

ISBN (print) 978-1-4766-7020-1
ISBN (ebook) 978-1-4766-3286-5

LIBRARY OF CONGRESS CATALOGUING DATA ARE AVAILABLE

BRITISH LIBRARY CATALOGUING DATA ARE AVAILABLE

Front cover image of Benedict Cumberbatch (as Sherlock Holmes),
and Martin Freeman (as Dr. John Watson) (BBC/Photofest)

Printed in the United States of America

*McFarland & Company, Inc., Publishers
Box 611, Jefferson, North Carolina 28640
www.mcfarlandpub.com*

Sherlock and Digital Fandom

The Meeting of Creativity, Community and Advocacy

JENNIFER WOJTON *and*
LYNNETTE PORTER

McFarland & Company, Inc., Publishers
Jefferson, North Carolina

ISBN (print) 978-1-4766-7020-1
ISBN (ebook) 978-1-4766-3286-5

LIBRARY OF CONGRESS CATALOGUING DATA ARE AVAILABLE

BRITISH LIBRARY CATALOGUING DATA ARE AVAILABLE

Front cover image of Benedict Cumberbatch (as Sherlock Holmes),
and Martin Freeman (as Dr. John Watson) (BBC/Photofest)

Printed in the United States of America

McFarland & Company, Inc., Publishers
Box 611, Jefferson, North Carolina 28640
www.mcfarlandpub.com

Acknowledgments

We thank Benedict Cumberbatch for his brilliant portrayal of Sherlock. Without him, this book would not exist. He also made our research a lot more entertaining and easier on the eyes.

We especially acknowledge the many fan sites and fans whose fiction, art, blogs, and digital discussions provided examples for this book and provoked our own discussions and commentaries about what it means to be a fan. We hope it is evident throughout the book that we enjoy studying and interacting with this fandom and thank the many kind, knowledgeable fans, cast, and crew met at special *Sherlock* events.

Table of Contents

Introduction

"Someone who is FIAWOL (Fandom Is a Way of Life) invests
the majority of [her or his] time and energy on fandom and
fannish pursuits, often making long-term commitments (e.g.,
running a convention, being a Usenet/mailing list/commu-
nity/forum moderator for years, etc.), and forming their
strongest social bonds through fandom."

—Fanlore.org

Terms like *aca-fan, fan-scholar,* and *scholar-fan* are ubiquitous in fan
studies. They are often used to help define the subject position of academics and fans. For the purposes of this book, as authors, we feel com-
pelled to disclose how we identify and what we perceive these identifications
contribute to our individual authorship, our partnership, and our methodology because of the tensions inherent in these different groups acting
and interacting, especially in digital spaces. These tensions range from
fans feeling animosity toward academic researchers invading their spaces
and using them and their creative or critical works as objects of study to
academics whose investments in popular culture may lead to criticism
from more traditional academics, most often aimed at discrediting the
focus on popular culture artifacts.

Aca-fans is an older term popularized by both Henry Jenkins and
Matt Hills; we prefer to use the newer *scholar-fans* to refer to academics
who participate and have a vested interest in a fandom but whose primary
motivation for their investment into fandom comes from scholarly purposes, goals, and interests. *Scholar-fan* was coined by Jenkins and now is
more commonly used. In addition, differentiating between "fan" as an
identity and "fan" as a practice, according to Paul Booth, is important if
academic scholars want to "see what is particularly 'fannish' about a range
of practices" (3). Fan, as an identity category, as Hills explains in several

1

works, is linked to fan "affect," to the indelible feelings of attachment that fans have to the object(s) of their affection, whereas fandom, according to Booth, relies on the practices "around which fans can structure particular meanings in their lives" (3). Kristina Busse categorizes these definitions as "fannish identity and fannish behaviour" (388). In this book we focus on fannish behavior and comment on fan identity only to differentiate it from common practices of digital culture at large or to note how fannish identity may influence praxis in digital spaces.

The acronyms *FIAWOL* (Fandom Is A Way Of Life) and *FIJAGH* (Fandom Is Just a Goddamn Hobby) are indicative of fan identities more than fan practices. They often indicate the level of investment one has in fandom and are a generally snarky way to separate identity groups that are unlikely to be able to find common ground. Fanlore.org provides a humorous but enlightening example: "We tried living together, but I'm FIAWOL, and she's FIJAGH—it just didn't work out." However, some partnerships, such as this book's authors', works well because of this balancing difference, as the following "biographies" illustrate.

Jen Wojton, FIJAGH: *Fan-scholars,* as coined by Hills, generally refers to fans who use their expertise to critically examine and contribute to an understanding of popular culture texts within the fandoms to which they subscribe. Whereas some fan-scholars (e.g., Hills, Porter), indicate that they are invested in a fan identity, others (e.g., Wojton) make clear that, although they may mimic fan behavior in their research, fandom is not their way of life. As opposed to the self-identified fan-scholars who acknowledge that fandom is a way of life for them or the scholars who make note of the extent to which they are removed from fandom and, consequently, fan practices in their methods, I represent a new category of academics who are fascinated by fandom but do not consider themselves fans of anything. Because of my position as a student of fandom and an academic scholar, my methodology and perspective are different than that of scholars who are personally involved with one or more fandoms.

Prior to investing my time and energy into researching online fan culture, as represented by the fan communities organized around the BBC's television series *Sherlock* (2010–present), a modernized adaptation of Arthur Conan Doyle's stories created by showrunners and frequent scriptwriters Steven Moffat and Mark Gatiss, I would have, without compunction, claimed to be a fan of Sherlock Holmes. I have read novels and short stories by Conan Doyle, and I am always interested in the many adaptations of his characters. I have realized, however, that it is unlikely that those invested in fan culture would consider me much of a fan. I am interested in *Sherlock*-related primary texts, but I have never interacted with or contributed to any fandom (digital or face to face) in any significant way, and I don't purchase any memorabilia. I relay this information guiltily because, during my research, I have gained so much insight by examining the myriad ways in which fans constitute and contribute to a robust, insightful, and thriving community online. When I began research for this book, I wondered if I would become more heavily invested in fandom on a personal rather than only on an academic level: someone for whom fandom is a way of life, or if I would remain someone for whom fandom is just a goddamned hobby. Because I identify as FIJAGH, what bearing would my lack of fannish experience have on my research? Could I possibly evolve into someone for whom FIAWOL? Would I want to? Essentially, how might my subject position affect my research?

As an academic, I can easily recognize my fannish tendencies and practices, although they have been cultivated by academia rather than by media and/or fan communities. Both academia and media fandoms continue to shape and be shaped by the digital spaces that they inhabit. My interest remains rooted in fan culture as it is mobilized in digital culture. I am a fan of scholars and scholarship about digital culture and fandom rather than a member of any particular media fandom. I have contributed to and consumed academic blogs, attended conferences, and geeked out upon meeting or interacting with authors whom I admire online. I distinctly remember that, during a graduate class, one author we had read and posted about on our class-generated public blog actually responded to some of our posts. We were giddy. I felt particularly proud to have received a long, thoughtful response to my post from the author of the work we were studying, as well as a profound pressure and responsibility to respond in kind, although I also felt "out of my league" as a student. As an English major in the 1990s, I did not have that kind of access to authors because digital technology and culture had not evolved enough to make such easy access possible and investment in conversation between students and professional authors was not perceived as equally valuable anywhere outside the classroom. Currently, my life's work and my identity as a teacher, scholar, and student are vested in those practices that help me to engage with other thinkers/creators and to interact with their works. That is not so different from the practices of media fans, and because digital technology affords participants unique ways of interacting with both texts and those who produce those texts, there is much common ground.

Lynnette Porter, FIAWOL: Although I have been an academic for decades, my fannish interests go back much further. My first television crush was Speedy Alka-Seltzer, the singing, dancing commercial icon. Somehow, my paternal grandmother got me an autographed glossy black-and-white photograph from Speedy. I was an incredibly thrilled two-year-old. Early on, I was a fickle fan. By the time I was three, I preferred *The Quick Draw McGraw Show*, starring Quick Draw McGraw and Baba Looey, who visited a local shopping center to promote the show. Of course, I had to meet him. Those formative experiences set the tone for much of my life. Merging fandom with academic writing began, for me, in the late 1970s, long before popular culture or media studies became possible majors. Yet, by the time I was an undergraduate minoring in radio/television/film, I learned that not only journalists or critics wrote about filmic texts. I began to write about *Star Trek* films and *Starsky and Hutch*. Once I became an assistant professor on the road to tenure, I could more easily do more than just write about what I viewed on screen. More disposable income meant traveling to fan conventions was possible, and greater access to computers allowed me to share information with other fans in the U.S. In the past twenty years, I have become increasingly invested in traveling to fan events and using the information gathered there to inform my academic writing about actors, directors, films, television series, and fandoms. I also just have a good time. As mostly a fan who later wrote about my experiences, I have attended conventions for *Quantum Leap, Star Trek, Lord of the Rings (LOTR), Doctor Who, Torchwood,* and *Sherlock*. I have interviewed actors, directors, and crew members as part of my research for books or articles. I have spoken as an academic expert at Dragon Con and Creation Entertainment's *LOTR* conventions and, as a member of the Tolkien Society, at a London fan event. As an author, I have participated in book signings at many fan conventions. As a result of my travels and shared love of a fandom, my friends are an international group, and we catch up through participation in digital communities. In the past decade, my passive research in physical archives has been enriched by my daily online research into fandom and my fannish pursuit of information about my current television or cinematic interests.

However, my identity as a scholar-fan can make me uncomfortable because of tensions between fandom and academia. When I attend an event as both a fan and an academic, I find myself code switching between interacting with other fans as a fan and using fan jargon or acting as an author/academic who is perceived as an outsider; that switch is automatic, depending upon with whom I am speaking. However, I also consciously "code switch" my appearance at events. When I participate only as a fan, I may wear a fandom t-shirt to identify myself as part of the group. When I sign books or participate in a panel, I wear business casual to reflect my affiliation with academia and, consequently, am treated differently than I am as a fan. Similarly, when I taught a *Sherlock*-themed humanities course, I wore a different *Sherlock* t-shirt each class day, much to my students' amusement or enjoyment. It seemed important that I establish an identity in the classroom not only as a teacher/author but as a fan of what I was teaching. However, because I did not change clothes before teaching other courses, I often was subjected to a raised eyebrow or sarcastic remark by faculty outside my department who did not think my *Sherlock* shirt appropriate attire for a professor. My role as a scholar-fan incorporates my identities as an academic and a fan, but this lifestyle engenders tensions between my colleagues and me—whether they are academics or fans.

Whereas the partnership between the authors of this book (FIAWOL and FIJAGH) has been built on respect and appreciation for our different subject positions and has resulted in insights that could only be produced by working together, these biographies explain part of the dilemma in studying or being part of a fandom, as well. Tensions exist between academics and fans, but different subgroups within a fandom also feel tensions between them or between them and the depictions of fans in mainstream media. Digital communities of *Sherlock* fans often express their displeasure with mainstream media depictions of them or public perceptions of fans or fandom that do not correlate with their fan identities. Contrary to what the mainstream press most often reports, a fandom is not homogenous or necessarily comprised of young, apparently sex-crazed women living vicariously through the exploits of beloved characters or the actors who portray them. As one example of such a media portrayal of fandom, a 2014 *New York Magazine* interview with *Sherlock* star Benedict Cumberbatch showed staged photographs of young female fans with their faces pressed against the window of the actor's car, as if they are pushing against the glass in order to be closer to the object of their affection (Yuan). However, the *Sherlock* fandom, which is the focus of this book, consists of a wide range of fans, who, despite their different demographics and purposes, share one feature: They can often be recognized by their commitment to the ethos of fandom as detective work in a more self-reflective, self-referential way than other fandoms. As discussed later, *Sherlock* fans are recognized—and sometimes derided—for their desire and ability to analyze clues and share their findings with others.

Sherlock fans feel an affinity for Sherlock in his role as a consulting detective. However, this fandom is debunking the notion that Sherlock Holmes is the world's only consulting detective. Detective-fans may not consult with clients, but they do consult with each other to share insights and decipher clues found in episodes and interviews with cast and crew. They celebrate minutiae within an episode and pull the thread of dialogue, costume, or set design to unravel a larger mystery across episodes or seasons. They delight in imagining what takes place outside the camera's focus and fill gaps between what Moffat insists is the important stuff—the plot points and character development happening on camera. At Sherlocked USA, Moffat explained that the filmed scenes shine a spotlight on the most important aspects of the story. Everything else is unimportant background. For fans who want to know information such as how Molly Hooper (Louise Brealey) and Sherlock salvage their friendship after a cruelly manipulative phone conversation ("The Final Problem"), this missing scene needs to be added in order for fans to have closure not only about this episode but about the ongoing relationship between these important characters. Fans filled the gap not only through creative outlets like fan fiction but also detective work such as tracking down and sharing tweets in which Brealey addresses Molly's feelings in the aftermath of the conversation. As well, comments Moffat made at Sherlocked USA were quoted in fans' convention reports shared among Tumblr sites; the showrunner's perception of scenes, often quite different from fans', provides more clues into how and why episodes were structured a certain way and what and how much information was designed to be given to viewers. Although other fandoms also revel in learning insider information, *Sherlock* fans are particularly adept at ferreting out information to support or debunk theories and to return to earlier episodes or interviews as they piece together the series' complete "truth."

Yet another way in which at least a segment of the *Sherlock* fandom is unique beyond their interest in deduction and high degree of digital interaction is the way they interpret Sherlock's sexual orientation. Although most television fandoms ship (i.e., promote the sexual relationship of) same-sex characters, whether they are depicted as homosexual on screen, *Sherlock* fans go beyond the expected Johnlock (John Watson/ Sherlock Holmes) interest or fan fiction. Some analysis in later chapters is specific to the depiction of characters who may be interpreted in different ways, depending upon a fan's ideal image of characters or the series. For example, when audiences encounter Sherlock Holmes, as portrayed in *Sherlock*, it seems impossible not to notice his lack of a romantic partner because of the extent to which coupling is the default expectation in U.S. culture, as well as other cultures in the more than 180 countries in which *Sherlock* is broadcast. In addition, a "love interest" story line is certainly prime fodder for television series to explore. As a result, some fans interpret Sherlock as having an off-camera sexual relationship with John or another character, such as Irene Adler. However, other fans read Sherlock's lack of overt interest in a sexual partner as his asexuality. Certainly the ambiguity and innuendo that many viewers enjoy in episodes can lead to a variety of interpretations. For providing the opportunity for a non-heteronormative character to figure as the male lead in a series, the creators and scriptwriters of *Sherlock* deserve praise, although, to be fair, Sherlock's lack of interest in sex and romance does align with the canonical version of Sherlock Holmes. However, in *Sherlock*, the title character's sexuality and relationship status often come under scrutiny from characters in the series as well as the show's fans. Because of this emphasis on Sherlock's sexual orientation and sexuality in four seasons' episodes and a special, an important aspect of *Sherlock* fandom is its reading of the title character, which may not coincide with co-creators Moffat's and Gatiss' or actors' interpretations. Therefore, Sherlock's sexuality and fan responses to it, whether through fan fiction or asexual advocacy, is necessary to understanding a large segment of the *Sherlock* fandom.

Popular culture artifacts, like television shows, are certainly ephemeral, but they are also pervasive and can have a lasting impact on the general public's perception of characters, in canon and adaptation, and the social themes incorporated within episodes. Especially when a television show breaks from the norm and includes characters who challenge typical heteronormative views/values, there is an opportunity for the show to become more than mere entertainment. In addition, because of the prevalence of digital texts—including news articles, interviews, video or audio clips, promotional photos, and stories—being archived, the characters, plots, and information about a television series long outlive the actual number of years it is broadcast. Television series that have an impact on popular culture, like *Sherlock*, transcend their initial broadcast dates and become cultural touchstones that have meaning for fans and academics alike.

Although analyzing or even reporting digital artifacts created by *Sherlock* fandom is one method of studying it, theory developed within the scholarly area of fan studies underpins our approach. In this book we analyze four distinct but interconnected types and sites of interface among fans, advocates, mainstream media, showrunners, and celebrities: mainstream media articles related to *Sherlock* and those officially associated with it; social media; single-owner or small group-operated fan websites; and fan fiction and associated comments. This interdisciplinary project draws on the work of fandom/digital culture scholarship (e.g., Henry Jenkins, Matthew Hills, Paul Booth) within a broader framework informed by scholars of digital culture and queer and feminist ideologies (e.g., Donna Haraway, Lee Edelman, Lauren Berlant), as well as emerging scholarship on asexuality, which is informed by queer and feminist perspectives (e.g., Erica Chu, Julia Decker, Jacinthe Flore).

This show and its corresponding digital artifacts, which are often created through interaction/negotiation between showrunners and fans, can inspire the public in general or a fandom specifically to think more critically about representations of sexuality, gender, friendship, and family (both birth and extended) relationships. Fan artifacts, as well as the series itself, also inspire prolific web-based and in-person responses from fans that range from immediate emotional messages to deeply personal self-reflections and critical dialogues from fans and non-fans to creative or advocacy works, all which are studied in the following chapters and illustrate why *Sherlock* fandom is both unique and representative of fandoms in general. These texts, involving several print and visual technologies, are particularly useful and timely for studying digital communities and digital culture and constructing an understanding of the ways in which fans represent, consume, transform, challenge or champion, and disseminate ideas related to both their fandom and to what it means to be a fan in the digital age.

1

Fans and The Powers That Be
Interaction and Common Awareness

Fan culture and mainstream entertainment media can shape and be shaped by each other through digital interactions and negotiations. These interactions have the potential to foster community building and advocacy efforts within digital spaces and beyond them, as well as create tension and lead to unproductive competition. The traditional boundaries between fans and entertainment professionals—sometimes referred to in fandom as "The Powers That Be" (TPTB)—have been breached as each group works to engage the other while pursuing their separate objectives (e.g., social change, personal and professional acceptance and/or acclaim, commercial profit).

The fact that fandom has gone digital is not disputed among fan-scholars, scholar-fans, or even the casual television-viewing public, but the extent to which *Sherlock* fans interact with the series' creators, media critics, journalists, and each other often receives more publicity because of the show's international popularity and because *Sherlock* fans are detectives in their own right. This fandom is robust and active; they have become a cultural force.

One Example: Digital Interaction Surrounding "The Final Problem"

The ways in which fans respond online to *Sherlock* vary greatly. However, the number and variety of digital responses—within moments or hours of the broadcast of a new episode—illustrate the richness of this fandom's participation and the need many fans feel to connect/share experiences with other fans and potentially the series' cast and creators.

When new episodes are about to be broadcast, the number of official (i.e., BBC), mainstream media, and fan communications increases exponentially. As only one example, in January 2017, mainstream media produced dozens of promotional interviews and articles before the Season Four premiere episode was broadcast by the BBC. In addition to mainstream media's publicity for "The Six Thatchers," fans interacted with online publications and each other in several ways. They participated in online polls hosted by newspapers. During the British broadcast hours before viewers outside the U.K. could watch the episode, many fans produced a constant stream of real-time "spoiler" tweets. Bloggers posted unofficial reviews on Tumblr and fan sites in other domains, and especially those fans unhappy with the episode's character developments (e.g., the birth of Rosamund [Rosie] Watson, the death of Mary Watson) wrote "fix it" fan fiction. Such responses by a digital fan community might be expected and are common within *Sherlock* fandom.

For several reasons, the digital fandom and mainstream media became even more active as the final episode of the season neared its broadcast date. Many viewers anticipated that the Season Four finale might be the series' finale, as a result of the lead actors' global film and television stardom and busy schedules that make scheduling time for *Sherlock* almost impossible. Thus, the show generated additional mainstream media news articles in anticipation of this important episode. When the episode was leaked online, reportedly by Russian hackers, mainstream media and fan communication went into overdrive.

Producer Sue Vertue immediately tweeted the problem to fans and implored them not to seek out or view the hacked episode: "Russian version of Sherlock TFP ["The Final Problem"] has been illegally uploaded. Please don't share it. You've done so well keeping it spoiler free. Nearly there" (Molloy). Instead of Vertue going to newspapers or entertainment media to alert fans about the hacking, she wrote directly to her fan followers on Twitter, knowing that the word would soon spread.

Next, fans and the series' official voices published persuasive reasons why the most dedicated viewers should or should not see the episode a day early. For at least some fans, Vertue's praise of fans not posting or sharing spoilers likely was yet another reason to stay away from the Russian file or social media spoilers, though the counter-cultural ethos still runs deep in well-developed fandoms, so just as many were likely drawn to the spoilers *because* of Vertue's praise. Nonetheless, many fans wanted to see how the season ends before the majority of viewers awaiting the episode on BBC or, in the U.S., PBS could view it; some used Google

Translator to help them understand the Russian-language dialogue. Although quite a few fans found (and shared information about) the hacker site before it became international news, mainstream media found out about the illegal link when Vertue tweeted fans. Articles touting headlines like "Sherlock Series Finale Leaked Online" (*The Telegraph*) and "BBC's Sherlock Asks Fans Not to Spoil the Series Finale for Everyone After It Leaks Online: Talk about a 'Final Problem'" (Hegarty; *Digital Spy*) made fans around the world aware that the episode was available if they could find it and wanted to be spoiled. The thousands of times an article was shared (the statistics posted next to the social media icons by which readers could share the article) indicate how far the message spread.

The question arises whether so many fans would have tried to locate—or succeeded in finding—the hacked episode if the BBC official *Sherlock* account (@Sherlock221B) and Vertue had not made the information public. The *Sherlock* account asked fans to ignore the file "illegally uploaded online" "if you come across it," implying that they did not want fans to seek out the episode and hoped they would avoid online discussion of it or its content. The #KeepMeSpoilerFree hashtag at the end of the official message seemed designed to create a strong community within *Sherlock*'s large digital fandom who wanted to wait to see the episode on television. Both Vertue's and *Sherlock*'s tweets ignored the fact that many detective-fans would not resist the challenge to find the episode once they knew it existed and to decode the dialogue to understand what was happening. Fans' Tumblr sites quickly became repositories for spoilers and comments about what would become a controversial episode that fans interpreted in myriad ways, depending how they had read "clues" about John Watson, Molly Hooper, and Sherlock in particular.

Suspicious fans even questioned whether the leak was legitimate or just a marketing ploy to create more interest in the episode or to provide an excuse if ratings were lower for this episode because too many people watched it early. *Sherlock* received additional press (and the conspiracy theory was disproven) when Russia's Channel One published an apology "for any inconvenience this leak has caused" and noted that it had been cooperating with BBC Worldwide "from the moment we were alerted to the appearance of the leaked episode" (Dowell). Channel One's initial investigations suggested that an outside party had breached the system.

Although the overnight television ratings for "The Final Problem" were indeed lower than expected (with only 5.9 million U.K. viewers), the composite ratings including downloads on BBC iPlayer increased the viewership to 9.1 million (Lodderhose)—further indication of *Sherlock*'s digital fandom, who might prefer seeing the episode first or again online rather than during a scheduled television broadcast. The ratings also reflect the power of the digital media fandom, who decide when and how they want to view a television episode. How much the online leak really affected the ratings is unknown, but fans who did not like the episode and watched it online or in the U.K. and posted comments or spoilers may have affected other "spoiled" fans' decision whether or when to watch "The Final Problem" on television, outside the U.K. in particular.

To spoil or not to spoil other fans is a choice that viewers able to see an episode earlier must make especially when television has become a collective viewing experience via Twitter. During the BBC's broadcast, fans interacting with others on Twitter fell into two camps: those eager to share their comments and thus posting spoilers as they watched the episode, although they know that Twitter can be seen around the world and spoil fans not yet watching the episode, and those who posted messages proclaiming they would stay offline because they did not want to be accidentally spoiled and/or complaining about those who were tweeting spoilers. The running commentary provided by tweets in real time made following the episode's basic plot relatively easy. (Lynnette Porter, following the Twitter feed five hours before watching the episode on PBS, easily figured out the plot.) The plot details and emotional responses mirrored the episode's ups and downs (and, according to many, holes in logic) to the extent that watching the episode might have been superfluous for those unwilling to spend an hour and a half to see firsthand what had been described on Twitter. After observing the very active #Sherlock tag during the broadcast, Jane Atkinson (@northernbetty) tweeted "Amazing that so many languages are tweeting about #Sherlock at the same time. Truly a global water cooler moment." Although discussion about the episode was vibrant during the broadcast, the problem of instantaneous digital discourse—spoiling viewers who could not see the episode during the tweetstorm and creating a "haves/have nots" dichotomy by viewing region—became an equally important tweetable topic.

Within ten minutes of the conclusion of the U.K. broadcast, the *Telegraph* and *Digital Spy* posted their reviews—which could be another source of spoilers for fans around the world awaiting the episode's television debut in their country. Half an hour after "The Final Problem" ended, *Metro* ran its weekly audience-response poll. This highly unscientific poll is interesting in that the series' fans could easily skew the results if they wished to do so, especially in light of professional critics' mixed reviews that were popping up online around the same time. All fans had to do was vote as many times as they pleased. Without having access to the IP addresses of those who voted, for example, or another way to identify respondents who voted, there is no way of knowing how many fans voted multiple times and skewed the results, but being able to vote several times likely was a temptation at least some fans could not resist. (Porter participated in the poll five times from the same IP address to test the assumption that multiple votes would be possible, although she did choose the most positive response each time—something a *Sherlock* fan is likely to do.)

Yet another way that the digital community responded to "The Final Problem" was through fan fiction, with a number of stories "fixing" problems authors felt needed to be addressed. As discussed in detail within the fan fiction chapter, these stories appeared about the same time as the majority of reviews—within a few hours of the U.K. broadcast. As soon as authors could physically write and post a story, they did so.

In the days following "The Final Problem," *Sherlock* fandom split into several factions, depending upon the way they had understood the characters' development during the previous seasons leading to the Season Four finale. Whereas some fans read the ending as hopeful for future Johnlock (i.e., an intimate relationship between John and Sherlock) or asexual Sherlock living with heterosexual John while sharing baby-rearing duties, others felt betrayed by Mary's voiceover that "who you are doesn't matter" and what they perceive as the queerbaiting that denies Sherlock and John a happy ending. Others sought hope in Molly and Sherlock admitting their love for each other, albeit under horrific circumstances. However, likely a greater number disliked Molly's scene and the possibly final way in which the series depicts her. Just as critical fans tweeted Vertue and Mark Gatiss to complain about the finale, so did many Molly fans contact Brealey, who, with the assistance of supportive fans, defended her character and defied personal attacks on her performance. Those not looking specifically from a relationship perspective berated the series' depictions of mental illness, queer characters Eurus Holmes and Jim Moriarty as the series' villains, and disturbing use of canon, notably the transformation of the warmest expression of friendship between canon Holmes and Watson in "The Three Garridebs" into a cruel execution. Twitter and Tumblr became the primary platforms for virulently protesting the "groundbreaking" series' most recent, and possibly final, episode. Gatiss and Vertue received hundreds of angry tweets to the point where Gatiss began blocking people. More than 5,000 fans, though not the 7,500 needed to send a petition to Hartswood Films, the BBC, Steven Moffat, and Gatiss, supported it on

Change.org ("Make Hartswood Films, BBC, Gatiss, and Moffat Answer for the Queerbaiting of Sherlock"). The petition begins by thanking the people working behind the camera to create *Sherlock*—series' co-creators Moffat and Gatiss, producers at Hartswood Films, and episode writers (who frequently are Moffat and/or Gatiss)—for four seasons (seven years) of "beautiful cinematography, glorious and witty dialogue, and gorgeous characterizations of Sherlock Holmes and Dr. Watson" ("Make Hartswood Films"). In particular, the writers of the petition quickly draw attention to the series' history of references to "queer literature and history, queer coding, and subtext" that Sherlock and John might someday be more than just great friends, especially if or when their sexual relationship is more overtly depicted on screen. Despite these references, the petition explains, the potential queer relationship between Sherlock and John never was realized in television canon within four seasons of episodes. The problem, the petition states, is that "thousands of LGTBQ people, including youth, were drawn to the series for the hope of representation and a happy ending" ("Make Hartswood Films").

The Season Four finale, "The Final Problem," is singled out for the petitioners' specific ire. Not only is the promise of a homosexual relationship between Sherlock and John unfulfilled by what many fans perceive as the series' final episode, but the content of that episode is especially homophobic. As the petition delineates, "two sadistic villains"—Jim Moriarty and Eurus Holmes—are confirmed as queer characters, making the depiction of gay characters not only the opposite of "groundbreaking" in a positive sense on television but, worse yet, returning the characterizations to the mid–20th century, when gay characters (if they were there at all) were most likely evil and immoral and receive their "just" fate—death—by the end of the story.

Although Moriarty is brought back from the dead in flashback sequences during "The Final Problem," he can be cited as an example of an evil, immoral, and ultimately dead queer villain. Eurus survives physically, but her mental state is shattered, and she is permanently incarcerated; only her brother Sherlock can "save" her in any way—and, as the petition has described him, Sherlock is a closeted character. Perhaps the petitioners have not linked Sherlock's repressed sexuality as being "good" in opposition to "bad" queer villain Eurus' openly expressed sexual memories as an illustration of societal disapproval of openly gay characters. Nevertheless, these fans clearly explain their displeasure and anxiety about the effects of queerbaiting on an audience looking to *Sherlock* as a positive representation of queer characters and being harshly let down by the plot and characterizations in "The Final Problem."

The petition ends with a demand for the previously thanked creators, producers, and writers to explain themselves and their rationale for queer-baiting throughout the series and causing harm to the viewers who look to *Sherlock* for positive representation of queer characters. Online exchanges like this petition, as well as tweets, directed to TPTB exemplify how fans perceive their power and attempt to leverage it, but it is also clear that the scales are tipped in favor of TPTB. They can ignore these types of messages and cannot be "forced" to respond, no matter how much publicity a flurry of fan messages receives in mainstream media.

Not all fans reacted negatively to "The Final Problem," and Vertue, *Sherlock*, and Gatiss also received positive tweets thanking them for the series or apologizing for fans sending abusive messages. A few tweets even warned angry fans that, although constructive criticism was all right, vilifying the show's creators or actors was not; the argument was not that such messages could be emotionally or psychologically damaging and were wrong to send (i.e., the argument used against trolling fans) but that Vertue, Gatiss, or other cast or crew might not continue to interact online with fans if they receive hate tweets. This is evidence of how fans are very aware of the tenuous nature of digital communication with showrunners. Fans must "behave" in certain ways if they want to continue to have any kind of access to TPTB.

Within a week after "The Final Problem" was broadcast, Gatiss and Moffat visited Cambridge University for a Q&A session. In an interview before the session, the showrunners were asked about fans' highly emotional responses to the episode. The interviewer from *The Cambridge Student* asked about the series' representation, because—for better or worse—that seems to be fans' biggest issue with *Sherlock*. Gatiss explained that "I don't see why a programme has to become the kind of grail for anyone's expectations. I just don't think that's fair. The show is extremely popular, and we do our best in every way we possibly can." Moffat added that "The ticking boxes exercise is never going to work, because it ends in what you call tokenism" and noted that he could more easily represent greater diversity in *Doctor Who* than in *Sherlock*. The interviewer concludes that "Moffat and Gatiss find it difficult to strike the balance between entertainment and representation, and that if they had to they would always choose the former over the latter" (Dickenson).

Because the digital fandom has always gone to social media to interact with TPTB, it is not surprising that angry fans chose this medium to immediately express their feelings—or that fans with a different opinion about the episode might try to serve as mediators between one part of the fandom and TPTB. Whereas fans use social media as a one-way communication vehicle to "talk" to TPTB, Moffat and Gatiss use "traditional" media—such as newspaper interviews—to explain their position and, in the process, gain support. Choosing "traditional" media as an outlet for the content that they want to be most widely received also adds to the establishment of a hierarchy.

TPTB's Access to Mainstream Media and Public Opinion

Although Twitter has been an often-used forum both for official personnel—actors, showrunners, producers, directors, and specialists who compose music, design sets or costumes, or create special effects, for example—and fans to "toss" messages at each other, directly or indirectly, the communication often seems one-sided as far as power relationships go. Either the official voice of the series can send a message and ignore replies hashtagged or reposted to it or respond, most often to criticism, and then disappear. In 2012, Moffat decided to leave Twitter after receiving complaints about *Doctor Who* and feeling picked upon. A *Hypable* article summarizes the reasons why Twitter and Moffat were not the best social media combination for a healthy relationship with fans. For example, Moffat "has struggled to find the right tone on social media" (Byrne-Cristiano). Like many in the entertainment industry, he sometimes chooses words that seem argumentative or condescending to fans, which only enflames fans' anger, not only about their original point of contention (e.g., a character's portrayal) but about the way they are being treated by TPTB. The tone of messages, especially those limited in length by a social media platform, is often hard to interpret. Engaging fans, instead of enraging them, often requires more diplomacy than can be easily expressed in a tweet. Furthermore, knowing to whom to respond and how often to respond becomes difficult when someone like Moffat cannot easily discern who is an ardent fan with a real concern and who is a troll harassing him. There may be no single correct answer to the question of how to handle fans' messages, and a public misstep can lead to further problematic social media interactions. Personality also comes into play when TPTB attempt to interact via social media with fans with a range of interests and levels of communication skills. As the *Hypable* article notes, "Moffat has also been accused of being overly sensitive to constructive criticism and mistaking it for rudeness" (Byrne-Cristiano).

However, Moffat's partner, Hartswood Films producer Vertue, has kept her Twitter account and occasionally posted messages regarding Moffat. After he deleted his account, she tweeted that Twitter was "a distraction" for the busy showrunner. As a result, when complaints about *Sherlock's* third and fourth seasons were posted on Twitter, fans wanting to make a showrunner aware of their displeasure either tweeted the official BBC *Sherlock* account (@Sherlock221B), Hartswood Films (@Hartswood-Films), Vertue (@SueVertue), or, even more often, showrunner/actor Gatiss (@MarkGatiss).

In the past, especially in the series' early days, Gatiss teased upcoming *Sherlock* plots or locations or helped to promote the series. However, he turned to mainstream media to vent his frustration when the number of negative tweets began making news or seemed overwhelming. A *Huffington Post UK* interview included the comment that fans who find "The Final Problem" too confusing should "[g]o and read a children's book with hard pages if you don't want to be challenged. We're making the show we want to make. We don't make it a certain way because fans are pressuring us" (Frost, "'Sherlock Writer Mark Gatiss"). This claim—that the showrunners make the episodes they want to make—underscores the power that showrunners have compared to fans, even if ratings and high numbers of fan complaints might peripherally influence a network's decision to renew a series.

As long as *Sherlock* continues to make money, especially through global sales, the BBC will likely continue to greenlight new episodes. With Martin Freeman's and Benedict Cumberbatch's schedules full of film or television miniseries projects up to two years in advance, the news in mid–2017 that *Sherlock* likely would not return (at least not for several years) indicates the BBC's continuing interest. The series' stars have higher wattage now that they are members of high-profile film franchises like the *Avengers* (including Freeman's role in the *Black Panther* and Cumberbatch's in the *Doctor Strange* films), as well as award-worthy dramatic miniseries (e.g., *Fargo, The Hollow Crown*), but as long as they are willing to return to *Sherlock* and can find mutually possible breaks in their schedules, the series has the possibility to return. By then, the *Sherlock* fandom may have even less clout and be less vocal after years of hiatus, and the showrunners will, once again, produce stories that please them and that they believe others will enjoy, even if they do not seek audience (or specifically fan) input.

To be fair, Gatiss did not only respond to fan complaints about Season Four. He also felt a *Guardian* critic too harshly claimed that *Sherlock* was becoming James Bond; the showrunner sent a Bondesque poem to the "Letters" section of the critic's newspaper. Unlike the response to fans, which did not go over well because it seemed condescending, the poem "went viral," Gatiss reported in a later interview. "I had more attention from that than I have from any interview I've ever done. It was in the *New York Times* and *Vanity Fair*" (Fleming, "Mark Gatiss and Ian Hallard"). This is one of the few times in which the tables turn and fan voices get mainstream attention, though part of the attention is garnered because of Gatiss' reaction. When Gatiss angrily responds to fans, he seems to be superior and fans unsophisticated in their understanding of the text. When he responds more creatively to a professional critic, he engenders support and gains positive publicity. This comparison illustrates the recurring power differential in the social media spaces afforded both TPTB behind a television series and the fans who reach out to them.

Amanda Abbington and the Twitter Conflagration

As noted earlier in the chapter, fans often turn to Twitter when they want to communicate with TPTB. Gatiss was the first to tweet fans, intriguing them with tidbits from filming the first seasons' episodes, and, when Moffat killed his Twitter account, Vertue stepped up with official news regarding *Sherlock*. Although Freeman and Cumberbatch have, to date, not established a Twitter presence, Amanda Abbington (at the time Freeman's partner) became another official voice for the series when she joined *Sherlock* during Season Three. At first, Johnlock fans resented the addition of character Mary Morstan, who would wed John Watson, but the character and Abbington gained a friendlier fan following as the series progressed—and when at least some fans could surreptitiously send messages to Freeman via Abbington.

Yet, for all the pleasant messages Abbington sent to fans, she failed to grasp the nuances of communication with fans, much less the hierarchy among fans. Although the actor has power over fans by choosing whether and how much *Sherlock* information to parcel out, fans better understand the impact that Abbington's words can have on fandom and the repercussions within fandom when Abbington expresses her displeasure.

A case in point is the May 11, 2016, Twitter conflagration when Abbington tweeted a photograph of the first page of her shooting script for the fourth season's second episode. The cast had met to read through the script before filming began the following week. She captioned the photo "This just happened." The seemingly innocuous twitpic to alert fans to the start of the next episode's production generated the expected interest among Abbington's followers, many who immediately retweeted the photo.

When Abbington tweeted a photo of the front of her read-through script, some fans immediately reacted as if the image were a clue about the second episode. One fan applied a filter to the image to enhance the text (Reetu Kabra, reprinted in the blog "Benedict's Third Testicle"); in so doing, a few words from several lines on the script's second page were revealed: "eyes, up, Collects himself. Looks to the, stay close to his face, cut to." Even the most dedicated Sherlockian likely would not be able to deduce the plot of the episode based on these few words. Abbington, however, snapped upon seeing what had been done to the photo she had tweeted.

According to fan culture theorist Matt Hills in "Psychoanalysis and Digital Fandom: Theorizing Spoilers and Fans," fan-created spoilers represent a paradox for producers: Producers do not like spoilers because they see them as "a form of damage to the commercial value of a property." However, producers often view official spoilers (released by the producers themselves) as "enhancing brand value" (108). What this "info-war" reveals about spoilers, according to Hill, is that "it isn't the spoiler per se that is industrially opposed ... but rather its unofficial informational scope, scale, and lack of professional propriety. Unofficial spoilers threaten producers with a lack of mastery and control over the presentation of what they consider *their* narratives" (108). This info-war is less about spoiling a consumer's enjoyment of a show and more about control of a commodity. This is made very clear by Abbington's disproportionate reaction to a fan's enhancement of her twitpic, because that enhancement reveals nothing about the show.

Her initial tweeted responses were to castigate the fan who posted the enhanced photo (e.g., "Stupid fucking cretins put a filter on my photograph. What? You can't wait. You have to fucking spoil it for everyone else? Arse holes.") and then to stop posting information about *Sherlock* (e.g., "Won't be posting anything else about Sherlock then. Ruined that shit"). In this way she placed blame on fans who took her photo and used it in a way she had not expected (thus potentially freeing her from any backlash from her employers) and tried to control (at least in the future) what fans can know about filming by not providing any information at all.

However, Abbington also understands the power of Twitter to generate interest in the series and her role in it; in 2016, *Sherlock* was entering its fourth season and a fourth year's-long hiatus between new episodes. Keeping fans engaged with the series and encouraging their interest in episodes scheduled for broadcast in 2017 is likely another reason why Abbington and other *Sherlock* insiders continue to use Twitter as a means of disseminating information about the series. Recognition of Twitter's value in promoting the series likely helped influence Abbington's further tweets in response to the "leaking" of words from the script.

After several angry tweets on May 11, Abbington eventually admitted she "may have overreacted" and backed off from swearing at fans. She likely anticipated that her "hug" added to an apology ("Sorry about that, folks. Really") would restore the status quo and end any animosity between groups of fans or between official *Sherlock* source(s) and extremely invested fans. Because Abbington is a celebrity with thousands of follow-ers, her tweets carry more weight with fans. When she attacks fans, she may inadvertently activate a troll network eager to go after the offending fans. Of course, these "uber fans" or "super fans" do not consider them-selves trolls in the traditional sense. They may feel it is their responsibility, as devoted fans who "take direction" from the content of celebrity tweets, to police the fandom and destroy those fans who have annoyed or threat-ened the celebrity. Uber/super fans following Abbington's tweets on May 11, for example, not only wanted to defend her through their righteous anger on her behalf, but they likely sought her approval for their actions. In fan parlance, they wanted a "cookie" as a reward for protecting the celebrity.

Through a series of tweets, Abbington engaged primarily with one fan, Andressa, about the results of the actor's angry tweets among *Sherlock* fans. When Andressa and a few other fans attempted to explain to Abbing-ton that her tweets could incite violence against the people who enhanced the photo, the actor did not seem to understand the power of her tweets. She merely stated that what others do is not her fault. Although Abbington is right in thinking that she cannot control fans' actions, she nonetheless should understand that, by calling fans "cretins" and swearing at them, she potentially has the power to emotionally wound fans who are trying to do what the *Sherlock* community encourages: uncover and disseminate information about episodes in production. By baiting fans, Abbington might anticipate that at least a few among the thousands of her followers might take the bait and use her photo to gather more information than she anticipated. As well, nothing in the plot was revealed by the photo's enhancement. Abbington acted more upset that fans would attempt to spoil the plot rather than reacting to actual spoiled information. She also seems unaware that uber/super fans may turn on other fans within the community to ostracize them or even attempt to emotionally or psychologically destroy them for participating in the fan community in a way that an official source did not anticipate or approve of. Losing control of the official message she wanted to send to followers is likely the real issue at the heart of Abbington's Twitter meltdown.

In light of trolling and other online abuse directed toward fans, those *Sherlock* fans who contacted Abbington about her tweets potentially inciting troll-like fans to attack others are not only brave, but their actions are necessary to make celebrities aware of the ramifications of social media. Actors such as Abbington may use Twitter to promote themselves or their projects, but they may not consider how their messages may affect individuals within fandom. Twitter-savvy fans have taken the responsibility of educating actors about the ways in which social media works and why celebrities, in particular, should think about the ramifications of their words before they tweet. In this way, fans are helping to create a safer space within social media for open discussion and sharing of information about *Sherlock*, even in those types of sites with structures more likely to permit individual users to be targeted and attacked by those who disagree with them.

Andressa used her tweets to educate Abbington about the nature of Twitter and fan communities. Through her tweets, she may be perceived as advocating a kinder, gentler Twitter, but she also attempted to educate an official *Sherlock* source about the potential ramifications of Twitter communication sent from that source. Through a series of tweets, Andressa first wrote that "When you snap like that, people go after the fan who started it. That's why it's so bad." Abbington replied directly to Andressa (but the message was retweeted thousands of times) to ask how that was her fault. Andressa next explained that "All I said is: it happens. It sucks. Please try to take a deep breath before tweeting, because it can get really awful" and added in another tweet that she had also tweeted Gatiss that "Sometimes what [fans] do with your words isn't your fault, but if you can prevent the consequences, PLEASE do." Abbington further commented that she is a supporter of free speech, and the conversation ended, from her perspective at least.

"Educating" Abbington seemed a more positive approach and one that generated a more emotionally moderate response from the actor. A tweet earlier in the day by Natalie K complained directly to Abbington "Not a fan of actors who refer to their fans this way" and reposted the "cretins" comment. Abbington replied "Stop following me then." The actor, however, did respond to Andressa's thoughtful comments and participated in a brief conversation via a series of tweets. Although Twitter is often not conducive to thoughtful discourse and is limited to short responses instead of lengthy messages, at times it may be useful as even a limited forum for some type of "advocacy" (e.g., be polite, think before you tweet) against bullying or trolling. This discourse also educates celebrities about the nature of Twitter and the ramifications of their messages directed to their fan base.

The discussion did not die on Twitter or Tumblr; thousands of notes, retweets, and posts reflected on what Abbington had tweeted and how fans responded. One fan blog, Benedict's Third Testicle, reprinted not only Abbington's and Andressa's conversation but the running commentary by other fans who posted their responses to a blogged discussion. Choppedcreationcheesecake, for example, posted a lengthy commentary (more than 200 words) about Abbington's lack of understanding of fandom and Twitter. The fan blogger summarized problems with Abbington's tweets directed to fans, such as unnecessary insults, mistakes or misreadings of context, and apologies after the actor either cools off or comes to understand the context differently. In addition, Choppedcreationcheesecake more importantly discusses the resulting within-fandom conflicts that can (and often do) arise and cause personal harm to individuals. The blogger explains that, after Abbington insulted fans who analyzed and reposted the script page she had intentionally posted on Twitter, "some of the Uebers [*sic*] on Twitter immediately whole-heartedly repeated her insults and celebrated them." When the actor calmed down and apologized later, however, the Ubers, whose "goal is to always, always uncritically [*sic*] agree with anything their star does and says ... celebrate[d] her some more for having the guts to do that" (Choppedcreationcheesecake). The fans who felt bad by being called out on Twitter as the reason why Abbington claimed she would no longer share information about *Sherlock* may have received a belated "group" apology from the actor but did not receive one from the Ubers. Within *Sherlock* fandom, the faction of uber fans/ super fans may still feel superior for aligning their views with Abbington's changing perspective and staying on the actor's good side, and the Sherlock-styled sleuths who analyzed the insider information provided by Abbington and shared their findings still are marked as "bad" fans for angering Abbington—no matter how the situation turned out.

In conclusion, Choppedcreationcheesecake commented on Abbington's response to Andressa, who had tried to explain to the actor just how seriously fans take her tweets: "AmA [Amanda Abbington] really doesn't get fan mechanisms, does she? ... When you call a fan out and call them names, the other fans will go after the person you called out. If you don't get that then you really, really don't understand your own status and how a fandom works."

Site owner/moderator Ballsy further discussed the ramifications of this series of tweets making the rounds of #Setlock and the *Sherlock* fandom: Abbington "seems completely unaware of her power within this fandom. There are ubers out there who consider themselves the self-appointed fandom police.... They are not pleasant, and they feel fully justified in ruining the lives of those who they feel don't comply with their fandom policies." Ballsy noted that uber fans/super fans want to receive praise or thanks from, in particular, *Sherlock* star Benedict Cumberbatch for their "protection" of him against the actions of other fans. Although Abbington has a supporting role in the series, she still has a great deal of power over fans. Ballsy wrote that when Abbington tweets insults toward a few individuals, the actor "might as well have issued direct orders to the Ubers to attack this fan," which is what happened in this situation.

In a final statement directed to Abbington (who likely would never read it, although hundreds of *Sherlock* fans following this or other fan blogs likely would), Ballsy reminded Abbington to be more sensitive about what is written on social media, because cyberbullying must be taken seriously, and the actor should remember how she felt to be victimized online. The blogger referred to Abbington's receipt of death threats made via Twitter in 2013 and 2015 when her character was introduced as John Watson's love interest and later became his wife; Abbington screen-captured the threatening tweets and then tweeted that she had forwarded them to the police, along with information that identified those who threatened her. Ballsy cautioned not only Abbington but any of TPTB about their use of social media when addressing fans, explaining that "There are too many amongst this fandom (it happens in others too, it's a thing) that are way too willing to attack others, for a cookie [i.e., praise].... The Sherlock team need to be more cautious.... Cyberbullying has claimed victims."

Although the conversation about the way that official sources and fans interact, and the ramifications of these interactions, began and ended within one day on Twitter, the discussions within fandom continued several days afterward and included much longer, more thoughtfully written and likely edited responses. Forums such as fan blogs are far more conducive to further discussion. Whereas Abbington, for example, may have considered only the immediacy of Twitter in sharing her emotional responses to what she perceived as accidentally leaked information,

Sherlock fans continue to discuss, share, and archive information so that it becomes a close-to-permanent record of fan activity.

Abbington, like other official personnel working on *Sherlock*, seems to have difficulty discerning between baiting fans and sharing information with them. Fans also post and repost messages on blogs like Sophie Hunter Gossip Blog and Benedict's Third Testicle, among other fan sites, to complain about baiting and the increased lockdown of information from the *Sherlock* set. Abbington may not have understood that her message would become part of an ongoing discussion about baiting fans.

Like many representatives of official, sanctioned information networks that try to control the amount and type of information disseminated to the public about their product or business (in this case, *Sherlock*), Abbington may assume that consumers (in this case, fans) will be pleased with whatever information is provided to them. In fan culture, however, tracking down information and being the first to share it with other fans builds credibility. Thus, the fans who applied the filter and shared what amounted to only a few indecipherable words from an official script likely did so for three reasons: (1) they want to know first what is happening on the *Sherlock* set and within the plot, (2) they want to be recognized as Sherlock Holmes–type fans who are technologically savvy enough to decode information others cannot, and (3) they want to be enhance their credibility within fandom by becoming (or maintaining their status as) a go-to source of information.

Showrunners' Use of Sherlock *to Illustrate Perceptions of* Sherlock *Fans*

Sherlock's showrunners, especially Moffat, are very much aware of the fan community's presence on social media. Moffat makes use of this knowledge in unexpected ways that have resulted in fans being referenced on the show and, consequently, having an influence on the mainstream culture that consumes it. He knew, for example, that fans spent much of the two-year hiatus between the broadcast of Seasons Two and Three theorizing about how Sherlock survives a fall from a hospital roof, as shown in "The Reichenbach Fall." Moffat also had become aware of fan fiction pairings not previously shown in the series. Furthermore, although Moffat and Gatiss have often said that they are Sherlock Holmes fans, which is why they wanted to write their own "fan fiction," they are decidedly different kinds of fans than those who are most vocal within the digital community. Moffat, like members of the public or mainstream media who only observe *Sherlock*'s digital fandom and at least sometimes subscribe to popular interpretations of "obsessed" fans, either validated devoted fans or upset them because of his interpretations of typical fan behaviors, as illustrated in "The Empty Hearse."

When Moffat wrote Sherlock's "return" episode to begin Season Three, he incorporated scenes that specifically reference fans or respond to fan expectations regarding Sherlock's potential romantic relationships. A fan theory about Sherlock's survival became the basis of a "theory" scene in the episode. According to this fan theory shown on screen, Sherlock and his apparent nemesis Jim Moriarty (Andrew Scott) are really working together to fake Sherlock's death by setting up a dummy to fall from the roof. While Sherlock mimics sorrow during his phone conversation with John right before the Sherlock-dressed dummy falls, Moriarty nearly spoils the ruse by giggling. Sherlock shushes him, the pair lock eyes, and they move toward a kiss. Although the scene is abruptly cut before the kiss takes place, this "theory" scene illustrates Sherlock in a homosexual relationship—something that many fans portray in fan fiction, discuss on fan forums, and would like to see become televised scenes.

"The Empty Hearse" also depicts fans of Sherlock, who are included as part of the show, mimicking the community of real-world *Sherlock* fans who obsessively follow the series. During "The Reichenbach Fall," Sherlock is glorified in London's media for the high-profile cases he solves; by the end of the episode, however, Moriarty has manipulated the media into turning against Sherlock. Nevertheless, Sherlock's media popularity has garnered him many fans who refuse to believe that he is anything less than a hero. In "The Empty Hearse," a group of fans meets to discuss what happened to Sherlock and postulate whether he is still alive and, if so, how he survived the fall. The meeting only breaks up when every fan's phone starts buzzing at once with the news—spreading quickly via social media—that Sherlock has returned from the "dead." Such a meta (i.e., self-referential) scene that illustrates how real-world fans of the series become highly invested in the characters indicates that Moffat, who wrote this episode, recognizes fan devotion to the series (or Sherlock) and the immediate connection among fans through social media.

Within one episode, Moffat acknowledges fans' intense investment in Sherlock Holmes (or, in the real world, *Sherlock*) fandom. This acknowledgment is evidence that the showrunners pay attention to fan activity in a critical way, and that fans directly influence the content of the show, which suggests a concomitant relationship between showrunners and fans that even extends to content.

There is no denying that the kind of fan practices shown in "The Empty Hearse" and evidenced in the real world during #Setlock (i.e., traveling to filming sites to watch the cast and crew at work) have affected the content and even the practices of filming *Sherlock*, which is significant in and of itself. More importantly, a shift in the perception and recognition of fan-produced knowledge systems demonstrates the extent to which empowered fans in digital spaces are creating new ontologies, negotiating many aspects of media culture—from "spoiling" to helping celebrities to recognize the kind of impact they have in a digital environment. Simply put, fans have a significant impact on media culture, while creating and maintaining creative and knowledgeable online communities that also influence cultural practices beyond those traditionally associated with fan culture.

Booth and others rightfully claim that fan practices are being emulated by the media industry in order to capitalize on fan-based knowledge systems and practices. He also asserts that "by retaining ideological and textual concomitance, contemporary fan work negotiates the boundaries between producer and audience while still maintaining a reverence for those boundaries.... Fannish work, in subverting the system, may support it" (15).

Interaction Between TPTB and Fans at Sherlocked USA

Whereas the previous sections detailed digital communication between fans and TPTB, fan conventions offer a different type of communication experience: face-to-face meetings. The tenor of conventions differs from the previously mentioned digital communication because fans pay quite a bit of money and the point of a convention is to get insider information, merchandise, and face time with venerated celebrities. This leads to the convention environment generally being non-critical, whereas in online environments fans feel entitled to express unfavorable opinions and criticisms freely. At a convention many intermediaries control access to the guests and determine which fannish behaviors are acceptable, unlike in the uncensored online environment. The convention experience, with the opportunity to be in the presence of those responsible for bringing Sherlock to life, cannot be reproduced in an online environment. Even so, digital communication plays an important role in the convention process for fans who share information with others via social media. The result of this communication is usually broadcast to the digital community as soon as possible after the encounter, adding to fans' credibility within the fandom and enhancing *Sherlock* insiders' reputation with fans.

During Sherlocked USA, nearly six months after "The Final Problem," the fan attendees happily mingled with TPTB and shared their love of *Sherlock* with like-minded fans. It was clear that the guests understand that the *Sherlock* fandom thrives in a digital environment. Host/panel moderator Tony Lee frequently warned guests that innuendo would lead to new fan fiction. A Mycroft Holmes/Mrs. Hudson pairing became more likely after Gatiss commented on the sexual tension between the characters. Gatiss and Scott mentioned that they would like to play Mrs. Hudson, leading to more plot possibilities. A Mrs. Hudson spinoff series was proposed during several panels; in one version, the series would star Mrs. Hudson as a detective, whereas in others she would keep Moriarty in line (he is afraid of her) or she would be Mycroft's boss. Whether sexual innuendo or creative spinoff concepts became part of a panel's commentary, Lee's follow-up statement was always similar to "You don't know what you've done" (to which some guests smirked, "Yes, we do") or an estimation of the number of fan fictions that would soon be written. Everyone, it seems, understands fans' creativity in writing fan fiction and expects whatever transpires during a panel discussion to immediately be shared online, shortly followed by a wealth of new stories.

However, actors' and showrunners' awareness of *Sherlock's* digital fandom goes further than fan fiction. Several times Lee instructed fans what to tweet (or not tweet), when to take and post photos, and why electronics should be shut off during panels. He noted that guests might not say anything "off the record" if fans tweet information that panelists might not want documented. Similarly, any type of recording is prohibited at conventions. The threat held over fans eager to share "insider" information is that guests may not attend future conventions (i.e., may stop interacting face-to-face with fans) if they feel uncomfortable about the digital fandom.

Announcements on the first full day of the convention reminded fans that guests who are on break or seen outside the convention floor should be left alone. Apparently, groups of fans, eager to talk in person with those they had only seen on screens or communicated with via Twitter, had already surrounded a few actors walking through a lobby or standing in an elevator. Some fans did not seem to understand the difference between an official *Sherlock* insider's public persona—the personality on display during panels, photo or autograph sessions, or run-ins on the convention floor—and the private persona once the guest is "off the clock." Not every guest is or should be as witty in person and on the spot as he or she is in carefully worded tweets or sound bites. However, one of the most coveted types of proof of a star encounter is the selfie, and fans sometimes forget the "do not approach" rule when they see actors or showrunners outside of scheduled convention activities.

A meet-and-greet with Andrew Scott illustrates the importance of star selfies in a digital community. Fifteen fans who paid $185 for a 45-minute conversation with the actor were asked whether they preferred talking longer with Scott or taking a selfie with him. Selfies won and within a few minutes were distributed across social media. Interest in meeting a *Sherlock* star, especially one as popular as Scott, increases the number of times a photo is shared, liked, or commented upon. For example, Lynnette Porter's Facebook post of her selfie with Scott garnered 89 Likes, which is dozens more than any previous photo or comment in her multi-year history on that site—not bad considering that her page is not designed to attract *Sherlock* fans. Those *Sherlock* fans with a concentrated following of other fans often received hundreds of Likes and Shares.

VIPs who paid the most for Sherlocked USA tickets and gained greater access to stars through private receptions and photo ops shared official photos, as well as selfies, on Tumblr blogs, Instagram posts, and tweets about encounters with actors. Within a day of a post, if it contains interesting or controversial gossip, the information is retweeted, reblogged, or otherwise shared and discussed on other fans' sites. A post about a comment Wanda Ventham (Benedict Cumberbatch's mother) reportedly made about her son's marriage, reposted to fan sites Sophie Hunter Gossip Blog and Benedict's Third Testicle, for instance, was dissected, and fans commented or shared the discussion.

The convention atmosphere is generally positive, with complaints reserved for the way queues are handled or another management issue. Because the actors and showrunners can choose to mingle in hallways with fans as they move from one event to another, fans may get the impression that the amount of interaction with TPTB has few limitations. The reality is that the guests are usually protected against any fan interaction that might become inappropriate or dangerous. Although guests sometimes walk alone to or from the convention rooms, they most often are escorted, which helps to maintain a discreet distance between fans and guests. Time with guests is severely limited—although a guest can decide to take more time to chat if he or she wishes; convention volunteers are far less likely to chide an actor or a showrunner than a fan for slowing a queue. A table or a stage usually provides safe distance from overzealous fans, and the speed and monitoring of queues and panels help maintain each guest's safety. Even the types of questions asked during panels can be carefully controlled. Before Sherlocked USA, fans submitted questions online for panel discussions. A selection of questions, likely vetted by convention management, was given to Lee to ask guests, and, because the list of questions was inevitably too long for the session, only randomly selected questions ended up being asked. Instead of complaining about the ways that their interactions with TPTB are controlled, however, most fans seem grateful to have even limited face time with celebrities.

Perhaps because TPTB recognize the expediency of digital communication and fans' willingness to share either good or bad stories about showrunners and actors, even those who had complained about fans in mainstream media or chosen not to interact with fans online seemed genuinely interested in greeting fans in person. Gatiss and Moffat were a big hit in their panels, and Moffat, in particular, earned a great deal of goodwill by spending time chatting with fans getting his autograph. The assembled cast and crew made a point of thanking and applauding the fans before they exited the stage one last time. Such face-to-face interaction not only leaves fans with a positive impression of *Sherlock* insiders, collectively or individually, but also increases the likelihood that fans will share positive experiences online. Those who cannot attend an event like a convention often ask "What is he/she like?" when someone reports meeting a star. One of the first comments to Porter's posted selfie with Scott is "Is he as lovely in person?" Of course, no one can get to know an actor during the brief second needed to take a selfie or longer conversations made possible at a convention, when the actor's public persona is on display. Nonetheless, the afterglow of connecting even briefly with a star usually leads to a positive response to questions about what the actor is really like.

The digital fandom and, more importantly, awareness of it by showrunners, cast, and crew, is confirmed at events like conventions, where fans and *Sherlock* insiders understand the power of digital media. When Gatiss asked fans at a Sunday morning panel why they were not in church, Lee quipped, "This *is* their church." The level of obsession with *Sherlock* and its showrunners, producer, designer, and actors evidenced at Sherlocked USA would lead those only observing the fandom to conclude that fandom is akin to a religion promulgated by zealots. However, despite guests' jokes about fans' propensity to share everything online, these insiders also recognize the bond among fans. While saying farewell during the closing ceremony, actor Alistair Petrie (Major Sholto) commented on the convention's real purpose for fans: community.

Sherlock elicits a variety of highly personal and emotional responses from fans, who often choose to share their responses with TPTB and other fans. Whereas digital communication permits and often encourages conversations online and, if possible, in person, perhaps its greatest strength within *Sherlock* fandom is its ability to validate fans' readings of characters and the series, especially when it contradicts the "official reading" promoted by TPTB. As examined in the following chapters, this fandom's strength comes from its ability to make *Sherlock* personal and to become empowered—with or without the blessing of TPTB—to use *Sherlock* and Sherlock as a catalyst for change.

2

"Traditional" Fan Works in a Digital Community

For generations, fans have been writing and archiving creative works about their favorite television characters. In the 1960s, fans typed stories or photocopied art, bound collections, and either traded or sold fanzines at conventions or mailed them to subscribers. During the early 2000s, as more fans worked online, fan fiction archives became popular as one way to turn "traditional" fan works into digital texts and, later, art including animation and video. Instead of communicating with other fans primarily face to face, they advertise creative works internationally and instantaneously online. However, as a 2017 *Forbes* article reminds readers, fan fiction authors still follow many of the "traditional" practices of those who came before them. Although fan fiction provides a creative and often a cathartic outlet for all writers, many begin their careers by "donating" their work to other fan-readers but go on to make money as professional authors. Some examples held up as role models are Lois Bujold McMaster (author of the sci-fi series "The Vorkosigan Saga") and Diane Duane (author of *Star Trek* novels). At least a few *Sherlock* fan fiction authors who post their stories on Archive of Our Own (AO3) note that they write fan fiction under a pseudonym but also write and sell their work professionally under their real name; sometimes they provide links with announcements of the publication of a new novel. The *Forbes* article praises one *Sherlock* fan fiction writer in particular: series showrunner Steven Moffat, who is quoted as affirming that he "refuse[s] to mock fan-fiction because I'm a man who writes Sherlock Holmes fan fiction for a living" (Cuccinello).

Not everyone on the *Sherlock* team perceives fan fiction as positively. During an appearance on *Top Gear* in 2013, Benedict Cumberbatch talked about fan fiction and the way his character was often treated by authors.

He mentioned "a load of fan fiction which has me [presumably he meant Sherlock Holmes] and John Watson floating in space on a bed handcuffed to one another ... not just with handcuffs, either." Just as Cumberbatch showed his awareness of fan fiction, so were fan fiction writers paying attention to everything he said during the *Top Gear* interview. From Cumberbatch's comment and a fan fiction writer's inspiration was born "XO," a quirkily entertaining fic about Sherlock and John trapped on an alien spaceship and forced to have sex with each other.

The subject of slash (i.e., same-sex) fan fiction came up again during an *Out* interview in which the interviewer seems to encourage a less-than-flattering depiction of fans or fan fiction in the way he prompts Cumberbatch's responses. After the interviewer suggests to the actor that writing Sherlock and John as a gay couple might, by removing women as potential partners, defuse the sexual tension felt by young female fans, Cumberbatch agrees that fan fiction is "about burgeoning sexuality in adolescence, because you don't necessarily know how to operate that. And I think it's a way of neutralizing the threat, so this person [i.e., Sherlock] is sort of removed from them as somebody who could break their heart." The interviewer further describes fan writers as the "rapacious slash fiction community that has turned his chilly, acerbic, and distinctly asexual Sherlock into a lustful cock monster" (Hicklin). Although a few fans might be interested that the interviewer labels Cumberbatch's character as "distinctly asexual," many who read Sherlock that way likely would be just as thrilled to learn the interviewer's definition of *asexual* as they were to read his description of the *Sherlock* fan fiction community.

For *New Statesman*'s Elizabeth Minkel, the issue is not so much that Cumberbatch—or anyone associated with *Sherlock*—is aware of fan fiction devoted to the series' characters. The stories are not written for TPTB. What does matter to Minkel and fan fiction writers is that "two middle-aged men with very large platforms were sitting at a table pathologising teenage girls' sexuality—and making a whole load of potentially harmful assumptions about a topic they know literally nothing about"—and if they know nothing about this topic, then they should not be discussing it during an interview. Articles about a high-profile actor who, at the time, was promoting more than one movie, only provide a broader public readership with more misinformation about fan fiction and fandom. That fan fiction writers often respond to fans' experiences as marginalized segments of society surprisingly was not mentioned in *Out*, a publication that emphasizes LGBTQ advocacy. (To be fair, later in the *Out* interview, Cumberbatch discusses and seems disgusted by Hollywood hypocrisy in making gay actors fear they will never be cast if they come out; the actor also describes discrimination against boys outed at his school and his attempts to stand up for equality. He may not have been as judgmental about fan fiction writers if he had been informed about the composition of an AO3 membership survey.)

In contrast to the negative interpretation of fan fiction in *Out*, in her article, Minkel summarizes its significance: Fan fiction "gives women and other marginalised groups the chance to subvert the mainstream perspective, to fracture a story and recast it in their own way." She directs readers to a 2013 AO3 survey of its membership to support her description of fan fiction writers. In a survey of 10,005 AO3 members, resulting demographics indicate "typical" writers and readers. The average age is 25; 38 percent of respondents self-identified as heterosexual; 54 percent self-identified as a member of a gender, sexual, or romantic minority; more respondents self-identified as genderqueer than as male ("AO3 Census"). Based on the number of queer fan fictions written by members of the *Sherlock* fandom and the positive comments associated with non-heteronormative stories, it would not be surprising if *Sherlock* fans who are also AO3 members have similar demographics.

Since 2010, *Sherlock* fans have taken fan fiction and other creative works online. AO3, the largest online archive of fan works (primarily fan fiction) has, as of July 2017, more than 96,000 stories about Sherlock Holmes as he is portrayed on various television series. The stories are published in several languages, with more added daily. English-language stories dealing only with *Sherlock*, not canon stories or those dealing with other adaptations, posted by July 2017 number nearly 89,000.

One hallmark of fan fiction, in general, is that stories regarded positively by readers must, regardless of the creative license taken in representing circumstances, times, and places outside the universe of the show, remain relentlessly attuned to detail and faithful characterization in order to establish a kind of fidelity with the show and characters that fans recognize and appreciate. Stories that do not adhere are called out in the comments and generally voted down, and stories with a high degree of fidelity are praised and fans express appreciation for the pleasure they derive from recognizing and interpreting those details. As one might expect, *Sherlock* fans are particularly critical and seem to relish pointing out flaws and oversights as they read. Conversely, they take pride/pleasure in deducing/decoding connections that are implied in fan fiction stories.

Only one of many examples of a fan fiction writer's knowledge of

Sherlock and ability to "deduce" characters like Sherlock is evident in "Boyfriend Material," by Poppy Alexander. By Chapter 58, published in July 2017, the story had earned more than 3,100 comments and more than 1,200 kudos on AO3; fan-audience response is clearly positive toward this continuing saga of the Boston Brawlers professional hockey team, led by Captain John Watson and goalie extraordinaire Sherlock Holmes. Details from canon, such as John achieving the rank of Captain during his military service, have been incorporated into the hockey genre when John is made the captain of his team. Fans especially like this kind of "insider" detail that harkens both to canon and *Sherlock*. Even as a goalie, Sherlock uses his deductive prowess to determine the most likely moves by the opposing team's players and thus is able to make amazing saves. However, Alexander needs more than a clear, fluid, engaging writing style and knowledge of the characters in this television adaptation (e.g., John's failed dating history, as detailed in *Sherlock* episodes; Sherlock's past substance abuse; Sherlock's reliance on technology to immediately find information online). She also needs to be able to write about Sherlock's deductions in a way that makes his thought processes seem logical and different from other characters'. Being able to think like Sherlock and explaining his deductions plausibly to fans highly critical of inaccurate or illogical plots or character traits is crucial to success as a *Sherlock* fan fiction writer. When Poppy Alexander introduced a storyline of two hockey fans writing a blog that implies a sexual relationship between Sherlock and John, she has John read the blog—and thus includes a meta element to the story. The blog looks like it was written by extremely enthusiastic fans "squee"-ing about the players' personal relationship and using fan language and emoticons. With this addition to her story, Poppy Alexander illustrates her familiarity and the story's fidelity to hockey, characteristics of Sherlock and John as depicted in *Sherlock*, and fannish behavior. This example illustrates a fan fiction author's mastery of more than one community's subcultural language and interests, which broadly reflects how demanding the writing of effective, popular fan fiction can be.

Because of the strong commitment of *Sherlock* fans to establishing fidelity while creatively expressing alternative fictions, those who consume and make comments about stories become synchronous, active participants in the creation of the paratexts associated with the fan fiction stories themselves. Fan reader reactions/comments help to create the genre in a palpable way, which happens seamlessly and efficiently in digital spaces. Fan readers' position as concomitant creators of these texts is significant in understanding how and why these types of fan works have been around so long, are so well loved, and have flourished in an online environment.

As only one example of the use of digital media to synthesize personal feelings about a Season Four episode, within hours of the U.K. broadcast of "The Six Thatchers" and before the episode was broadcast in the U.S., six fan fiction works referencing this episode were published, including very short stories (a few hundred words) and one plot and character analysis. All of these entries attempt to make sense of the death of a major character and the separation of John Watson and Sherlock Holmes. Another 33 stories were posted on January 2, 2017, the day after the episode was broadcast; most of these deal with Johnlock (i.e., the platonic or sexual pairing of John Watson and Sherlock Holmes) and are tagged as "fix-it fics." By January 3, about half of the more than 50 stories uploaded that day reflect the newest episode. Considering that by that time the episode had generated 8.1 million viewers in the U.K. (by far outdistancing Queen Elizabeth's holiday message in holiday viewing, per the BBC), fans, as well as more casual viewers, were very interested in eyeing the first new regular episode in three years.

In this episode, Sherlock adds to the vow he made in Season Three's "The Sign of Three" to protect the Watsons (John, Mary, and the forthcoming baby). In "The Six Thatchers," Sherlock and John better understand Mary's former life as a freelance assassin, and Sherlock vows to protect her if she returns to London after running through various countries in an effort to draw a murder-minded former compatriot away from her family. Sherlock specifically says that she only needs to stay close to him so that he can protect her. However, after standing next to Sherlock while confronting her former shadowy employer, Mary jumps between Sherlock and the bullet meant for him. As a result, she dies, conveniently in John's arms after he, Mycroft Holmes, and New Scotland Yard's Greg Lestrade arrive late on the scene to capture the government employee who freelanced as an assassination broker. Heartbroken John angrily warns Sherlock to stay away, leading Johnlock fans to immediately want to reconcile the duo. They do not want to see Sherlock suffer the loss of John's friendship, and writing fan fiction in the episode's aftermath provides a way for writers and readers to make the friends' separation fit fans' "head canon" (i.e., the way fans believe the characters should behave and the direction the series should take). For many fans, John and Sherlock belong together under any circumstances, and "The Six Thatchers" disturbs their view of the series. Fan fiction allows fan writers to fix the situation.

The *Sherlock* fan fiction archive houses many works that serve a variety of purposes within fandom. Some stories focus on character relationships and, as in the case of "The Six Thatchers," re-establish the status quo between John and Sherlock or create plots in which the relationship is tested or strengthened. In many stories, these characters fall in love or decide to embark on a sexual relationship. Although various pairings of characters are often featured in fan fiction, especially a same-sex sexual relationship, known as slash (e.g., Mystrade [Mycroft and Lestrade]), or romance (e.g., Sherlolly [Sherlock and Molly]), the main focus in this chapter is fans' description of the relationship between Sherlock and John, in whatever form it takes.

Many stories, such as the previously mentioned "Boyfriend Material," fit into the alternate universe (AU) category. AU stories often place the characters in different professions or time periods while finding a way for the friendship/love/sexual relationship to be established. Crossover AU stories allow writers to merge *Sherlock* with other literary or cinematic texts or other fandoms (i.e., have them "cross over" to another text or fandom). All these stories are often highly creative because they escape the limitations of the series' canon while ensuring that John and Sherlock are recognizable from the series. AU fiction has become so popular that it warrants its own art and has developed a subgenre of fans. Artist Fox Estacado, who is also active in *Sherlock* fandom as a member of the well-known Three Patch Podcast group, celebrates the diversity of Sherlock fan fiction with a poster entitled "A Study in AU!Sherlock." Among the 12 drawings of famous AU versions of Sherlock, he is pictured as a ballet dancer in mid-leap, a shirtless stripper poised against a pole, a zombie, and an android. Perhaps the strangest AU is tunalock, with Sherlock as a fish wearing a scarf. Estacado also sells "Ask me about my ship" t-shirts with a flip-up side showing a Johnlock drawing. Her collection of other Sherlock prints further shows that AU fan fiction has developed a devoted fan following willing to buy art and other merchandise to support this subgenre of *Sherlock* fiction.

Yet another category of works is nonfiction; fan writers analyze the series and develop theories about where it is headed or what is going on with specific characters in the long-term trajectory of multiple seasons' episodes. Although clearly not fan fiction, these analyses provide ideas and explanations that may be useful to fiction writers, which justifies their inclusion in a fan fiction archive. As a creative work, such analyses allow writers to share their insights with other fans and create scholarly essays that likely would not be published by mainstream academic journals, often because the writers are not students of media studies or are not academic professionals.

A final category, discussed in detail in Chapter 7, is fan fiction that promotes advocacy, often regarding Sherlock's sexual orientation (most often written in this category as asexual Sherlock stories) and inviting comments about the character's or the fan's sexual orientation and experiences (e.g., coming out to friends or family, being misunderstood, facing violence because of one's orientation). Such stories may provide educational content or make readers aware of asexuality. Links to advocacy sites or information about asexuality sometimes accompany the stories or comments about the plot or character interpretation. In this chapter, these categories of fan works published in AO3 are examined in light of their content and their use within the *Sherlock* fan community of fan fiction readers and writers.

The Nature of Fan Fiction Communities

Most fan fiction communities have a relatively low threshold for entry. Anyone with an Internet connection and basic digital navigation skills can submit and post comments, although not all posts receive attention and feedback. Posts also may be censored at the discretion of the site's moderator, and AO3, for instance, tries to moderate users' behavior so that the site is free of bashing, doxxing (i.e., revealing someone's true identity in order to threaten or harass the person and, often, his or her family), or discriminating against users.

The digital community is responsible for which stories or information is deemed important and valuable. Stories or comments that strike a positive chord with readers may be rewarded with hundreds of kudos, hearts, or positive posts that support what the writer has done with a character or a plot point or address another reader's response to the story. Authors of fan fiction may solicit feedback, although simply the act of posting a story to an archive like AO3 means that readers can provide comments without direct solicitation from the author. Comments sections often make readers and writers feel that their contributions matter, because exchanges in which readers thank the authors and authors express their appreciation for their readers are commonplace. This perception of meaningfulness in their work is a tenet of "participatory culture" per Henry Jenkins and is, in part, responsible for how or why online communities thrive. A high number of comments or kudos can contribute to a text's popularity and consequently bolster authors' and readers' perceptions about their work. Stories are awarded status based on the number of views, comments, and kudos, so readers directly influence the popularity of the story. As well, many readers post recommendation (rec) lists of their favorite stories, often organized by theme, with the result that some writers achieve a great deal of status within the fan fiction community.

The way in which favorite stories are promoted within the community via kudos is similar to readers' good word-of-mouth promotion or independent reviews of well-written, professionally published stories that consumers post on sites such as Amazon or Goodreads. Unlike professionally published stories, however, fan fiction is not subject to the same editorial scrutiny as texts submitted to editors and marketers working for a publishing company. The fan community, therefore, has much more influence about what is considered "good reading," because readers looking for a topic (such as asexuality) in AO3's vast archive of *Sherlock* stories often search secondarily by the number of kudos given to a story (in order to avoid poorly written stories) or the name of an author who regularly receives a high number of kudos.

Because the stories exist in digital sites, they may be extensively organized by keywords and archived so that readers may search by commonly used tags. Authors who post stories add tags so that their work may be easily found by readers or other authors seeking stories about a particular topic; no one but the author has the digital capability to categorize a story or provide any warnings about content (e.g., a note that a story includes a topic that may trigger discomfort in readers, such as torture or infant death). Additionally, authors in AO3 may alert readers that a story describes adult sexual content, but there is no warning, for example, that a story is about a character's sexuality. Topics about sexuality are so common within AO3 and other fan fiction archives that many readers expect the majority of stories to include some type of sexual activity, whether it is described explicitly or implied as part of a character's relationship. Stories discussed in this chapter, for example, often include a variety of tags related to the type of relationship (e.g., asexual Sherlock, bisexual John, first-time, marriage) that alert authors and readers to the subject matter. The stories analyzed in the following sections illustrate the variety of topics and purposes that fan fiction provides to the *Sherlock* fandom, including supporting new ways of reading the characters, expanding the *Sherlock* universe to include new professions or geographic locations, and even advocating greater representation of asexuals or understanding of asexuality.

Johnlock (Slash or Gen) in Popular Fan Fiction

In particular, slash fan fiction has benefited from the move from paper to digital prose as a means to reach more readers and have a greater impact, even secondarily, on advocacy. When fanzines were available only in print, a person wanting to participate in reading or commenting upon the stories had to seek those individuals who were in the know, thus risking judgment, especially if the stories deal with a slash relationship. When print was the dominant format for fan fiction, readers could not anonymously search for stories about homosexual, bisexual, or asexual characters, much less find links to related sources of information or become involved in anything but a face-to-face conversation about asexuality.

According to Francesca Coppa's essay, "A Brief History of Media Fandom," "[t]he movement of media fandom online as well as an increasingly customizable fannish experience, moved slash fandom out into the mainstream" (54). In fandom's past, slash zines had been quietly sold at conventions, sometimes literally under the table. Digital fandom has opened the likelihood for fans being able to find fiction forums and archives that specialize in slash. Fans who do not want to read slash have many other places to read non-homoerotic fiction. Thus, fans with similar tastes in fiction can interact with those who share their interests. As Coppa notes, "slash-friendly discussion lists allowed these fans to consolidate and talk openly to each other; many began to articulate their reasons for slashing, reading strategies, and politics" (54).

Sherlock fans with access to the Internet have not faced the restrictions inherent in reading printed fanzines or possibly justifying their selection of reading material. Since a very robust international fandom has become devoted to *Sherlock,* the series' messages about sexual orientation and non-heteronormative relationships have been particularly inspiring to fan fiction communities.

In the case of fan fiction, the creators and readers of these texts are most often heterosexual women whose desire to indulge in fantasies about homosexual couplings position them as queer. As well, taking "control" of characters via fan fiction can empower writers to explore relationships or activities that they would not in real life or even in another publication format.

Michel Foucault asserts that studying discourse may reveal important shifts in the "mechanisms of power" and social control. What is of paramount concern for Foucault is not to assess whether sexual acts are accepted or prohibited but to "define the regime of power-knowledge-pleasure" and to investigate who controls or, more specifically, which institutions control the discourse about sex and what affect this discourse has on the locus of power. Because computer-mediated texts afford writers relative anonymity and foster insular communities, people often feel freer to express desires in online communities that they might normally suppress. For example, women find a place to express and consume nonnormative desires in the supportive, insular communities who create, disseminate, critique, or simply passively read fan fiction. These actions and the positive reception that they receive empower those who participate to re-examine mainstream culture's dictums about what is acceptable sexual expression or even what are appropriate definitions of relationships.

Foucault's ideas about discourse as a system of rules that dictate individual truths can reveal some interesting ways in which online communities may become the arbiters of new rules and shifting individual truths. For example, while dominant discourse tries to enforce one objective truth (e.g., *Sherlock*'s creators and actors insisting that both Sherlock and John are heterosexual and merely feel platonic, brotherly love for each other), this objective truth is always situated within the framework of the subjective "faith" of its constituents in what is being posited. Fortunately, according to Coppa, "Media fandom may now be bigger, louder, less defined, and more exciting than it has ever been. Arguably, this is fandom's postmodern moment, when the rules are 'there ain't no rules' and traditions are made to be broken" (57). For example, AO3 stipulates that any type of story is allowed within an adult fan fiction community and that bashing or harassing writers for their plotlines or characterizations is forbidden in order to promote a mutually supportive creative community. Members "police" comments and report trolls who only post hurtful comments. Authors' right to create and share stories that may support or refute the "official" view of characters' sexuality, however, is not challenged on AO3. The following examples of Johnlock include both slash and gen (i.e., general or non-sex-specific) stories that illustrate the wealth of creative fan responses to the television series' canon.

Johnlock is not limited to stories set within the parameters of the television series. Many AU stories also are slash and have additional tags to identify them (e.g., parentlock, in which John and Sherlock eventually decide to raise a child or children—John's, Sherlock's, a blended family, a family with at least one adopted child). A further extension of this AU category, perhaps fulfilling some fans' wish for John and Sherlock to have children within a heteronormative setting, is the Omegaverse, where

Sherlock or John is able to bear the other's child, although each retains male sexual characteristics.

Both "The Blog of Eugenia Watson," a multi-chapter story receiving, by July 2017, more than 87,000 hits since 2014, and "The James Holmes Chronicles," earning more than 79,000 hits since it began in 2013, deal with adoption of a child. Both stories continue to receive thousands of hits per year and have earned more than 2,700 kudos each. In the former, author Mad_Lori, a highly popular writer in this fandom, creates a scenario in which Sherlock and John live across the hall from John's ex-wife and mother of his teenaged daughter, Eugenia. Sherlock, who first taught Eugenia to play chess, pays for her chess tutor and eventually adopts her so he can parent her during international tournaments. During one trip, Sherlock is kidnapped by shadowy figures determined to influence how the world is run and who want brilliant, problem-solving Sherlock to further their cause. Of course, after months in captivity, Sherlock manages to return home. Throughout the story, not only at the heartfelt reunion of this family, Sherlock's and John's deep bond helps them both parent Eugenia, who fiercely loves all her parents. In this slash story, John is bisexual, and Sherlock is only attracted to John.

"The James Holmes Chronicles" involves topics like child abuse and recovery, which might trigger detrimental responses in readers. Nonetheless, this series has become very popular. The author, prettyvk, slowed the publication of later chapters because of family responsibilities (according to her comments about the story), but the multi-chapter story concluded a first arc, and chapters have gradually been added to the second arc. James is Jim Moriarty's son, who Sherlock rescues, physically and emotionally. He provides the stability of his and John's home at Baker Street but alone adopts James. Sherlock's uncertainty about parenting, as well as John's calming influence, bind both "parents" and child. Although John and Sherlock are not married, they both are involved with James' welfare, and, just as in the television series, John often explains and illustrates the emotions that Sherlock has difficulty understanding or interpreting.

All these AU parentlock stories or series become "alternate" because of a change in the Sherlock-John relationship and the inclusion of a child who becomes theirs. In these stories, only the family dynamic differs from television canon. Sherlock still is a detective who, often with John, solves crimes and has clients. John and Sherlock still bicker and misunderstand each other at times while remaining loyal to each other.

During Season Four, fans could interpret "parentlock" as part of the television series' canon. As a single parent to baby Rosamund (Rosie) following the events of "The Six Thatchers," John struggles with parenthood. Fan fiction published while Season Four episodes were being broadcast often portrays Sherlock as loving Rosie, whether he is babysitting her (as shown in a scene from "The Six Thatchers") or helping to raise her (as suggested by the concluding montage in "The Final Problem"). Parentlock, set in an alternate universe or broadly within the plot of Season Four, is a consistently favorite fan fiction (sub)category that either embraces a non-heteronormative family or reconstructs reality to make John and Sherlock more heteronormative.

The television series consistently toys with the idea that Sherlock might be sexually interested in women. For example, in the fourth season, Irene Adler's name comes up a few times. John hears her signature orgasmic text tone on Sherlock's phone while the two are working through their estrangement in light of Mary's death. Sherlock admits that Adler texts him, but, for the most part, he ignores the messages. John insistently tells Sherlock that he should answer the texts and pursue the relationship, because it, like his marriage to Mary, could be over all too soon ("The Six Thatchers"). In "The Final Problem," Sherlock is goaded by his newly revealed sister Eurus to play one of his violin compositions for her. When he begins to play Irene's theme, first heard in the second season episode "A Scandal in Belgravia," Eurus asks if Sherlock has had sex, because the passion-infused music indicates he has. Sherlock, characteristically, does not reveal his level of sexual experience or his orientation, but the implication of his continued contact with sexually interested Adler is that the two may be in or on the verge of a heterosexual sexual relationship, despite Adler's lesbian orientation or apparently long-standing partner. However, the end to the fourth season provides an additional, perhaps alternate, interpretation of Sherlock's sexuality or preferred type of love relationship, which does not include Irene Adler.

According to some fans interested in Johnlock, the Season Four finale, "The Final Problem," makes parentlock television canon. A closing montage shows Sherlock taking Rosie from John to point out something to her. The next image is of Sherlock handing Rosie to John, who smiles at his growing baby girl. The family (because it is revealed in this episode that Sherlock considers John to be family) seems at home on Baker Street, the base from which Sherlock and John, audiences are led to believe, continue their case-solving adventures together. Because the montage seems to be set months after Mary's death, it suggests that, at least while Rosie is a baby, she and John spend a great deal of time with Sherlock and may live in 221B. The episode's glimpse of potential parentlock encourages and seems to validate this fan reading of the series.

Meta and Other Nonfiction Creative Works

A nonfiction category nonetheless included within the fiction archive is tagged "Meta." The articles include everything from analysis of a single episode to a running commentary about the meaning of episodes within the series' themes, from exploration of a single item (e.g., John's RAMC mug and what it indicates about his military service) to a character's long-term development, from details about a location or setting to clues about characters because of their clothing. *Sherlock* fans often assume there are more clues to the plot because this is the story of a brilliant but, as later episodes illustrate, sometimes fallible deduction specialist. As Mark Gatiss noted before the fourth season debuted, "people also find things that aren't there.... And then miss the blindingly obvious things that are there. People read an awful lot into it" (Sommers). Meta articles encourage this close reading of the series and discussions of what the scriptwriters and showrunners intend, and more than 690 have been published by July 2017. They help writers to develop theories (e.g., M theory, referring to the many characters whose name begins with M and their connections) and provide supporting evidence. Authors of meta articles, who also write fan fiction, supply other authors with guidance to improve their stories (e.g., ways to write realistic BSDM, facts about the British school system). They also present technical information and point out plot holes, which can fuel the creation of additional fan fiction.

One example of a highly popular meta article (nearly 12,000 hits within 3 years) about the content of an episode and its ramifications is "Let's Play Murder," which attempts to answer the question of whether Mary Watson aims to kill Sherlock or, as Sherlock later explains to John, whether she actually knew how to shoot Sherlock in the chest while giving him a good chance of survival. (Sherlock is declared clinically dead in the hospital but miraculously hauls himself back to life after a lengthy post-shooting visit to his Mind Palace in "His Last Vow.")

cookieswillcrumble, writer of this multi-chapter meta, is a surgeon who also has taught anatomy to university students. This *Sherlock* fan includes both screen caps from "His Last Vow" and detailed anatomical drawings to support her argument that Sherlock is very lucky (and his love for John miracle inducing) not to have died from the injury or complications that could/should compromise his survival. In later chapters going off on a tangent from the original argument, cookieswillcrumble analyzes John's curriculum vita (CV) and his credentials as a doctor. Based on her knowledge of and experience with British medical education, she raises questions about the short CV and John's compressed time frame for his internship. Perhaps, according to this meta, John does not act as "doctorly" as he should and might not be as all-knowing as viewers expect him to be. By balancing the fiction of *Sherlock* with the reality of Sherlock's gunshot wound, cookieswillcrumble helps readers understand how much creative license the scriptwriters have taken—and how much weight is being given to Sherlock's love of John as the "cure" for a fatal gunshot wound. The reader-friendly presentation of a highly technical explanation of Sherlock's injury and prognosis earned this meta more than 640 kudos by July 2017, making it one of the most-favored metas in the archive.

A popular meta representing another type—advice to writers—is wordstrings' "An Open Letter About Fic Writers to Fic Readers," which, by July 2017, has received nearly 780 kudos. It provides insight to the practices of fan fiction writers and ways to meet reader expectations while not compromising the writer's vision or pressuring the writer to change a publishing schedule or the direction the story is taking. This meta is a short list, but the tone and quality of the advice reflect the ideal relationship between writer and reader and encourage writers and readers to follow its advice.

These examples highlight the important role of meta articles within a fan fiction archive. They may serve different purposes, but they ground the series and fan fiction within the reality of writing.

Conflict with Mainstream Media Representations of Fandom

As potentially empowering as fan fiction communities may seem as safe spaces for creative, free expression, an example of mainstream media's intercession occurred when Caitlin Moran, a U.K. journalist and autobiographical author, brought fan fiction to a question-and-answer session with *Sherlock*'s lead actors, following a public screening of an episode in 2014. She asked Cumberbatch and Martin Freeman to read the story aloud, like a script, claiming that it was innocent. However, as the actors read their characters' dialogue, it became apparent that the story was, as much fan fiction is, sexually graphic. According to *The Daily Dot*, the writer of the fan fiction, Mildredandbobbin, was "mortified." Mildredandbobbin told the *Daily Dot* via Tumblr that she was "appalled" that Moran had used her work "for cheap laughs" (Romano). Although the writer enjoyed the relative freedom, anonymity, and popularity afforded in a digital community, her work had become, out of its original context, the butt of a mainstream media joke (as often occurs when a fandom is discussed publicly by those who are not involved in it). This exposure to the censure of the creative discourse of fan fiction reinforces Foucault's and others' perceptions regarding the power of dominant discourse to subvert (e.g., make fun of) alternative epistemologies.

There is some good news, however, for those fan fiction writers vested in minority voices. This incident has also inspired at least a few fan fiction writers to "come out of the closet," to claim their works publicly and take a stand for their value. As Brooke Magnanti reminded *Telegraph* readers after this incident, "*Sherlock* itself, the show, is also fanfic ... based after all on Arthur Conan Doyle's beloved character." Simply because Moffat's and Gatiss' adaptation is sanctioned by the BBC and broadcast worldwide gives it public acceptance does not mean that others' reinterpretations of Conan Doyle's characters should be suspect or dismissed simply because they do not have the backing of a broadcast network. Magnanti notes the possible outcomes of Moran's "outing" of a fan fiction writer in a public forum: "It's entirely possible that thanks to *Sherlock* fanfic, someone who never before considered writing professionally might decide to give it a try. It's also possible that some who considered doing so may now be scared to, fearing the long memory of the Internet and the ridicule they might receive." Her final advice to fan fiction writers illustrates the power of digital fan fiction communities and the support they receive from within those communities: "[T]o those [fearful writers] I say: forget the haters, sally forth and conquer all worlds. There is nothing shameful about stretching your wings."

Given the potential power of advocacy through fan fiction and comments/links to outside sources of information, fan fiction writers can play an important role not only in the expansion of a fandom and maintenance, through archives, of a series' enduring popular culture legacy but in the empowerment of individuals. Fan fiction can be much more than entertainment or creative interaction with a beloved series like *Sherlock*, although these functions are worthwhile; it can foster a supportive community and allow writers and readers to "spread their wings" to soar in new directions.

3

Beauty and the Beastly
Navigating Fan Websites

Long gone are the days of a single, unified fan club devoted to a television series or an actor, one that typically published a newsletter or fanzine and organized group communication to send to a star's management. Digital fandoms are oriented far more toward individuals, who publish their own information and decide how best to honor or adore the object of their affection.

Members of a digital fandom like *Sherlock* visit many web platforms daily, some people spending hours seeking, reading or viewing, creating and publishing, and sharing information. Much of the communication with other fans does not require a great deal of thought or preparation—such as the production of a 140-character (plus graphics) message that can be sent instantly to followers or Twitter at large and automatically reposted on other social media sites. Fans can volley dozens of messages daily in response to mainstream media sources of news, interviews, and reviews; new *Sherlock* content; messages from the series' official voices (e.g., tweets from Amanda Abbington or Sue Vertue); and other fans' comments. Communication requiring more time or thought, such as a video or a textual blog, is technically simple to publish. Many fan sites promote daily blogs, a feature that helps to grow a fan's reputation as the blog gains followers. Fan sites without new content for a few days may lose visitors—many who might never return—and decrease the fan's credibility or status within the digital community, so there is a lot of pressure on content creators. Archival websites require continuing management and maintenance, sometimes for years, which is certainly a great commitment of time and energy.

Sherlock Holmes and Benedict Cumberbatch fans who added *Sherlock* as a secondary fandom have developed sections within their long-running fan sites just for *Sherlock*, but their Sherlock Holmes fandom—and websites—likely will continue long after this television adaptation. Sherlock-Holmes-Fan.com, for example, is dedicated to all Sherlock Holmes fans, whether they encountered the Great Detective "on TV, in a movie, or through his stories." The website has a tab for BBC *Sherlock*, but that section is only one among many.

Fan sites also have become more than mere websites; they embody a complete web presence. Whether a group-run, semi-official site like Sherlockology or an independent individual fan's site, the website is usually the largest repository of information about *Sherlock* or Cumberbatch. It also may be the most permanent among associated social media sites affiliated with a website—although "permanent" is a misnomer in a digital fan community. In addition to the website serving as a blog or art space and archive, fans' web presence frequently includes at least one social media site like Twitter and a page-format site like Facebook. Tumblr became a favorite place for *Sherlock* or Cumberbatch discussions and the even more frequent sharing of photos, videos, and animations. For example, in addition to the Sherlockology website, in 2017, fans running the site also monitor and produce content for Twitter, Tumblr, YouTube, Instagram, Pinterest, and Twylah. The content varies in size and format (e.g., prose, still graphic, animation, video), depending on what is appropriate for that platform. However, the topics of digital conversation often overlap. Although individuals may not opt for as broad a coverage on as many platforms, most fans with a website devoted to fandom set up interlocking links—where one site feeds information to another—or post icons to connect one site with another; in 2017, Instagram, Twitter, and Tumblr tend to be favored. The Cumberbatchweb fan site, which has unofficially served as a link between the actor and fans to announce news about Cumberbatch's participation in events, began as a result of the fan's love at first viewing of *Sherlock* and the actor portraying the title character. According to the FAQ page, 225,000 unique visitors check the site each month, with 260,000 followers across all social media platforms: Twitter, Tumblr, and YouTube. However, Twitter is linked to more web pages on this site, and recent tweets are directly fed to the website. Both Sherlockology and Cumberbatchweb have become go-to sites for fans of, respectively, *Sherlock* and Cumberbatch. Each provides a different focus, tone, and style of content geared toward the needs of different groups within fandom. Each requires a great deal of work to provide a visually interesting, newsworthy site that is updated frequently. Because these sites were not created and are not being maintained by the BBC, Hartswood Films, or anyone associated with Cumberbatch, the fan labor is "free," donated by fans to their "hobby" interest; the sites are not intended to generate income for those who developed them. However, to defray the costs of maintaining a web domain and server, both sites display Donate buttons where fans can provide financial support. Not all fan sites do so, but those with heavy traffic often need financial help in keeping a site up and running, especially when it has become an archive as well as a news source.

The tension between the industry of all things *Sherlock* and fans laboring for the love of their favorite show has led Paul Booth to observe that

> fandom and the media industry must exist together; one necessitates the other. Media play is finding those nuanced moments when fandom and the industry are discursively interactive. Those moments reveal sites of power struggle, where sometimes fandom asserts itself and other times the industry claims ownership.... Media play happens because of the emotional connection to a media or text.... Fans become part of the industry just as the industry relies on fans.

Booth's observation accurately positions fans as both having power and as being reliant on the media machinations associated with the objects of their affection. These negotiations very often take place in both overt and covert ways in online spaces where fan voices are amplified in certain circumstances through the digital platform and because of the kind of notoriety that the products these fans produce and maintain have gained.

Copyright Ownership and Violations: Tension Over the "Ownership" of Digital Information

Although television series generally benefit from a fandom's enthusiasm and support, the balance of power regarding the ownership of texts, including images on any platform, legally is tipped to the creator of the text. The publicity photographs and videos produced by the BBC to promote *Sherlock* are owned by the network, for example. When Cumberbatch is interviewed on a chat show, the program is copyrighted by the creators of that show. However, digital fandom more commonly operates on a principle of open sharing. A tweet, blog, or post that other fans find interesting or newsworthy is shared with others. The mere presence of retweet, email, reblog, and other share-type icons encourages fans to immediately take content from one site and share it via their own. The idea that someone else may "own" that information and not want it distributed freely and free of charge seems foreign to the concept of a true digital community. The following examples illustrate the potential for conflict within the *Sherlock* digital community when not every fan who has created content (i.e., taking and posting a photograph, writing a blog or a story) wants it reposted somewhere else. More formally, the owners of information that makes money for them (e.g., photographers who sell images to publications, television production companies, networks, authors with books about *Sherlock*) are likely to assert their copyright ownership and stop the illegal sharing of information.

Many fans gladly post photographs they have taken at conventions or to red carpets, and they do not mind if their sometimes grainy or blurred photos or selfies are cross-posted on numerous fan sites. In fact, these images document an encounter with a famous person and can increase a fan's recognition within fandom and status as someone who not only attends an event but has met a star. Although the photograph owner's work has been taken, most likely without permission, and pinned on someone else's Pinterest site or added to a Tumblr collage, the fan-owner does not mind because the photograph does not infringe on his or her right to make money from that photograph. Unless the site where the fan-owner posted the image automatically holds the copyright to whatever is posted, then the fans who share the photo on numerous fan sites do not have to worry about a copyright violation.

What is more important, however, is that many fans who routinely copy and paste photographs from one fan site to another or give unofficial "copyright credit" to the fan site originally posting the image do not realize that they are breaking U.S. copyright law. (Other countries have even stricter definitions of what is copyrightable and what constitutes a violation.) Because graphics are a key part of most fan sites, especially on Tumblr, copying and sharing images is common, and most people do not stop to ask whether they can use an image on their site.

Two examples within *Sherlock* fandom illustrate some common misuses of copyrighted photographs and the consequences. A flurry of messages was blasted in July 2016 when one fan's posted photo was "borrowed" by numerous other fans without the photograph owner's permission. She did not want the photo spread across fandom and sought to have the image removed from sites by reporting a copyright violation. The resulting discussion was posted on the Merely Contemplating fan blog and reposted on Cumberbatchweb, where it was likely to reach even more readers because it is a leading fan site for Benedict Cumberbatch. Under the blog heading "OK, I received the final copyright violation warning," blogger larygo admitted that she had posted a photograph of Cumberbatch and Freeman, in their roles as Sherlock and John, which was taken by a fan during the public filming of a *Sherlock* episode. The photo originally was posted on the fan/photographer's site, and those fans following the #Setlock hashtag had viewed or shared it. However, because the photographer did not want the photo to be distributed, larygo received a copyright violation from Tumblr, the site's second such violation. The blogger warned other fans to remove the photo from their sites.

larygo's strategy had been to cite the location where she pulled the image, but that did not prevent a copyright violation notice. The blogger also felt victimized because the fan/photographer did not contact her first to ask that the photo be removed and instead resorted to contacting the web host about a copyright violation. Furthermore, larygo noted that the photograph was on many other fans' Tumblr sites, providing a possible rationalization for posting the copied photo in the first place and perhaps indicating the fan's frustration or displeasure with feeling singled out for a violation. The blogger further justified her fannish behavior by commenting that "the picture was beautiful so I couldn't resist.... I guess I have to be super-extra careful from now on; The next warning would terminate this blog. So if I disappear without warning in next few months, you'd know what happened. ~~God it could happen anytime~~" (larygo, "Merely Contemplating").

In reply, fans blogged their sympathy and reported that owners of other Tumblr sites also had to remove the photos. A few sites even had been deactivated as a result of receiving multiple copyright violations. Instead of feeling that the fan/photographer was morally or legally right in seeking copyright protection for the photograph or applauding the justice of the web host's policy on copyright violations, most commenters expressed their sorrow about the missing sites with posts such as "This is really sad. Hope [the fan] can activate her blog again, so many wonderful pics there" (elennemigo, "Merely Contemplating"). The discussion ends with a warning for fans not to repost the photographs from only this fan/photographer—not to stop "borrowing" photos from any site, fan or professional, without copyright permission.

One of the most interesting points from this discussion is that some of these *Sherlock* fans have received previous copyright violation warnings yet go on posting photos illegally. At least one commenter seems almost unable to control a proclivity for posting others' photos, even if it means that the website will be deactivated. After all, posting photos on Tumblr is "what fans do." Within fandoms, copyright violations are perceived mostly as a nuisance rather than a deterrent, and the belief that anything online is fair game for more than Fair Use is hard to change.

Even Cumberbatchweb, a longtime fan site with a seasoned webmaster who should be familiar with copyright restrictions, provided a cautionary tale. In a 2014 blog post and response to another fan's question about copyright, Cumberbatchweb described an interaction with a photographer requesting payment for images of *Sherlock* star Cumberbatch posted on the fan site. The webmaster had to pay the photographer a fee for the photos and subsequently deleted professionally taken images from the site. In response to the more recent conversation about copyright, Cumberbatchweb reminded other fans that "Any time you post or re-blog an image on tumblr that you don't own the copyright to and haven't licensed it's a breach of copyright and the photographer can come after you for both the license fee and damages" ("Merely Contemplating").

Cumberbatchweb discussed the right of professional photographers, who earn money by selling celebrity images, to protect their livelihood but wondered why an amateur photographer, who was not attempting to sell the #Setlock photos, would not want the images freely shared. Fan/ photographers do not face a loss of income if other fans repost their photos. Cumberbatchweb's comment implies the question, Why wouldn't a fan want his or her work shared across fandom, with or without permission? This question underscores many fans' reason for participating in fandom: sharing information. A secondary reason for wanting one's work shared with others, especially if one's name is attached to the work, is credibility and status within fandom. That someone would not share one or both of these reasons for posting a photograph may be difficult for many fans to understand. That may account for the sadness and shock/fear (the "omg" and "this is serious" comments, in addition to the "signal blast" reposting this discussion on many fan sites) that portray fans who illegally post images as the "victims" and the image-owner as someone creating a problem for fandom.

Professional sources of information such as the BBC, Hartswood Films, professional photographers, and publishers of for-profit publications may choose whether to go after individual fans who post images (most often) or scan entire articles without paying for the right to do so. Fan sites that help promote the series while illegally posting a few photos of the actors in costume may be ignored by *Sherlock*'s creators—the harm in alienating fans would outweigh the "good" of stopping the copyright violation. However, professionals who work independently, as do many photographers and writers, are far more likely to track down copyright violators—because their livelihood depends on the marketability of their work. In these cases especially, the law sides with the creators of information, not the fans who like it so much they want to share it with everyone free of charge.

Fans' Go-to Sites for Sherlock *Information*

From most to least official *Sherlock*-related websites, the following are designed either for (in the case of official websites) or by (in the case of semi-official or purely fan sites) *Sherlock* fans. All official sites and the semi-official site Sherlockology are included in this list. Unofficial fan sites listed here are ones with which most *Sherlock* fans are familiar because the fans maintaining these sites have more interaction with the series' insiders. For example, the Baker Street Babes have participated in official panels for BBC- and Hartswood Films'-promoted fan conventions like Sherlocked USA and have gained access to actors for their podcasts (e.g., Lara Pulver, Louis Moffat). Although Cumberbatchweb is not formally sanctioned by Cumberbatch or anyone professionally associated with him, this fan site is the oldest and arguably the most extensive site about the actor's roles, awards, and public appearances. Thus, the following range of websites encompasses the sites where fans return frequently to find new content related to *Sherlock*.

The BBC's Official Sites

As is typical of any BBC television show, the network keeps a web page active as long as a series has not been canceled. The *Sherlock* page is basic: a two-line series' synopsis; listings where viewers can see episodes on iPlayer (for U.K. fans) or BBC television or buy them online; news about the series (e.g., the Webby award, an interview with guest star Toby Jones, a discussion of #SherlockLive); photo galleries and video clips; and links to other sites, such as John Watson's blog. The background images feature Sherlock and John in 221B Baker Street, and the interface is easy to use. The design is a standard format for a BBC One television series, and it does what a broadcaster's page is expected to do: direct audiences to episodes first and provide promotional information to encourage fans to keep watching whenever new episodes arrive.

What was more interactive and special about *Sherlock*'s BBC web presence was the number of websites created early in the series to attract members of the growing digital fandom and provide them with additional content. These digital paratexts are evidence of showrunners leveraging the affordances of digital media in order to connect with and engage fans, and in doing so, these official sources mimic fan practices and co-opt what has traditionally been the territory of creative, enthusiastic fans. For example, Joe Lidster, who later developed the materials for the interactive Twitter game #SherlockLive, developed the content for four websites referencing characters and events from the series: The Blog of Dr. John H. Watson, The Science of Deduction, Molly Hooper, and Connie Prince. Of these, the longest-running blog was John Watson's, which periodically provided episode-related content up to Season Four, when a notice announced that it, too, would no longer be updated. Although the other series-related blogs began strongly, with high-quality content mirroring their characters' personality, they had much shorter lives related primarily to first-season episodes and were not as popular as John Watson's blog, with its details about cases and snarky comments posted by, for example, Harry Watson, Mike Stamford, or Sherlock.

The blog of Molly Hooper refers to "The Great Game," and Molly's diary-style blog, full of kittens and hope, includes nine entries from January 27–April 2, roughly encompassing the time she falls for Sherlock but then meets and dates Jim from IT. The January 28 entry gushes over Sherlock, who she does not name (until she slips on March 25): "He's so intelligent it's like he's burning. And he's so cool but not really. And he's fit. Oh, he is really fit. And I can't stop thinking about him." The tone of Molly's prose mimics not only the style of effusive diary-writers but also some types of fan fiction. Especially during the first season's episodes when Molly merely fawns over Sherlock, this blog succeeds in mimicking Molly's tone but also imitates some fans' practice as they write stories representing Molly. This practice becomes a "which came first" scenario in which fan and official content creators' praxis is intermingled.

Moriarty insinuates himself into Molly's life via a comment in the March 25 entry, as soon as Sherlock is mentioned. By March 30's series of messages between Molly and Jim, their romance is blossoming, but one day later Molly posts a frantic message in the hope that Jim will contact her or come to work. Apparently during an argument, Jim reveals that he is gay. The blog ends abruptly on April 2 when Jim turns out to be far more interested in crime and Sherlock than in her and Molly realizes "It was a lie. Everything he said." Although Molly's blog ends badly, the content provides details that fit between the scenes of "The Great Game." In this way, Molly's blog not only serves to provide *Sherlock* fans with additional background to enhance their enjoyment of the episode and become more involved with the series, but it once again mimics fan practice. Fan fiction regularly provides scenes missing from episodes that can help tie together the televised narrative. "Missing scene" fics are popular because they provide closure for fans, as does Molly's blog.

By providing links among the Connie Prince, Molly Hooper, and Science of Deduction websites as supplementary information to the first season's finale (at a time when no one knew if *Sherlock* would be successful enough to receive a BBC order for more episodes), the BBC ramped up interest in the episode and courted members of the series' digital fandom. Each character seems "real" because his or her voice, through content and comments, sounds just like an episode's spoken dialogue. The design also matches what viewers know of the characters' personalities. By designing websites specifically to coincide with "The Great Game," the BBC encouraged fans to "play" online and act as if Connie Prince, Molly Hooper, and Sherlock Holmes are real people with whom they can interact. However, this level of interaction did not occur during Season Two. Only The Science of Deduction and John Watson's blog continued past "The Great Game."

Like the Connie Prince and Molly Hooper websites, Sherlock's The Science of Deduction adds online content to enhance the digital fandom's enjoyment of "The Great Game." Sherlock invites visitors to help him solve a short series of Hidden Messages sent anonymously. In case fans of Molly's blog did not find Sherlock's, Molly attempted to solve one of the Hidden Messages and provides a link from her blog to Sherlock's. However, Sherlock's blog does not end after this episode, and its content spans about five episodes during Seasons One and Two.

For example, during first episode "A Study in Pink," John admits he checked out Sherlock's website. Sherlock is quite proud of his analysis of 243 types of tobacco ash, but John finds it boring. When fans visit The Science of Deduction, they see a DELETED!! link to the analysis—Sherlock's response to John's reaction. Without knowledge of the scene from "A Study in Pink," this deletion lacks context and is no longer humorous, so the fan-centric nature of these types of activities is tantamount to their success. Links also were made to John's summaries of cases (such as "The Blind Banker") presented in episodes; however, by 2017, several links were broken, indicating the BBC's lack of maintenance of the series' additional website content. One of the last references to an episode occurs in the Forum section, when a child asks Sherlock to help her find Bluebell, her pet rabbit, which is featured in the Season Two episode "The Hounds of Baskerville." Elsewhere in Forum posts, Sherlock complains that everyone prefers to read John's blog; therefore, he does not need to update his website. Logically, once Sherlock fakes his death at the conclusion of the following episode, "The Reichenbach Fall," The Science of Deduction would not be updated. However, it could have been revived during Season Three but was not. John Watson's blog continued through Season Four's "The Six Thatchers," and Sherlock occasionally and humorously commented on his friend's case descriptions and personal revelations.

Perhaps the series' popularity no longer required online games or additional content in order to keep fans interested, or perhaps a cutback of BBC resources may have doomed continuing interaction between television episodes and websites. The BBC's motivation for creating and maintaining digital paratexts is generally related to income. This limits the sites' viability in a way that fan-created texts are not limited because fans' motives are based on their passion, without concern for monetary gain.

The Blog of Dr. John H. Watson gained quite a fan following. Because, in the series, John's blog serves several purposes and John frequently is shown typing entries or bickering with Sherlock over a case title or description, this website was always likely to capture the most attention. It is the blog most faithful to John's character, episode plots, and the John-Sherlock friendship, and its existence in digital space makes the characters viewed on screen seem part of the real world. As such, the entries do more than entertain fans—the posts allow fans to become part of the series, just like the clients and other characters who comment on John's blog in an episode. Because blog entries provide John's perspective (and additional between-scenes details) for all episodes into Season Four, they also function similarly to fan fiction by providing banter among characters and filling gaps between scenes or episodes. For example, in a response to John's blog after his marriage to Mary Morstan, Sherlock calls the couple's honeymoon their "sex holiday." The term gained such popularity among fans who read John's blog that it later appeared in several fanfics. This entry also illustrates how life goes on for John, Mary, and Sherlock between televised episodes and helps fans feel that they are a part of the same digital world.

Although Mary's death and John's resulting abandonment of Sherlock provide a good reason for John to stop posting this blog, fans felt let down at its conclusion. A final post once Sherlock and John reunited and began their adventures again at the conclusion of "The Final Problem" would have provided better closure for fans, who checked the blog to see what John or other characters had to say about the latest televised case. As well, the blog provides additional comment about cases either referenced within an episode, such as "The Aluminium Crutch" in "A Scandal in Belgravia," or forming the episode's plot and given its title, such as "The Empty Hearse." John's blog not only bridges gaps between televised scenes but attempts to break the fourth wall and provide a realistic website experience for fans. It also heightens fans' awareness of John's and Sherlock's friendship through emotional entries, such as John's grief and eventual coming to terms with Sherlock's "death." The tone and level of detail keeps fans returning to the blog to revisit cases and glean more details about the characters' lives.

John's blog, both online and as depicted on television, has been so carefully scrutinized by fans that when John is shown typing his blog in "The Six Thatchers," fans complained that he is trying to type on a .jpg of the blog, not a text page (Freeth). Some took to Twitter with comments like "That awkward moment when John Watson is typing on a jpg image file ... #Sherlock #SherlockSeason4" (Minn). The blunder was covered in mainstream media, complete with a clip and highlighted photos showing the .jpg file's title. Media coverage illustrates *Sherlock* fans' attention to detail, even a tiny one on a televised computer screen that is not the camera's focal point. However, it also disappointingly supports fans' concern that John's blog was no longer considered an important part of the series and would not be continued online. A Reddit conversation about the blog included comments that Sherlock is rumored to tweet during Season Four, and the blogs no longer were needed as additional digital content (asdfreoiuzqwert) and, because the blog is a stand-in for the books Watson writes in the canon stories, that John may resort to another electronic format instead of a blog (lambrinibudget). Fans also wondered if the blog entries would be continued in the series and had only been discontinued in real life (lambrinibudget). That fans continued to discuss the blog and want to see additional entries well into Sherlock's fourth season indicates their interest in additional digital content supplied by official sources. Highly positive fan responses to #SherlockLive—as well as a fan-voted Webby award—should be a big hint to television broadcasters and production companies that a digital fandom like this one craves additional online content, particularly when more interactive elements fit well within the series' continuity. Interactive digital content also reifies the value of the creative praxis of fandom as effective and engaging enough to be co-opted by official *Sherlock* media creators.

Hartswood Films

Although Hartswood Films has produced other successful television series (e.g., *Coupling, Men Behaving Badly*), *Sherlock* by far exceeds previous productions. Not surprisingly, then, the Hartswood Films website provides the most information about *Sherlock*. Notices about the series' nominations and awards adorn the page. For fans, seeing *Sherlock* from a business rather than a story perspective adds another layer of knowledge to their understanding of the series.

Sherlockology

Shortly after *Sherlock* debuted in the U.K. in summer 2010, a small group of British Sherlock Holmes and *Sherlock* fans launched the website Sherlockology. It provides information about the television series, as well as Sherlock Holmes. The site includes a variety of content appropriate for fans of both Holmes and *Sherlock*, attracting not only the appreciation and attention of an increasingly large fan base but also of the producers of *Sherlock*. The showrunners became aware of Sherlockology because of its knowledgeable, professionally designed content and respectful attitude toward the series. By 2013, when *Sherlock* began filming its third season's episodes, fan volunteers from Sherlockology met with BBC representatives to discuss the website. The meeting led to this website being granted a semi-official status not offered to any other fan site. Although this seems like the ultimate goal of a fan site, this kind of status has benefits and drawbacks.

In recognition of Sherlockology's special status as a fan-operated website with insider access to the showrunners, producer Vertue wrote a promotional blurb for the website's home page: "Thanks Team Sherlockology for all your dedication, hard work and sleepless nights in getting your website to this level of class, accuracy and information. Certainly takes a lot of heat off ME having to do it!" (Sherlockology, "Sue Vertue, Hartswood Films"). By listing her name and the production company on this fan site, Vertue alerts anyone visiting the site that this group of fans achieved a new level of connection with the showrunners and cast. This statement increases the website's status (and that of its volunteer staff) and indicates that the information presented on this site has the blessing of the showrunners.

It also makes observers question the extent to which fan labor is being exploited by corporate entities. Sherlockology does not make a profit.

According to Bertha Chin in "Sherlockology and Galactica.tv: Fan Sites as Gifts or Exploited Labor?" using this kind of fan labor for the purpose of promoting the show is not as simple as the pure exploitation that is suggested by Vertue's comment, which acknowledges that the services that Sherlockology provides are the domain of her job as producer. However, fans who contribute to their fandom, according to Chin, participate in a "gift economy" in which the exchange for their labor is often pleasure and recognition. In the case of Sherlockology, the endorsement by Vertue is major recognition. In an attempt to re-frame how fan contributions are traditionally perceived as tertiary, Chin looks to the fans who create the content for their perception of the value of their fan-driven works. In an interview with Sherlockology founders/operators, Chin reports that they feel they are contributing to fan culture in a significant way and that is what is rewarding, not that they are serving the publicity machine for *Sherlock*. Fans who operate in online communities are often vested in more than just the object of their affection; they are focused on community building, though it is equally important to keep in mind that, as Hills explains, "commodification is—perhaps counter-intuitively—the glue that binds" the "affective fan labor" and corporate goals (Doctor Who 63).

The shift to a sanctioned website also indicates an important change in the content provided to fans via Sherlockology. Although the fan volunteers could still technically create any type of content for their site, they began to be provided information that no other fan site (or fans in general) could learn elsewhere. Thus, Sherlockology has become a means for showrunners, to a certain extent, to control the type of information presented to fans through a frequently visited website, as well as Sherlockology's social media presence. If Sherlockology would violate the trust in which the BBC and Hartswood Films has placed in it not to divulge spoilers (i.e., information about upcoming episodes not officially released to the public), for example, the team likely would find its access to actors and producers abruptly curtailed. However, in theory, Sherlockology can publish whatever it likes on its website. The variety of content illustrates the mediation between an international fan community desiring the latest in-depth information about Sherlock Holmes, *Sherlock*, or actor-related projects and the showrunners who wish to court fans but present only the amount and type of information they feel is beneficial to promoting the series.

Since its status change, Sherlockology has become, as its home page notes, "The Ultimate Guide for any BBC *Sherlock* Fan." Articles located under the News & Events menu illustrate the special relationship that the website has with the BBC and Hartswood Films and directs fans to unique content related to the series. The article "Sherlock: The Abominable Bride—Set Visit" is one example of the way Sherlockology's writers balance fans' enthusiasm for the series and desire to know the latest information with a more reserved journalistic style. The set-visit report was published on January 2, 2016, the day after the television special "The Abominable Bride" had been broadcast in the U.K. and U.S. and had begun to be distributed internationally to cinemas to reach an even wider audience. The date of the set visit, however, was February 3, 2015, nearly a year earlier. Although Sherlockology staff were invited to the *Sherlock* set for an exclusive behind-the-scenes visit, they were not allowed to publish the set report until after the episode had been broadcast. (Similarly, Sherlockology carefully times its episode reviews and avoids releasing any information that may inform fans of narrative content before an episode's release date.)

The set report offers tidbits that fans cannot read anywhere else. Along with journalists also invited to the set, the Sherlockology team explained that, upon arriving in Bristol, where filming was taking place, they and the journalists were "all herded into a relatively small holding room, where representatives from the BBC hand[ed] us various sheets of paper that we [had] to sign to prevent us saying anything about this trip until we're told that we can do so months later" (Sherlockology, "Sherlock: The Abominable Bride—Set Visit Report"). This comment underscores to readers two important facts about Sherlockology: it is granted the same status as professional journalists' publications, and the site is restricted in the same way as other mainstream news media and is not unregulated like most fan sites. The Sherlockology team interviewed cast members and showrunners and, eventually, presented their interviews online as part of the set report. Just like other journalists, they were not restricted as to the types of questions they could ask, so, on behalf of fans, they could pose questions that their readers would like to have answered. The only restriction in this case was the embargo on publication until the episode had been broadcast so that no spoilers would be published in advance. In addition to cast and crew interviews, the report features photographs taken on set that day, providing a unique "fan" perspective on the set visit and information that journalists did not publish in their publications. Sherlockology also maintains a more awestruck tone in the narration and a minute-by-minute account of the day's activities, a voice and organizational structure unlike the reports that typically appear in newspapers or magazines for a mainstream audience of casual *Sherlock* viewers.

Sherlockology resembles a mainstream news publication; however, unlike a mainstream media outlet, Sherlockology represents *Sherlock* fans and designs its graphical and textual elements for fans, with puzzles, calendars, and wallpapers, as well as extensive prose details about set visits and special events—all types of information found on typical fan sites rather than in journalistic articles. As well, Hartswood Films occasionally creates contests for Sherlockology followers and provides exclusive *Sherlock* prizes.

Sherlockology toes the line between being a site produced by ardent fans who provide inside information to other fans who lack the staff's access to *Sherlock* and serving as a quasi-official site supporting the BBC and *Sherlock's* producers by being deferential to showrunners, cast, and crew. The published description of the Sherlockology team's visit to the Cardiff set during filming of "The Empty Hearse" serves as an example of how these tensions play out. The Sherlockology team was left alone in a waiting room (green room) with a script on the table. The report of their temptation allows fans reading about the set visit to put themselves in the staffers' place:

> We resist the urge to look.
> Yes, we want to know, but with all the cast and crew working so hard, our conscience makes it clear that the solution [to Sherlock's return from the "dead"] deserves to be discovered while watching it on screen in the final cut [Sherlockology, "Sherlockology on Set"].

This paragraph echoes Moffat's and Mark Gatiss' attitude toward spoilers—that fans should not reveal anything about an episode before its broadcast. It also reassures the BBC and producers that the Sherlockology staff can be trusted.

Other details in the Sherlockology set report are likely to interest fans heavily invested in the series: "We do not miss the opportunity to get some advanced information on Sherlock's costume and particularly his new scarf. Benedict was given three to choose from, we're told." This type of detail is unimportant to casual viewers, and mainstream media seldom use a first-person narrative in their set reports.

In a *Telegraph* article about a set visit during filming of "The Abominable Bride," for example, journalist Tim Martin includes interviews with the series stars, referring to Benedict Cumberbatch as "Cumberbatch" rather than the familiar, fannish use of "Benedict" favored by Sherlockology. The article's emphasis on descriptions of what took place on set is used as transitions between interviews with cast members. The following description of the lead actors preparing for a scene illustrates a third-person, objective style typical of newspaper articles and different from Sherlockology's fan narrative:

> As Cumberbatch and [Martin] Freeman prepare to return to set, they mutter about the show's excursion into period drama. Freeman laments the fact that he can't get dressed by himself, while Cumberbatch has period arcana to deal with, including a fancy meerschaum pipe that is, he notes darkly, "a pyrotechnic pipe" [that might explode if he smokes it] [Martin].

The *Telegraph* article, like Sherlockology's report, provides details to interest highly invested fans, but the journalist does not include references to himself and merely reports what took place. Martin may or may not be a fan of the series or its actors, but readers cannot tell his bias from the style or content of his report.

Just as Sherlockology's behind-the-scene reports differ in tone and style from the majority of newspaper reports, so does the Sherlockology team's style differ from highly invested fans' reviews, either pro or con. The Sherlockology spoiler-free review of "The Empty Hearse" covers the plot's main points and assures fans that they will be satisfied with the episode. Unlike other fan reviews, Sherlockology's was posted before the episode was broadcast (indicating their special fan status) but did not reveal any surprises about the story or characters. The team's review is positive, interspersing supportive but unrevealing phrases like "making a triumphant return," "infused with uproarious comedy, wicked and knowing writing," and "brilliant" performances throughout the review (Sherlockology, "Sherlock S3E1").

In contrast, fan sites known for being pro–Cumberbatch or –*Sherlock*, such as Cumberbatchweb, offer gushing reviews presented in first person. Within one sentence, Cumberbatchweb describes "The Empty Hearse" as "emotional, exhilarating, audacious, and thrillingly clever." She also bases the review on the way she would have written the episode: "It's just chock full of so many lovely moments it's really hard to know where to start. If I had sat down before the episode aired & written myself a little checklist of things I'd like included in the episode ... the resulting list would have looked a lot like The Empty Hearse." In short, Cumberbatchweb gives a positive review because "The Empty Hearse" meets her expectations as a fan; she does not provide an objective assessment of the episode.

Cumberbatchweb's review also describes "Benedict's parents [who guest star in this episode] ... exuding warmth from every pore." Cumberbatch is "beyond brilliant," and Freeman is described as "fearless, brave, funny and very touching." This review with its superlative adjectives, use of first names, and comments about the lead actor's parents, not their characters, is typical of positive reviews posted on personal websites celebrating a series or an actor. The length of Cumberbatchweb's review is twice that of Sherlockology's and considerably longer than journalistic reviews, primarily because of effusive word choice and strings of superlatives. As these few examples illustrate, Sherlockology provides a midpoint between gushing fan reviews and unbiased mainstream media reports.

In addition, the site continues to build a fan community beyond the explicit control of showrunners or the BBC because fans can contact Sherlockology directly and develop a personal connection to the website team through online communication channels. For example, fans tweet Sherlockology with their comments about an episode or news about the series or actors and within a few minutes can view their tweets published on the Sherlockology site as the result of a direct feed from Sherlockology's Twitter account to the website. An autofeed supplies tweets to the Sherlockology website, but the staff monitors the tweeted content and can remove any tweets they find offensive. Fans send email to the team and receive a personalized response.

Fans who visit the site are consumers of information (and possibly merchandise), and the tone of all information is positive toward the cast, crew, and content of *Sherlock*. Although fans may feel that Sherlockology provides them direct access to the showrunners, this "access" is carefully managed by the Sherlockology staff and always under the scrutiny of the BBC and Hartswood Films.

Baker Street Babes

The 12 women known within fandom as the Baker Street Babes emphasize their approach "to the fandom from a female point of view," as they engage in "fun, lively conversations about the canon, film and television adaptations of Arthur Conan Doyle's work, and associated topics." Although they are well known from their participation in fan conventions, where they often host an official panel in addition to a table in the vendors' room, or events involving *Sherlock*'s actors, such as attending *Hamlet* and reporting their fan experience during and after Cumberbatch's performance, their greatest contribution to fandom is more than 80 podcasts by 2017. Specifically within *Sherlock* fandom they have interviewed actors David Nellist (Mike Stamford), Lars Mikkelsen (Charles Augustus Magnussen), and Jonathan Aris (Philip Anderson), among others. However, because their focus goes beyond *Sherlock* to other adaptations, they also have provided fans with intriguing insights to web-based series and recent books about Holmes by interviewing web designers and authors. This diversity helps attract new listeners to the podcasts and encourage new site followers (who can donate money to help support the site). It also helps ensure that this website will last beyond *Sherlock*, although *Sherlock* fans can return to listen to older podcasts during hiatuses and after the series' demise.

The Baker Street Babes' popularity is not limited within fandom; members have been featured in mainstream media such as *The Today Show, New York Times,* and *USA Today.* Through these interviews, they professionally represent fandom to the public. Because they are well-informed about Sherlock Holmes and fandom and their enthusiasm as fans is genuine but not over the top (as many in the public may expect), the Baker Street Babes help dispel the public image of "crazy fans." Through a variety of fan-oriented events and public presentations, they live up to their mission "to help provide a bridge between the older and often intimidating world of Sherlockiana and the newer tech savvy generation of fans that are just discovering the Holmes stories for the first time" ("About").

Three Patch Podcast

Similar to the Baker Street Babes, the group known as Three Patch Podcast have become well known from their podcasts. They cleverly take their name from Sherlock's dialogue in "A Study in Pink," when the consulting detective reveals he is wearing several nicotine patches to help him think; the case is a "three patch problem." Each podcast begins with Sherlock saying this line before the series' theme music comes up—a link to *Sherlock* that grabs listeners' attention and affirms that the podcast is designed for this adaptation's fans. Not only does the group's name harken to the beginning of *Sherlock* but to Arthur Conan Doyle's canon story "The Red-Headed League," on which Sherlock's dialogue is based. In this story, Holmes explains that the case is a "three pipe problem." Because modern Sherlock has given up smoking (at least during the first episode), he turns to patches instead of a Meerschaum pipe for his nicotine fix. The group's name alone lets fans know that its members are familiar both with the series and canon and should have a unique, entertaining perspective on fandom and the series. The site also promotes itself as "The World's Only Consulting Podcast," reminiscent of Sherlock being the world's only consulting detective. The group consists of 19 consulting fans—or current staff—and 3 retired consultants who produce the episodes and meet with fans at conventions.

The Three Patch Podcast team consults frequently with other fans at roundtable discussions. Each podcast is lengthy—from 1.5 to 3.5 hours each—and covers several topics. Even when *Sherlock* provides no new episodes to discuss, the podcasts continue; for example, Episode 65, released in June 2017, describes the Sherlocked USA convention. However, this group does more than talk about *Sherlock*; they also analyze fandom and fans' lifelong bonds within a fandom. Episode 64A invites fans over 40 to talk about their experiences within fandom. As well, the previous episode, "When I'm 64," looks at aging from a multitude of perspectives: the effect of the passage of time on Sherlock Holmes; in *Sherlock*, Mrs. Hudson's defiance of television stereotypes of older women; and Retirementlock fan fiction, stories in which Sherlock retires, usually with John and often to a quieter life in Sussex. Three Patch Podcast notes in their purpose statement that they are "dedicated to the fandom culture, social issues, creative works and analysis inspired by and related to the BBC *Sherlock* series" ("The Three Patch Podcast"). Although they also host a series of separate Spoilercasts, the regular podcasts are spoiler-free and are as likely to include guests' discussion of personal experiences as to dissect a *Sherlock* episode.

Social issues come to the fore in several podcasts. As only one example, Episode 52 is dedicated to 221B Pride, in which, among other segments, "we celebrate LBGTQIA+ Pride" and "discuss fandom as a queer-friendly space." This group, more than most who create podcasts to educate as well as entertain fans, studies fandom and helps fans share a variety of creative, social, and political experiences.

During Episode 52, three *Sherlock* fans who self-identify as, respectively, trans, asexual, and bisexual discuss their coming-out stories and the way fandom helped them learn about their sexuality. As one fan states, "Fandom helped me discover 'Oh, transgender is a thing and maybe I can be that and it makes sense'.... Fandom helped me learn and discover my sexuality." Education and advocacy, as discussed in Chapter 7, are a strength of *Sherlock* fandom. When fans can hear—not just read about— other fans discussing their sexuality casually and openly, they better understand that coming out within a fandom can be a supportive experience and they can turn to fandom to learn more about sexual orientations and identities. Hearing someone discuss coming out can make the story seem more personal, as if the podcast speaker is talking to the listener. Also, the podcast's roundtable conversation format helps fans listening to an archived episode, even years later, realize that they are not alone in their coming-out experiences or in their search to learn more about their sexual identity.

Other Fan Sites

Although many individual fans also maintain websites devoted to Sherlock or Cumberbatch, they also band together—as Sherlockology's team did to create a fan site, without any expectation that its quality and depth would one day make it a semi-official site. Similarly, Cumberbatchweb has gained less official status but still receives information from Cumberbatch's management/PR people to pass along to fans. For this reason, Cumberbatchweb has attained a higher status than other fan sites for the actor. Not every individual- or group-created fan site becomes as well known by *Sherlock* insiders as well as fans or has been recognized for its quality and variety of content in multiple media. However, the websites mentioned in this section have attained that status—all because of the dedication, knowledge, and creativity of fans donating their time and resources to share information with other fans.

Digital Culture and Fan Interactions with Industry Insiders

As evident from this list, fan-based knowledge communities design their digital spaces and interactions in ways that reflect their affiliations and, more broadly, their goals. The dwindling divide between those who have been traditionally considered "producers" (e.g., actors, showrunners, production companies, broadcast networks) and those who have been traditionally considered "consumers" (e.g., fans) has led to particular ways for fans to assert their identity as fans and to contribute to a broader understanding of fan culture and community, especially as interactions transpire in digital spaces.

Unsanctioned fan sites may influence or undermine mainstream media's attempts to control digital content regarding a television series. As well, such fan sites may affect the showrunners' ability to control perceptions regarding the series or actors' ability to control public perceptions of their work or personal lives. This lack of control can be perceived as problematic when, for showrunners, controlling perceptions about their creation is an integral part of staying relevant and staying on the air, which is what allows them to continue profiting from their work. For actors, maintaining a positive public persona and avoiding career-damaging scandals is paramount to ensuring that they are bankable; not only talent or luck determines who is cast in career-making roles. Although what fans write in their blogs or tweet is not a primary factor in business decisions about an actor or a television series, fans are still consumers with the power to reach other fans, and *Sherlock*'s official representatives sometimes use mainstream media to counteract or contradict the opinions of particularly those fans who are most vocal. Fan criticism of Season Four *Sherlock* episodes, for instance, encouraged Gatiss to strike back in the mainstream press. Cumberbatch's irritation with fans who consider his wife and child (now children) as "PR stunts" is evident in his 2016 *Vanity Fair* interview (Schulman). If their websites and social media posts receive enough hits to attract the attention of mainstream media, fans garner a wider public audience and sometimes the perhaps unwanted or negative attention of showrunners or actors. Fans seem to understand that a loud enough group can encourage others to buy tickets—or not, lead a "save our series" campaign or let a series go quietly, and provide topics for mainstream entertainment news. Digital communities that take up an issue en masse know how to use websites and social media to get their message across.

The problem is that there is no such thing as a unified digital fandom—or any unified type of fandom. Digital communities, in particular, are made up of smaller, more insular subcommunities or even individuals with their own agendas or opinions. When subgroups or individuals begin to believe that their ideas are the only correct ideas and—as is being fostered within the political climate in the U.S. and U.K. in the mid–2010s—an "us" versus "them" perspective is the only viable reality, groups within a fandom attack and defend each other. As the following section illustrates, the dark side to the *Sherlock* fandom, as well as many other digital communities, is becoming increasingly problematic and violent.

The Dark Side of Digital: Trolling and Doxxing

In the best scenarios, fans help develop supportive communities; in the worst, they hope to undermine fans critical of the series or actors, sometimes in the quest to gain acknowledgment or praise from a favorite actor or showrunner. The Internet is a Wild West of unbridled opportunity for fans to post whatever they want, with seemingly little legal intervention.

Many fans are unaware of the laws that are in place in the U.S. or U.K. regarding anything from copyright violations to cyberstalking. They are shocked when the anonymity of digital communication is shattered, either by fans doxxing others (i.e., publicly revealing someone's true identity and personal information) or by law enforcement tracking down the source of threats or attacks. A fan-view of the freedom afforded by digital spaces often seems to come with no expectation of restrictions—or at least none that cannot be circumvented. Actions that fans might never take if they had to face their victims somehow seem okay in anonymous cyberspace.

An extreme example of interfandom fighting and the use of a digital community to be anything but supportive centers around the Fellowship of Erdemhart (TFOE) fan website. The site owner's opinions about Cumberbatch and his personal life, primarily his marriage, became part of the daily discussion of how his private life affects his performance in and availability for *Sherlock*.

In the latter half of 2014, little was happening in the Sherlockverse. The broadcast of "The Abominable Bride" was more than a year away, and #Setlock activities would not begin until January 2015. Cumberbatch fans within the *Sherlock* fandom turned their attention toward the actor's many other television or film projects as topics for fan blogs. A much higher level of scrutiny befell Cumberbatch—by entertainment journalists and fans alike—when the actor began participating in the Oscar campaign for the film in which he starred, *The Imitation Game*. During this period, he also was in the latter stages of filming television miniseries *The Hollow Crown* and facing interviews and publicity for the *Penguins of Madagascar* and *The Hobbit: The Battle of the Five Armies*. To fans' surprise, during this busy time, Cumberbatch announced his engagement to Sophie Hunter; the couple married a week before the Academy Awards in 2015. As a result of Cumberbatch's engagement and marriage, a schism developed within his and, to a certain extent, *Sherlock* fandom, and opposing groups often published their ridicule or anger on individual fan blogs. The subgroups became known as skeptics and nans or nannies. *Skeptics* are those presenting photographic evidence and textual analysis of the Cumberbatch-Hunter relationship to illustrate it as a public relations stunt gone wrong; *nans* or *nannies* are those who gush about the couple's love and seek to protect the couple's privacy at all costs. In addition to these categories of fans facing off regarding the *Sherlock* star's personal life, *stans* seem to believe that Cumberbatch can do no wrong, and anyone who implies or posts anything critical of him, his personal life, or his work must be at least publicly scolded and at worst obliterated from the digital community. Although *stans* (often equated with uber or super fans) is a common fandom term to denote those who go to extremes to meet or defend the object of their devotion, *skeptics* and *nans* are labels more specifically used in Cumberbatch or *Sherlock* fandom.

When some fans devoted not only to Cumberbatch but to policing the Internet to stop any negative discussion about him read some of TFOE's blog posts, they identified her as a skeptic and decided to harass or doxx her if she did not stop publishing her opinions. In her blog, TFOE discussed what had been done to her as part of the doxxing. Of course, cyberbullies warned her that they would "tell on" her to the object of her fan affection, Benedict Cumberbatch. They indicated that they would alert him and his management team to the blog. The real threat to a fan who goes to the trouble of creating a fan site and updating it nearly every day is that the star or celebrity will dislike them. Whereas many fans seek the celebrity's personal attention and want more than anything to be recognized and applauded for being such a great fan, that goal is based on the assumption that the star/celebrity will have only a highly positive impression of the fan and be pleased with his/her activities. For Cumberbatch to acknowledge his disapproval or dislike of an individual fan might be more difficult to accept than threats to that fan's life or lifestyle. Retribution from a star/celebrity seems more likely or possible than cyberbullies' threats to have someone fired from a job, banned from a theater, exposed to the police or other authorities—or even be killed. Unfortunately, these types of threats have been made to more than one fan within the *Sherlock* fandom.

As stated in TFOE's blog posts, she received death threats online, as well as in phone calls, after her private contact information had been made public. Even more potentially intrusive to TFOE's private life and that of her family, the harassment included threats to contact TFOE's local police department about her activities, although the blogger wondered why the police would be interested in a teenager's blog about a television star. The cyberbullies also threatened to call Child Protective Services because TFOE's parents allowed her to have a fan blog, and they phoned administrators from the Board of Education (TFOE, 9 Nov. 2015). In short, according to information from TFOE's series of posts, cyberbullies, in their attempt to "protect" Cumberbatch from non-threatening and unproven claims about his personal life as expressed on a teenager's fan blog, threatened to or actually contacted the authorities that they believed could squelch TFOE's speech by possibly incarcerating her, expelling her from school, and/or separating her (and possibly any siblings) from her parents.

The resulting discussion of doxxing among fans with similar "skeptic" blogs indicates the severity and prevalence of this problem. An anonymous commenter noted in the conversation taking place in the Sophie Hunter Gossip Blog (18 Sep. 2015) that anyone who expresses "radical" opinions in an online blog will somehow be punished for it by readers who disagree with the site owner's or commenter's ideas. (This comment refers only to chatter within fandoms devoted to actors, not "radical" opinions about, for example, potential terrorism. Most topics discussed on fan blogs do not involve life-altering or -threatening content.) Annashipper agreed, citing her experience with cyberbullies who partially doxxed her by analyzing information and photographs from her Facebook account. She listed other fans-with-blogs (e.g., wikianonbc, sophiehuntergossipblog, thefellowship-of-erdemhart, cumberbees, gatorfisch, carmen1969stuff, mimichanelle, ummzaksbest) who had been similarly doxxed. She questioned why some fans think doxxing is acceptable or why threats seem an appropriate punishment to "those who have it coming" because they post opinions disliked by these bullies.

As a result of being doxxed more than once (including multiple death threats), TFOE posted a farewell message before changing the content of her website only to photos of Cumberbatch and Sherlock. In it, she expressed her weariness with constantly being "devalued" for having a blog, and, "after the stress of real life and other stuff, it gets frustrating that not even in what was supposed to be a safe haven do I get any respite" (24 Apr. 2016). Like TFOE, other bloggers within *Sherlock* or Cumberbatch fandom simply disappear online after they have been threatened or doxxed; they delete their digital footprint as much as possible, destroying their creative works from blogs or archives and, if they choose to reinvent themselves under a different name later, attempt to hide any former identities or associations with factions within a fandom. Even when a blog, for example, is not deleted, the blogger usually resorts to removing all personal statements and eliminating the ability for future readers to post comments. When a web host cannot provide a safe space for the fans who post their information, harassed or threatened fans leave the digital community when they feel they have no other recourse or protection from cyberbullying.

That the Internet can be a scary place, in which doxxing and trolling often occur, does not lessen the fact that digital communities can be welcoming places that may educate, entertain, or encourage advocacy among their members. As noted in this and other chapters, websites run by a group (such as Sherlockology or the Asexual Visibility and Education Network) or a fan fiction archive (such as AO3) are monitored by more than one person who operates the site. The website may publish rules of conduct to determine who may upload or post information—and the consequences if the rules are broken. These fan-oriented sites encourage the community to help regulate behavior. Only registered users may post content to the Sherlockology site, for example, and they must abide by the legal disclaimer provided on the website ("Terms and Conditions"). AO3 members may be blocked from using the site and their posts removed if they verbally attack other members; a key line in the Abuse explanation in the Terms of Service is "We are most concerned with people who are actively and deliberately hostile to the community" (Archive of Our Own, "Terms of Service FAQ"). The structure of these types of websites helps ensure that, in *Sherlock* fandom, Sherlockology and AO3 are places where members can feel comfortable as part of the community and are secure from attack by trolls, for example. Sites operated by a single fan are more likely to become targets of doxxing, trolling, and other forms of harassment. Although fan-owners may block some users, if the harassment becomes prolonged and threatening, many fans facing this problem choose to shut down their sites. Infighting within the *Sherlock* fandom takes place among factions who differ greatly in the way they believe is best to "protect" the fandom, actors, or series from those they think are publishing harmful information. The "safety in numbers" approach seems more effective in maintaining a safe space for fans to discuss *Sherlock*. Sites with official or semi-official status and those with multiple webmasters or moderators are less likely to become the targets of trolls bent on destroying a person or a site. Keeping the community a safe space for visitors and members has been an important aspect of the sites discussed in this chapter.

4

#Setlock

In *Sherlock* fandom, the Twitter hashtag #Setlock is most often used to alert fans to public-access locations where the series is being filmed. #Setlock is perceived by many fans who can travel to those locations as a call to action. Once on location, they (sometimes literally) cheer on the cast and crew, take photos and videos, and report via Twitter what they have seen, heard, and done. Those who cannot see *Sherlock* filming in person may still consider themselves part of the #Setlock community because they scrutinize the reports, especially the visual evidence, and help interpret what was filmed as well as construct a plausible context for a scene within the episode or even the entire series. #Setlock best illustrates fans' participatory behavior within a subcommunity of the larger digital community of *Sherlock* fans. However, it is also one of the most controversial communities, leading to public discussion about the phenomenon and throwing a media spotlight on all *Sherlock* fans.

The #Setlock phenomenon began in earnest during Season Two with a special promotion for "The Empty Hearse," the first new episode after a long hiatus. In November 2013, a hearse drove around London; in the window was the episode's U.K. broadcast date of the episode and the hashtag #sherlocklives (Kemp). Fans who saw the hearse in various parts of London tweeted photos and news about the sighting, using both the #Setlock and #sherlocklives tags. The immediate fan response to the information helped promote the season premiere and generated excitement among *Sherlock* fans. During the filming of Season Three episodes and "The Abominable Bride" special, #Setlock became far more prominent. Fans learned from smaller-town newspapers where filming would take place outside of London or found the production team's coded road markers to alert vehicle drivers where to turn or park. The #Setlock community then planned when and how to travel to the next location, sharing information immediately via Twitter. Especially when filming took place (often at night) on North Gower Street in London, the stand-in for Baker Street, hundreds of fans gathered early and waited behind barricades for the actors to arrive. As a result, in Season Four, *Sherlock* officials took greater care to film less on location and more on closed interior sets and to try to stop the "advertisements" of where filming would take place, particularly in London.

The showrunners' great concern is that, when fans take photos or video of a scene filmed in a public location and share it immediately online, an episode's plot or casting choices may be spoiled for audiences who cannot see the finished episode until months later. Then, there are the practicalities of filming on location. For example, during outdoor filming of "The Empty Hearse" in a public square used for a bonfire scene, the camera could not avoid every fan standing in the background of the shot. As one entertainment news writer explains, "The crowds of onlookers were so difficult to avoid that the first episode of season three includes some accidental cameos from fans who were caught in the shot" (Baker-Whitelaw). Although being captured for posterity within a *Sherlock* episode may make some fans feel special or others jealous, the presence of people who are not characters or extras providing background actions appropriate for the scene can destroy the illusion being created by the *Sherlock* cast and crew. Fans who are not dressed appropriately for the scene or who are obviously watching the lead actors instead of reacting to the fictitious drama taking place can break the fourth wall just as surely as an actor turning to the camera and addressing the audience directly. While fan musings have always been a part of affecting how a show is perceived, for better or worse, #Setlock is changing the way that *Sherlock* is made.

Furthermore, Mark Gatiss notes that the "insider information" tweeted by fans watching a scene being filmed also "gives a lot away, which is a shame" (Jones, "Sherlock Fans"). Fans often share information about who is on set each day, indicating which characters are in a scene, what they are wearing, and what they are doing during a filmed scene. The surprise elements of a new episode—such as a dead character apparently returning to life—may not be quite so surprising if they are revealed months before an episode is broadcast, and the potential exists for audiences not being as excited about new episodes as they would have been if they had not been spoiled by #Setlock news or images.

Not surprisingly, fans who watch an episode being set up or filmed have a different opinion of #Setlock from those who make the episodes. One enthusiastic fan/blogger, hotsmugstache, who spoke to *The Big Issue* while watching on-location filming, explains the reasons why so many *Sherlock* fans are as likely to travel across a continent as across town because of #Setlock: "The most important part is the community experience.... The other big part, of course, is the game. It's the real, hard detective work of finding locations and analysing what is being filmed." However, even the most dedicated fan-detective cannot be completely spoiled by what can be seen at any location. "Even with all the information we gain from this really quite meticulous work, we still are nowhere near able to tell too much about the final plot of the series. In some ways we get the enjoyment of revelation twice"—once during #Setlock and once when the finished episode is broadcast (Lobb, "Benedict Cumberbatch").

On the other side of the camera, while trying to be kind to and express appreciation for their fans, the actors face the problem of "performing" for a crowd—a very different acting experience than they have on an interior or a closed set. Benedict Cumberbatch (Sherlock Holmes) worries about his performance when every take is scrutinized by a live audience. "It's sometimes a bit weird and confusing to know you can't really be off. Literally, if you trip up or if you raise an eyebrow, it becomes an internet meme" (Lobb, "Benedict Cumberbatch"). Gatiss reports that #Setlock fans once "broke into wild cheering when Martin Freeman [John Watson] opened a package of crisps on set" (Jones, "Sherlock Fans Say No to #Setlock"). Freeman's comment that "It's like trying to act at a premiere.... When we're [filming at] our stand-in for Baker Street, it is hard to do your job. And I don't love it" (Gill) instigated both a public debate about the appropriateness of #Setlock and Moffat's ameliorating comment in a later newspaper article that "We're all genuinely—including Martin, including grumpy old me—very appreciative that people love our show so much, we're thrilled by it in fact" (Holmes).

In addition to bringing *Sherlock* fans face to face with TPTB on location, #Setlock also illustrates the wide diversity of this fandom. Freeman adds that "We don't write the show just to please people who are fanatical about the show but to pretend those people don't exist would be crazy.... I have never known anything like ... the fandom of this show. But at the same time that's not the 12 million people who tuned in at Christmas." Trying to please both the #Setlock crowd who are obsessive about the show and a more passive at-home audience who look for entertainment instead of clues about the series' real meaning is sometimes a difficult balance. Freeman notes that "you have to do it for them [the at-home audience], while doing enough detail to please the people who know it way better than I do" (Lobb, "Benedict Cumberbatch").

Immediacy, not accuracy about the series' content, is paramount, and fans who know the latest filming news gain more status within the #Setlock community and probably the *Sherlock* community. Whereas other fan communities may have more formal membership (e.g., signing up for an account on Archive of Our Own, following a blog in order to contribute to a discussion), the #Setlock community does not. Because it is situated on Twitter, anyone can search for the #Setlock hashtag to find information about *Sherlock* filming; similarly, anyone can tweet using the #Setlock hashtag. The #Setlock community has fluid membership because this hashtag is often the only way to unite fans who want to communicate about *Sherlock* filming as it happens (or, following Season Four, sharing memories and favorite photos to relive their experiences with cast or crew). Fans who publish videos and photos more often than text and who go on location more often have become the "stars" of the #Setlock community, even months later when the archived texts and images provide a record not only of *Sherlock*'s filming but of the #Setlock community's activities.

Gaining Notoriety and Criticism for Fandom

By 2015, #Setlock had become so popular that even U.K. newspapers followed the tweets and debated the propriety of fan behavior regarding *Sherlock* filming. *The Daily Dot* defined #Setlock participation by stage:

> The first stage of [#Setlock] addiction is following *Sherlock*'s actors, writers, and behind-the-scenes crew members on social media. But let's be honest here, that's amateur hour. A more dedicated setlocker also keeps track of public casting calls and potential location rumors, just in case someone connected with the episode accidentally shares something—*anything*—that might contain some clues about the next episode. The top tier is for those who actually visit the set in person [Baker-Whitelaw].

This acknowledgment by the mainstream media is significant as it lends credibility to fan-created knowledge systems, which have been historically ostracized and portrayed as less critical and less worthy of attention.

Nevertheless, this media attention often follows well-ingrained patterns of criticizing fan behavior or underscoring how it differs from non-fans' public behavior. The *Daily Dot* headline, for example, identifies #Setlock fans as those "who stalk the 'Sherlock' film set" (Baker-Whitelaw). These fans are characterized as stalkers, a term that connotes deviant and psychologically aberrant behavior. However, actor Amanda Abbington (Mary Morstan Watson) told *The Big Issue* that the "people who come to watch us filming are sweethearts—99 per cent are well behaved and lovely. They are often really young girls, and they sit silently for hours to watch how it is filmed. We go over and talk with them and they get excited" (Lobb, "Amanda Abbington"). According to Matt Hills, in "Psychoanalysis and Digital Fandom: Theorizing Spoilers and Fans," fan behavior has been pathologized in ways such as the *Daily Dot* headline that are damaging to an understanding of fan-generated texts as more than just "equated with strong emotion" (106). Traditionally, fan-based texts have been seen as the creation of pathologically fixated authors and dismissed as the result of "unhealthy" fixation and attachment. Hills points out that whether notions about fan fanaticism are true is irrelevant. What matters is the extent to which researchers/scholars consider fan texts on their own terms to "help us unpack, challenge and contest cultural notions of fan abnormality" ("Psychoanalysis and Digital Fandom" 107).

While mainstream media often criticize fan behavior, they simultaneously rely on #Setlock to get unmediated content posted by fans on Twitter. Publications such as the *Radio Times, Daily Dot, Den of Geek,* and *Wales Online* have followed #Setlock and used information gathered by fans as the basis of their own highly clickable articles. Because *Sherlock* is often a hot topic in entertainment news, the media becomes influenced by #Setlock when writers incorporate second-hand information from fans visiting *Sherlock* filming locations. Instead of doing their own reporting or heading out to a filming location often far from London or Cardiff, reporters scan Twitter and other social media sites for the latest #Setlock news. In 2015, more than fifty articles, many repeating information from #Setlock tweets or actor interviews, alerted the general public to #Setlock and earned money for their publications from each click to an online article about it. From *The Guardian* to *The Hollywood Reporter,* with tabloid coverage in between, #Setlock was addressed or utilized by mainstream media.

The positive side for fans is that they receive public recognition, and those who are quoted within articles or had their tweets republished or followed by mainstream media writers thus could gain status (or notoriety) within the #Setlock community specifically or more generally within *Sherlock* fandom. This legitimizing of an Internet community as a source for critical information about the show demonstrates the extent to which a web-born community can gain both recognition and status, re-positioning fan culture and its spoils from the fringes to the mainstream. The media also continues to commodify/monetize fan-generated texts/knowledge in a way that benefits a commercial entity rather than the fans who are creating the content, except in raising their status among their peers.

Perhaps not surprisingly, *Sherlock* fandom through #Setlock has been dubbed a modern version of Beatlemania. Freeman has said, "I've got some great reactions to things I'm very proud of, but I don't think any surpass *Sherlock* in terms of critical acclaim and number of people watching—and just a general feeling that you're in a mini Beatlemania" ("Sherlock Like Beatlemania"). Abbington makes a similar comparison in her *Big Issue* interview (Lobb, "Amanda Abbington").

Many *Sherlock* fans do not want to be associated with a Beatlemania-styled fandom, however, and resent this repeated mainstream media claim. In a discussion about Abbington's interview, one fan expressed her discontent with being lumped into the mainstream media's depiction of *Sherlock* fandom as a bunch of screaming young girls. However, she admitted that, after observing fan behavior at the Barbican's stage door after Cumberbatch's performance in *Hamlet*, she realized that a segment of the *Sherlock* or Cumberbatch fandom is indeed made up of just that demographic. She acknowledged the diversity of fans within *Sherlock* fandom, writing that "just because it's not us, or we don't see it all the time, does not mean it doesn't exist" (The Sophie Hunter Hype Report). To actors like Cumberbatch or Abbington, who are faced more often with a contingent of young fans overwhelmed with emotion at seeing them in person, the fandom probably does resemble Beatlemania, even if a majority of fans are not part of this demographic or do not behave in the same way.

Whether Beatlemania is an apt description of all *Sherlock* fandom or even the entire #Setlock community, the actors' and mainstream media's perception that #Setlock is *only* like Beatlemania is to miss an important difference and to fall into the pathologization of fan behavior rather than to focus on fan-created texts. #Setlock features creative works such as real photos, creative manipulation of photos, all sorts of visual art, and video production. Between 2013 and 2016, the year of the greatest number of publications, #Setlock has inspired the creation of 76 fan fiction stories, demarcated with a #Setlock tag. As Francesca Coppa points out in *A Brief History of Media Fandom*, this phenomenon is not limited to *Sherlock* fandom:

> Media fans are making more kinds of art than ever before. Not only are they still writing fan fiction, but image manipulation software has also allowed for a more sophisticated visual art. Digital editing software has taken the fannish art of creating video ... to a whole other level.... And fans are continuing to create a rich

critical literature about themselves, and a tradition of fan meta-discourse continues to flourish online [58].

However, these fan endeavors are not always received well because of the kind of impact they may have on many aspects of the media that they venerate. *Sherlock* co-creator Gatiss mentioned to the *Radio Times* in late 2014 that #Setlock has changed the nature of the series. This statement supports the idea that fan activity, for better or worse, contributes not only to how the show/characters may be perceived but even how the show is actually produced. Gatiss explains, "When we were filming Baker Street exteriors last time, the fact you've got about 300 people behind crash barriers is ... interesting, [so] we have factored in trying to minimise large scenes outside If you're just drawing up in a taxi and running through a door, it's easier but large dialogue scenes outside are quite tough" (Jones, "Sherlock Fans").

#Setlock is controversial within *Sherlock* fandom, too. Not all *Sherlock* fans want to be associated publicly with the #Setlock community, even when it is not compared with Beatlemania. A January 2015 *Radio Times* online poll asked Is it acceptable for fans to attend #Setlock? More than three-quarters of the 5,000 fans responding to the poll (76.87 percent) answered No; only 23.13 percent voted Yes (Jones, "Should #Setlock Continue?"). A follow-up article included criticism of #Setlock by two *Sherlock* fans:

> Actors and crew should have the freedom to work without people spying on them and spreading spoilers about what and how and when and where they do it.... You don't spy on people working on the streets, do you? Nor tweet about how their job is done, right? If you did, they would also ask you to step back in order to get some privacy.

> I don't know why people can't let the actors and crew get on with filming.... They're distracting the actors from their job just by being there. They're spoiling upcoming episodes of Sherlock not just for themselves, but for everyone else as well [Jones, "Sherlock Fans Say No to #Setlock"].

By Season Four, #Setlock faced more obstacles regarding their access to on-location filming, which, as a result, gave them less mainstream media exposure and made them even more determined to find information about episodes that had not been previously published.

Attempts to Mediate Fan Behavior

Moffat has not wanted to alienate a large percentage of *Sherlock* fans by overtly discouraging #Setlock, especially when the series takes years-long hiatuses between seasons. During Season Four, TPTB tried more covertly to limit the way that information is distributed to fans and to film most often in remote locations where fans could not easily see what is going on (e.g., inside buildings, far away from fenced-off fan areas). This flies in stark contrast to the kind of reception received by Sherlockology, the semi-official *Sherlock* website operated by fans. Whereas Sherlockology is welcomed, #Setlock persists despite being discouraged. Sherlockology staff are pleased and express gratitude for the insider information they are given; #Setlock fans feel entitled to watch filming and to say hello to actors if filming takes place in a public area.

When the filming began for Season Four in April 2016, fans became concerned with Moffat's statement, widely carried in mainstream media, that this season's three episodes form "the story we've been telling from the beginning and it's about to reach its climax" (Ausiello). Many fans, as well as television critics, interpreted that statement to mean that the series would conclude in 2017 at the end of Season Four. Television critic Michael Ausiello added that "it's worth noting that [Moffat] has previously said that he sees the franchise carrying on 'for a long while.' When reached for comment, a [U.S. PBS] Masterpiece rep argues that the word climax can 'mean many things' and notes that Moffat 'likes to tease'" (Ausiello). Nevertheless, die-hard *Sherlock* fans began worrying and speculating online whether Season Four might be the finale of the much-loved series, especially in light of stars Cumberbatch and Freeman having much higher international profiles and plenty of film roles to take up more of their time. Thus, when filming began for Season Four, the #Setlock community looked forward to finding out juicy tidbits about the series that either would alert them to plotlines indicating the end is near or assuage their fears that this might not only be the beginning of the end of *Sherlock*, but of the vibrant #Setlock community.

Sherlock's production team, however, had different ideas than #Setlock fans about the amount and type of information that could be accessed by even as dedicated a group of fans as the #Setlock community. The first weeks of filming were completed on a closed interior set, and the only information tagged #Setlock came from the series' insiders, such as Gatiss and Abbington. In April, Gatiss tweeted a photograph of the back of Cumberbatch's head with the caption "Back!" He did the same with Freeman and Abbington. On April 14, Abbington tweeted "Lonnnnng day." Although fans frequently tweet Abbington as if she is a friend instead of a *Sherlock* actor, members of the #Setlock community have also tried to get her to spill secrets about filming. Such a #Setlock-tagged tweet posted on April 18 referred to a locked-down on-location filming site in Margram. (The #Setlock community had been alerted by photos posted by crew after filming took place, as well as fans living near the site, that trucks for *Sherlock* filming had been seen at that location. However, the information came too late for fans to congregate, and the filming was confined to a closed indoor location.) Josie (also known as ClaraOswald_12, a tag referring to Moffat's other television series, *Doctor Who*) wrote "The *Sherlock* filming that took place in Margram was a christening. That's all I'm saying." The tweet, sent to Abbington, earned the immediate reply "Or was it?" Similarly, on April 13, Abbington sent a friendly "Night night you lovelies," which could be interpreted as being directed to castmates or fans, before teasing "Tomorrow is a busy day." Both the #Sherlock and #Setlock tags were added to her tweet, ensuring that it would be seen by the community. This use of #Setlock by one of the show's celebrities is indicative of the extent to which #Setlock has gained recognizable status. The co-opting of #Setlock by official sources as well as measures taken to curtail unwanted fan behavior is evidence of officials attempting to manage #Setlock in a way similar to the handling of Sherlockology to make it a more palatable, less unruly fandom.

Unlike the #Setlock community's rapid sharing of information and plenty of first-hand opportunities to watch filming of episodes during Season Three in 2013 or for "The Abominable Bride" special in 2015, this time the number of sightings was greatly reduced by the showrunners and production company. #Setlock members had to pose questions to actors based on rumors rather than personal sightings of the actors at work, and many fans relied only on what Gatiss or Abbington tweeted under the co-opted #Setlock tag. By technically becoming a part of the #Setlock community and providing (non)information about filming, Gatiss' and Abbington's tweets seemed to be an attempt to redirect attention away from the fans and toward the series' cast and producers as the "real" source of content for this community. It also indicates that #Setlock content, which in previous years had resulted from information from fans who observed on-location filming and deduced plot details from what they had seen, would more often be limited to teases from official sources because fewer fans would have opportunities to watch the *Sherlock* cast or crew at work and confirm or deny what TPTB had tweeted. These changes altered the ethos of #Setlock, making it seem more a part of the official media. This change in status, which was clearly desirable for Sherlockology, was not as easily mitigated in #Setlock during Season Four.

For example, early in that season's filming schedule, a group of students from Into Film (a U.K.–based not for profit, educational organization supported by film agencies that helps young people 5 to 19 years old learn more about film) were permitted to visit the *Sherlock* set. They took a group photo with Cumberbatch, Freeman, and Rupert Graves (Detective Inspector Greg Lestrade). However, the photo, which was reportedly taken with the production company's permission (and the cooperation of the cast), had to be approved "by the studio," according to one student who visited the set. The group did not watch filming, but their presence on the set was embargoed, much like Sherlockology's set visit had been the previous year. Students were not allowed to tweet the photo, only to retweet it from their institution after permission was given to make the photo available to students. They also were not allowed to use hashtags to alert *Sherlock* fans to their visit. The tweets from one student (ffion@silvershuzuo) indicated the plight of many in the class who found themselves inundated with new followers once the photo had been retweeted. On April 20, ffion posted this notice regarding the photo that would soon be released: "Just a warning when I post the pictures with Benedict and the others please don't quote it with any hashtags thanks!!" A follow-up tweet the same day reports "I've just been told I'm not allowed to tweet the picture myself but I retweeted it!" Another student, Jean, tweeted similar information. At first, she gushed "It was amazing visiting the set of *Sherlock* today, I talked to Martin Freeman and Steven Moffat. And got pictures with Martin and Benedict!" When a Twitter friend asked if she could post the photos, Jean replied "not at the moment sorry, they have to be okayed by the studio before we can post them." The group photo was later released through a faculty member's Twitter account. Next to the twitpic was the note "Thanks @hartswoodfilms & Sherlock crew for inspiring our young filmmakers & supporting the work of @intofilm_edu" (Stevens). No hashtags for #Sherlock or #Setlock were included; the message was directed only to Into Film and Hartswood Films.

However, the Twitter-savvy fans of Cumberbatch or *Sherlock* were not under such strictures and gleefully retweeted the photo and students' tweets, adding the hashtag #Setlock to ensure that as many fans as possible found the image and reports of the set visit. In particular, Anything Cumberbatch (@Anythingbatch), reputed to be a Cumberbatch super fan, retweeted the image several times, each time adding the #Setlock tag. As might be expected, some fans scrutinized the photo, enlarging and cropping sections for discussion. During fan analysis of the photo of Freeman, one fan questioned (and had the message retweeted dozens of times) "Why is Martin's hair so.... Martin? He is in costume, yes?" (Michelle). Another fan demanded discussion of the fact that Freeman, apparently on the set as John Watson and not as himself, was not wearing a wedding ring in the photo. Sophie tweeted in all caps (i.e., shouted) to gain other community members' attention "WHY IS NO ONE TALKING ABOUT THE FACT THAT MARTIN IS WEARING JOHN'S CLOTHING BUT 'NO' WEDDING BAND." Because fan speculation was that, during Season Four, Abbington's character, Mary Watson, would be killed off (in part because the canonical Conan Doyle character dies), Freeman and John received a great deal of scrutiny as fans tried to determine if Mary lives or dies, John stays married, or the Watson baby is born and survives. Such discussion could not be controlled by Hartswood Films or the BBC.

The attempts to strictly determine the amount or type of information made available online via Twitter could not completely close down #Setlock information. Thus, even during a time when *Sherlock* filming became so tightly regulated that on-location information was severely limited and the filming kept as private as possible, #Setlock continued and followed its own rules, designed to circumvent what the showrunners wanted to happen. Fans eagerly shared whatever photographs they could find, attempted to clarify rumors, and analyzed every bit of information available, no matter how limited.

Even more creatively investigative #Setlock community members talked with sources who likely would not be "punished" for casually leaking information. The owner of Speedy's, a diner located next door to "221B Baker Street"—the North Gower Street filming location—let slip that filming would take place in late June 2016 at their location. It is doubtful that Hartswood Films would seek out another location for the exterior shots of Sherlock's home, which have become a staple in the series. It would also seem odd if, only in Season Four episodes, the familiar Speedy's sign and restaurant were missing from "Baker Street" if the producers sought another location in retribution for the owner leaking information to #Setlock. Lauren announced that she "just asked the owner of Speedy's" and found out on April 21 that on-location filming was scheduled at Speedy's on June 21 or 22. Within two hours, the message had been retweeted more than a hundred times through Lauren's and Anything Cumberbatch's Twitter accounts. Members of the #Setlock community immediately began to mobilize and plan for their location visit two months later. This single announcement during the early weeks of filming illustrates that, despite the dearth of location-specific tweets from official sources using the #Setlock tag, the fan members of the #Setlock community still found ways to circumvent the showrunners and track down at least some location filming. Even with control measures implemented by the production team, #Setlock continued as a viable community that could not completely be held to the "rules" set forth by official sources as to who would have access to information about *Sherlock* filming.

#Setlock and the Power Differential Between Fans and Official Sherlock Sources

The extent to which fans have become concomitant producers of texts and knowledge regarding the objects of their affection has ramifications for how fans and celebrities manage to negotiate a relationship that has distinct tensions and advantages. The fan/celebrity (unofficial/official) relationship is tenuous because, although actors and showrunners, presumably, have insider information that the fans want, those celebrities must mitigate their responses to avoid alienating their consumer base. Because celebrities are communicating via social media directly with fans and that communication is at the discretion of the celebrity rather than the official show's representative, there is room for negotiation between fans and celebrities. These negotiations imply that fans, as a subcultural community, have more to offer to the celebrities that they follow than might be perceived initially. These negotiations have the potential to lead fans who are adept at navigating the digital landscape to educate celebrities about the ramifications of their contributions to fan communities, as discussed in Chapter 1. Dedicated fans in digital spaces have the potential to moderate interactions in some surprising ways, which ultimately end up a testament to the power of online fandom to affect both the object of their affection and the digital culture that has evolved around it.

In the case of *Sherlock*, the insiders who share official information via Twitter may not yet realize the power or responsibility they have when they target fans interested in specific information about a topic (such as a beloved television series). These sources of official information also may not be as technologically sophisticated as fan users of the technology. Although the official sources of information about *Sherlock* control the amount and type of information they send, they seem to believe that fans will passively take that information and be grateful for it. However, fans in general, and *Sherlock* fans, in particular, certainly are not passive. After all, the #Setlock community is geared toward sharing spoilers.

5

Marketing Products and Events to Digital Communities

During a 2011 talk show appearance, Benedict Cumberbatch was asked about any desire to become the Doctor in *Doctor Who*, which, at the time, was *Sherlock* showrunner Steven Moffat's other BBC series. The actor had learned from watching David Tennant (the Tenth Doctor) navigate fandom, especially one in which children think of the actor as the Doctor. Cumberbatch also noted that he did not want to "take on the responsibility of being the Doctor outside of work and then seeing his face on countless pieces of merch" (Frevele). When that interview took place, Cumberbatch had completed the first season of *Sherlock*, which was just making its way around the world after its acclaimed U.K. debut during summer 2010; it arrived via PBS in the U.S. late that year.

Licensing of BBC products related to *Sherlock* was extremely limited at first, and vendors at *Doctor Who* conventions in the U.S., who also were selling merchandise related to other British television series, answered repeated inquiries about *Sherlock* with the same comment: they could not get a license or BBC-sanctioned products, although the market for *Sherlock*-themed paraphernalia was growing. Within a few years, however, Cumberbatch's face was on countless products and used to attract fan-buyers.

The actor's *Sherlock* fandom, by the way, also became part of the targeted market/audience for his later non–*Sherlock* projects, such as films (e.g., *The Imitation Game, Doctor Strange*) and plays (especially *Hamlet*). In fact, the Cumberbatch public persona became a marketable commodity, turning the actor's face and words into a "product," and public relations (PR) helped market the actor's "brand." During a January 2015 live-streamed conversation at the Adobe Summit in Europe ("Online Adobe Summit"), the actor confidently said he is proud of his brand, a recognition that his life and marketability as Sherlock have paid off not only for the BBC, Hartswood Films, and the series but his career advancement, no matter how he might sometimes regret the loss of privacy.

By 2017, when the fourth season was broadcast, finding *Sherlock* merchandise was no problem online or in brick-and-mortar stores, and Cumberbatch's photos and interviews helped to sell magazines and newspapers with news or gossip about the series. However, this chapter is focused on merchandise (i.e., tangible products and less tangible special events like conventions), not press-related marketing or PR strategies regarding the series or one of its leads. Nonetheless, the point must be made that the marketing of an actor, not just a character, is often geared toward a fandom, even peripherally, if the actor's face recognition can be used to sell tickets or increase viewership as well as make spinoff products desirable to fans.

The licensing of *Sherlock* to companies and availability of products to worldwide markets became prevalent after the series became a hit and had a demonstrated fandom wanting to buy merchandise. U.S. comic book stores, collectibles shops, science fiction/fantasy specialty stores, and U.S. mall favorite Hot Topic, for example, or U.K. specialty chain Forbidden Planet stocked everything from small, less-than-lifelike-but-cute Funko Season Two figures (e.g., Jim Moriarty, Irene Adler, Mycroft Holmes, John Watson, the expected multiple variations of Sherlock Holmes) to a Cluedo game specific to the series to an array of t-shirts, mugs, posters, comic books, jewelry, and buttons common to many television fandoms. PBS and BBC official online shops offer disc collections of episodes, sometimes with bonus items like busts of Sherlock Holmes and John Watson to encourage fans to buy more expensive editions. The fascination with Sherlock's blue scarf led to official *Sherlock* scarves, some featuring the 221B address or icons like the yellow smiley face representing the pattern of bullet holes Sherlock shoots in a wall of his flat to create the eyes and smile, with yellow spray paint adding the circular facial outline ("The Blind Banker," reproduced in "The Final Problem"). The BBC also has allowed authors of books about other BBC television series to write official companion books to *Sherlock*, and copies of Arthur Conan Doyle's novels or short story collections were republished to feature *Sherlock*'s John and Sherlock on the covers. Each BBC Books reprinted collection or novel included an introductory essay by Mark Gatiss, Moffat, Martin Freeman, or Cumberbatch. The variety of official merchandise expanded greatly once *Sherlock* became a global hit and fans wanted to promote their fandom at home and in public by buying, using, displaying, or wearing *Sherlock*-themed products.

However, creative fans did not let official merchandise become the only products other fans could buy. eBay, Amazon, Etsy, and Café Press, as well as individual fan sites and artists' sites, provide the electronic marketplace where fans sell unofficial products like custom-made knockoffs of Sherlock's Belstaff coat; t-shirts and other apparel; knitted or crocheted dolls dressed like Sherlock and John; buttons; drawings; paintings; and patterns for fans to make their own items.

Yet another category of merchandise comes from academia, whose scholars write essays for edited collections or author books about *Sherlock*, its fandom, or lead actors. Of course, non-academic, unofficial books also have been published, but academic books sold to fans as well as students and professors constitute a separate category of merchandise designed to attract a wide range of *Sherlock* fans. In this chapter, however, the focus is only on official and fan-created non-academic merchandise.

Official Merchandise

Products sanctioned through the BBC or one of its many divisions or offshoot companies for conventions, syndicated networks, or online or in-person shopping include merchandise closely related to the series. Some lower-cost items are generic enough to appeal to a wide audience of both ardent fans and more casual supporters of the series. For example, paperback reprints of the Conan Doyle stories, packaged with a cover photo of Sherlock and John and the aforementioned creator or cast introduction, are published by BBC Books and sold for under $11 each on Amazon. At the other end of the fan-buyer scale are limited edition, more expensive products aimed toward ardent fans. Matt Hills explains, in *Doctor Who: The Unfolding Event—Marketing, Merchandising, and Mediatizing a Brand Anniversary*, that fan consumers are often separated in categories that relate problematically to how merchandisers perceive their consumption. These categories are often based on overgeneralized notions of some fans as children or childish because they clamor for collectibles and other fans as adult/executive fans who look for merchandise that may be more expensive and is certainly more exclusive (60). This classification system is problematic in that it sets up a false dichotomy in which fans must be either children or adults because of the items they purchase. Adult-age fans may be perceived as "childish," lacking control or discretion when it comes to the objects of their affection, thus creating a generally negative stereotype. An example of merchandise designed to attract the "adult" consumer is as follows: Big Chief Studios was licensed to create lifelike character figures wearing replicas of costumes seen on the show. In an attempt to buy the limited edition 1:6 scale figures of Sherlock and John the moment they went on sale, fans queued online and waited sometimes hours to order the expensive collectibles (initially around $600 per John and Sherlock pair, accompanied by each actor's individually autographed and numbered metal ID plate). By 2017, Big Chief Studios had produced or was taking pre-orders for the original John or Sherlock figures (without autographed plates), Jim Moriarty, and Victorian "Abominable Bride" versions of Sherlock and John. The more recent latter figures in the numbered, limited edition, autographed set sell for £499 (including tax) or around $645 (using a May 2017 currency-conversion rate). Two hundred modern Sherlock figures were made for the autograph series, with another one thousand offered without the autograph; the latter line sold out. This example serves to further underscore Hills' analysis of "adult" merchandise being regarded as having a "cultural value" that is not found in more mundane artifacts. Although having exclusive, high-end merchandise is a selling point for marketers, academics should continue to look at the broad scope of fan consumption, including high- and low-end products, as significant markers of various kinds of cultural capital (Doctor Who 60).

As such, the following list of official (through the BBC) or licensed manufacturers' merchandise shows the scope of products available to consumers, which reflects how fan consumers are perceived by official sellers:

Action figures or
    collectible figures
Furlock teddy bear
T-shirts, sweatshirts,
    caps, scarves, and
    other clothing
Posters
Photographs
Books
Comic books
DVD/Blu-ray discs
    and sets
Busts or sculptures
Mugs or cups

Cluedo game
Key chains
Sculpted chocolate (i.e.,
    Cumberbatch's head,
    Cumberbatch as an
    Easter bunny)
Jewelry
Deerstalker caps
221B Baker Street
    miniature façade
Wallpaper
Buttons
Magnet

This list of toys and practical items reflects the value placed on quantity (i.e., mass production), as well as usability or a fan's visible association with, in this case, a television series (i.e., community, identity). It is very difficult for fans to avoid the "consumption as duty" (49) pressure of fandom, according to Linden and Linden; consequently, many different items at many different price points are offered, because it seems every conference attendee at least has to buy a t-shirt!

In addition to these types of merchandise, high-end products also include less tangible items like special screening events and conventions, which, considering the international *Sherlock* fandom, may involve hefty travel costs in addition to tickets. These types of "products" are examined in depth later in this chapter.

Community Through Consumerism

Purchases denote a monetary commitment and can be used to separate fans by financial status, but they more positively can also foster the loosest form of fan community. When fans spot someone wearing an "I Am Sherlocked" t-shirt in public, they likely feel a sense of comradery with the t-shirt wearer; they are part of the same fandom. It is not uncommon in a fandom for friendships to begin in this way. Products—especially wearable items and special events—can help develop small communities of individual fans.

Buying fan-themed merchandise is one way to connect fans who are interested in showing their support of an actor or a series and becoming an "insider" visible to other fans with the same fandom interests. Sharing reviews or posts about what has been bought can prompt fans' communication with each other via product comments or social media announcements touting a new purchase. Conversation threads congratulating fans on their purchases or asking questions about what was bought can evolve from a single enthusiastic statement about a purchase, most often made on Facebook, Twitter, Tumblr, Instagram, or other social media sites. Fans who want to help promote a product (perhaps more than themselves as owners of that item) post positive comments directly to the seller's website or review the product in a forum where more people are likely to see it. Even though these reviews or comments may not be directed specifically toward the fandom, they still indicate a tenuous link between an individual buyer and others who have purchased or want to purchase the same product. In this way fans are not only "brand advocates" but also a "brand community" that "co-create value" in line with their community goals but also work in service of a corporate entity (Hills, Doctor Who 74).

This communication, or even the fact that wearing a *Sherlock* t-shirt, for example, associates the wearer with the fandom, can convey status within the fandom. This is especially true of fans who travel long distances, at least once but often more frequently, to attend events where the series' stars will be present. Having a "moment" with an actor—to get an auto-graph, take a selfie, ask a question, say hello at a convention meet-and-greet—can make other fans envious and convey special "insider" status to those who have met the cast. Even having the financial ability to purchase a high-end product shows that having items reflecting interest in *Sherlock* is a priority; owning a limited-edition item is meant to indicate that some-one is much more heavily invested in this fandom than those who do not own exclusive merchandise.

The Divide between "Haves" and "Have Nots"

The positive aspects of community are sometimes offset by the divi-sion between "haves" and "have nots" within a fandom. For this discussion, casual viewers or fans who support the series primarily by watching episodes instead of buying products or attending events are not being considered because they are not part of this division. Their omission from this discussion, however, does not make them "lesser" fans—despite what some "haves" may write online about the "elite status" of being able to attend events anywhere in the world, meeting the actors many times, or buying the most exclusive tickets and products. Buying merchandise or paying sometimes quite expensive ticket prices for an event is not the only marker of "true fans" or "super/uber fans." As Henrik Linden and Sara Linden explain, "pilgrimages," requiring fans to spend money, time, and effort to visit the places where the "spirit" of their "idol" is most present, also increase the likelihood that one will be able to engage meaningfully with the object of their affection and lends a significant amount of status and social capital to those willing and able to sojourn (105, 106).

The have/have not divide is often expressed online as envy, even if a comment is positive in tone, such as tweets or posts along the lines of "I wish I could go, but I hope those who do have fun" or "I'd really like to have [insert product] but it's SO expensive!" Making merchandise exclu-sive, especially in association with events like conventions, is one way to encourage this divide, although manufacturers or event promoters likely do not intend to foster it. Instead, they see fans as a willing market for unique experiences or limited-edition goods, and the price tag determines who is able to enjoy exclusive merchandise.

Sherlock is often marketed this way with high-quality products that involve cast members. The collectible figures by Big Chief Studios, especially those that come with hand-signed autographs, are limited in number, which, according to supply and demand, results in a higher price. Similarly, a limited number of convention tickets for a special activity, such as a meet-and-greet with a few members of the cast and crew or a guaranteed photo op with a star, is more exclusive and justifies a higher price; after all, the stars do not have enough time (or likely energy) to sign autographs or smile through photo ops with every fan when thousands of fans attend an event.

In the U.S., the opportunity for *Sherlock* fans to meet the cast at formal events, on the street, or during filming is much less likely than for U.K. fans or "haves" who can afford to visit the U.K., have the leisure time to track down a current filming location, or hover in places the stars have been known to frequent, sites which Linden and Linden point out are attractive to fans on an "emotional level" (110). When London hosted official *Sherlock* fan conventions in 2015 and 2016, U.S. fans kept posting questions to Showmasters and Massive Events, the convention-management companies, about a promised U.S. convention. The convention planners did themselves no favors by announcing a U.S. convention a few years before one actually took place in 2017; the excitement initially generated by the official Facebook and website pages quickly turned to disappointment and mistrust when the convention planners reportedly ignored posts or email queries or hedged by indicating that they had not been able to find an appropriate convention site. Fans familiar with other fandoms' conventions frequently pointed out that most conventions locked in a venue and at least a few guests before announcing the event. Just as digital fan communities can spread good news at the press of a key or a vocal command, so can they immediately stimulate negative comments or doubt about the quality of an event or a product or a company's competence. Nevertheless, when the date and place for Sherlocked USA were finally announced, fans with the time and money to travel to Los Angeles quickly bought tickets and sold out the convention hotel.

A convention is an example of a limited event, and although the least expensive entry tickets (without any photo ops or autographs) to Sherlocked USA were a more affordable $126, the high-end VIP tickets with perks like photo ops with all guests, the closest seating at presentations, and face time with showrunners, cast, or crew member at an exclusive party cost $2,996. The type of badge/name tag attendees were required to wear clearly identified those who bought the most expensive ticket package; as well, their position front and center at every activity also pointed out to others just who had the available cash and *Sherlock* as a priority.

As the event neared, more ways for fans to spend their money were introduced. A series of meet-and-greets was announced, but instead of fans buying tickets, during the convention they signed an auction sheet listing the highest amount they would pay for joining one or two guests for forty-five minutes at a roundtable discussion. The number of fans per meet-and-greet was limited to fifteen. The Sherlocked USA website offered

> a rare opportunity to have time with the guest in a relaxed setting with just a few other people to share them with. These meet and greets are often a much more informal and relaxed atmosphere than that of the main event with discussion usually being more ad hoc and personal. At the end of the session there will also be a managed opportunity to get an exclusive selfie with the guest in the room! ["Meet and Greets"]

This description is designed to attract fans seeking that special moment with a showrunner or an actor; it almost promises a more intimate setting and an opportunity for a real conversation—possibly one that would endear the fan to the star or make the fan memorable long after the convention is over. Instead of being one among thousands of fans in a queue, those paying for a meet-and-greet would be part of a small group with special perks—digital documentation to be shared with others online about one-on-one time with a star through the "managed opportunity" for a selfie.

The convention atmosphere promotes consumerism, but the U.S. convention, at least to some fans, encouraged super-buying. At issue were the meet-and-greets for an extra cost. (Some meet-and-greets with other guests were free, and fans joined the conversation by winning a lottery.) Having to pay additional money, sometimes hundreds of dollars, for a short event seemed "too American" for some fans complaining about the set-up while queuing for photo ops. Rumors also suggested that the convention-management company had not made enough money, which is why Sherlocked USA was going to be a one-time event, whereas future U.K. *Sherlock* conventions were in the works.

The price each successful bidder paid for a meet-and-greet was determined by the price the fifteenth highest bidder agreed to pay, thus keeping the cost as low as possible for the lucky top fifteen. However, this process also encouraged fans who could spend more money to bid a high amount to ensure that they could enjoy a meet-and-greet with a favorite actor, such as Andrew Scott or Gatiss. These add-on costs not only determine who can participate in an event (i.e., "haves" who can have more) but can make attending a convention deceptively expensive for fans caught up in impulse bidding/buying during a convention.

During an online product or ticket purchase, fans are often encouraged to click a button on the receipt page to share news of their purchase on social media. Although some fans do so, more often they prefer to post the news on their website or favorite form(s) of social media. In this way they not only make others aware of fannish products or events but encourage others to buy the merchandise. In this way, fans act as "brand advocates," according to Linden and Linden, and as such are very desirable to merchandisers. Linden and Linden explain that "fans, not customers" are most encouraged because they help to establish the authenticity of the product through the perceived authority that is vested in "fan" as an identity; similarly, merchandisers prefer "brand advocates, not followers" because of the opportunity to exploit the "labor" associated with advocacy (31). In addition, fans posting news of recent purchases or plans to buy tickets or products also may attempt to increase their status/social capital within the fandom if they show that they can participate in more events (to the point that the actors and their handlers know certain fans by name) or buy the most exclusive merchandise. They may be perceived by some not only as "haves" but as super or uber fans for so prominently consuming fan-oriented merchandise so often. Within *Sherlock* fandom, some people who post frequently about their travels, purchases, or encounters with the cast members have become well known because of their frequent posts. Because of their posted selfies, super or uber fans even can be recognized by other fans. In this way the concomitant construction of fans as consumers of more than just goods, but as consumers of status via the purchase of goods, becomes clear.

"Haves" not only refers to fans with the greatest buying potential but also can include those with the fastest technology and the time (day or night, depending on the time zone when merchandise first goes on sale) to be online and the willingness to queue sometimes for hours. Fans who cannot take time away from their responsibilities to a job or family or who lack the technical skills or a high-speed Internet connection may be shut out or limited in their ability to purchase exclusive products. Thus, while a digital community may quickly promote or disseminate news about merchandise to eager buyers, technology may limit who has access to it.

Not only merchandisers urge buying as an affirmation of status; fans encourage each other to buy faster or more desirable merchandise before it is sold out. Before the doors to the vendor room were opened at Sherlocked USA, fans lined up to be the first inside so they would not miss out on the possibility of buying limited merchandise. As soon as the room was opened, fans ran toward the BBC's official merchandise table, which was quickly swamped, in some places five people deep. Tiny squares of carpet from the set, mounted and framed alongside a cast photo, sold quickly. Within a few hours, set designer Arwel Wyn Jones sold all the faded wallpaper he had brought from the set. Photos that guests could autograph, coffee mugs, t-shirts, prints, and the program cost far less than *Sherlock* filming memorabilia. When merchandise is sold at a special event, the objects have meaning beyond only being exclusive, collectible items. As Hills points out, event merchandise sales are likely to capitalize on "fan memories and affects" to "sell their memories—and desired imagined memories—back to them" (Doctor Who 73). These objects, regardless of their cost or rarity, connect fans to the event, not just to their fandom. Although the BBC-sanctioned vendors had the most business, independent artists also did well. One t-shirt and print vendor, selling her own designs, called home so her mother could bring more stock for the rest of the weekend. She had not expected such a rush on Friday night, the first evening of the convention.

To get rid of merchandise—including posters and banners placed in hallways—the convention-management company held a silent auction. Once again, fans clamored to see if they had a winning bid moments after Sherlocked USA's closing ceremony. Prices varied with the size and subject (e.g., Cumberbatch on a poster raised its price), but the majority of the almost-life-sized posters sold for around $100. The live auction brought in higher prices. Even books burned in 221B's explosion during "The Final Problem" fetched a good price. The highest bid ($2,000) went for a clapboard used during filming and later signed by several cast and crew members.

The promise of a limited-edition item or its availability only for a short time or during an event increases the urgency many fans may feel to buy it while they can; purchasing merchandise available only during an event further enhances fans' status because the purchase shows that they not only attended an event but had the funds to buy exclusive products. Higher auction or sale prices of products with limited availability offered on sites like eBay or Amazon may further indicate to fans the desirability of owning exclusive merchandise and sharing that information with other fans, although the attractiveness of such items might be diminished if they do not represent a connection to a memory of the event. Consequently, even though these items are often available online, the pressure to purchase them is highest during the event.

Furlock

The suspense surrounding a special announcement alerted the *Sherlock* fandom that something new and possibly very exciting was about to be added to the Sherlocked the Event convention slated for London in late 2016. An official tweet proclaimed "We have something very special to share with you tomorrow—all we can say right now is this ... #Furlock" (Sherlocked the Event). This style of announcement resembles the exaggerated language used to introduce a new guest (such as an actor or a technical specialist). When Furlock was revealed to be a customized teddy bear, Twitter erupted in a flurry of responses ranging from "disappointed" to "must have it."

This type of hype is commonly used by producers to engage fan consumers, but it runs the risk of making items seem less authentic and more commercial. Lesley! tweeted, all in capital letters like a printed shout, THEY MADE THIS ANNOUNCEMENT LIKE 24 HOURS IN ADVANCE THAT THEY HAD "EXCITING NEWS." Eszter Varga concurred: "You know a con organizer is fxxxing desperate for money when they announce the announcement for ... a toy bear!" Anything Cumberbatch laughed with a series of emoticons and added "Best not say what I think of #Furlock."

Nonetheless, other fans enthusiastically looked forward to embracing Furlock. The choice of a bear indicates the targeted segment of the *Sherlock* fan base that would be attending the Sherlocked convention in London and would want to have a cuddly toy (perhaps to substitute for cuddling Cumberbatch). As MarianneDupre explains, "we can't hug Ben, but we can hug this!" Enthusiastic tweets highlight the amount of interest in the first few days following the announcement. LisaMarie posted "Must have one" and included a heart emoticon. Justyna similarly tweeted "Oh hell yes!!!! Definitely need one!" More specifically, Beth wrote "WANT" five times, each in capital letters.

In fact, many positive tweets were split between "want" and "need/ must have," suggesting different levels of engagement with the product.

Some fans may *want* Furlock but be unable to purchase him, either because they cannot attend an event where he is sold or lack funds for the bear, even if a friend attending a convention could get them one or if Furlock became available online. A surprising number of fans tweeted they *must have* or *need* the bear, invoking the "duty to buy" paradigm previously mentioned. Fans looking forward to purchasing the bear did so presumably to add to their collection of *Sherlock* memorabilia, show support for their favorite actor (or own a substitute to love), or have the status of buying an exclusive product. After all, news of ordering the bear to be picked up at Sherlocked the Event routinely was posted on Twitter or Facebook (especially on the official event page), which let other fans know that this person could be in London (perhaps after traveling internationally) and buy the exclusive merchandise. Such a post implies status—money certainly, but also the willingness to participate as much as possible in "official" fandom. The reasons why fans feel they must have Furlock likely vary, but what is certain is that fans tweeting their desire for the product may believe that it is a must-have as a way to express their devotion to *Sherlock*. Especially after the product was first hyped and formally announced as something special, Furlock stirred up a sense of urgency within the fandom as those who wanted or "needed" the bear strove to ensure that they could get one.

Exclusivity as a Selling Point

The Facebook page "Introducing Furlock—The Official Sherlocked the Event" bear encouraged fans to pre-order or buy him (if he was still available) at the London *Sherlock* convention. The language on the site emphasizes the must-have status of the stuffed toy by proclaiming that Furlock is "[e]xclusive to Sherlocked" and a "limited edition" "officially licensed to Hartswood Films." Furthermore, the quality of Furlock ensures that he is far more than a convention trinket; he has been "produced by the Great British Teddybear Company." The exclusivity of the product and the reputed quality implied by the name of the manufacturer (apparent even to those outside the U.K. because of the company's distinguished name) justified its £39.99 price (approximately $51 U.S. in May 2017, but higher in 2016 when Furlock was first announced and the exchange rate was not as favorable to U.S. residents). At Sherlocked USA, the 12-inch tall Furlock could be pre-ordered for $59.99 (Eventbrite).

In addition, the "Fur" representing the product's teddy bear features was meshed with the "lock" look from the series' Sherlock. The toy's wardrobe was marketed to the show's fans quite specifically and reflects knowledge of fan discussion of Sherlock's wardrobe. In an early episode, Sherlock wears what fans dubbed "the shirt of sex," a deep purple shirt tailored to mold to his torso so tightly that its buttons strained (a common occurrence among Sherlock's shirts during the first season). Furlock similarly sports a purple shirt, coat with red buttonhole like Sherlock's Belstaff model, a blue scarf, and a deerstalker. The bear also was created to more closely resemble Sherlock's/Cumberbatch's long, thin face (although the bear lacks the actor's sharp cheekbones). Furlock's facial structure was noted in the advertisement as being "contoured to Sherlock's features." However, the bear's longer face and attire did not always make those fans commenting about the bear on Twitter think specifically of Cumberbatch's Sherlock, but they seemed to like the bear for himself and his association with Hartswood Films and *Sherlock*. His design also ensured that he would stand out from other merchandise sold at a *Sherlock* convention.

Although most comments noted in this chapter come from Twitter, some apparently were posted to the official Facebook page for the 2016 convention. However, according to one person posting a complaint, negative comments about Furlock had been removed from the page. (This complaint was subsequently unable to be located when Lynnette Porter went back to find it the day after she had seen the post.) If removing negative comments is indeed part of the marketing strategy for the Facebook page, at least a few people tried to alert other fans to this practice of ensuring that only positive Furlock comments could be read on the site.

Online commentary—pro or con—did not seem to affect sales appreciably, but sales may not have been as robust as expected. A later announcement in response to demand from outside the U.K. lessened Furlock's "exclusivity." The Facebook page noted the following: "For those of you unable to attend Sherlocked U.K., Furlock will be on sale from 1st October 2016 with worldwide shipping, and should stock still be available, he will also be available to buy at Sherlocked USA [in late May 2017]!" Furlock still was a limited-edition item, but with this announcement he seemed to be "devalued" as a leftover from the U.K. convention. He would be turned into a globally available product instead of being truly exclusive to the London event. Fans planning to attend the Sherlocked USA convention in mid–2017 also may have felt that theirs was less special because it did not offer a product created especially for that convention.

The fact that enough Furlocks were available after the London convention also indicates that the bear did not sell out there, perhaps because of his price as much as his appeal to the target buyers or because he could not live up to the hype and failed to remain authentically and meaningfully connected to discerning *Sherlock* fans. At least two Furlocks were held back from the remaining stock; it was announced before the fourth season finale that the official 2017 U.K. Sherlocked convention to be held in Birmingham would give away Furlock as a prize to two ticket-holding fans. The announcement on the U.K. convention's page was directed to fans who might not be as thrilled with Season Four as they had been with previous seasons; the ratings for the fourth season were the lowest in the U.K. of any season of *Sherlock*. (PBS did not release figures.) The episodes, dubbed "dark" in several interviews by the showrunners, made many fans worry about the content of the finale. Referring to this anxiety, as well as aligning themselves with fans, the Massive Events staff (planning the convention in association with Showmasters and Hartswood Films) posted on their website that "We feel we need a distraction whilst we await that third episode of season four and the Sherlocked team feel we can help!" Their message explains that, to win a Furlock, "you simply need to be a ticket holder to either the US or UK event by end of the day on Sunday 15th January 2017." The winners of the drawing that evening, one from the U.S. pool of ticket holders and one from the U.K. pool, were announced on Facebook on Monday morning (Sherlocked the Official Sherlock Convention–U.K.). Such an announcement potentially generated more interest in both conventions and perhaps forced fans still thinking about buying a convention ticket to rush to buy one before the deadline so that they could enter the drawing.

As is typical of exclusive items available only at a fan event—such as San Diego Comic Con, where exclusive editions of collectibles made specifically for the convention are in high demand—Furlock eventually became available in very limited quantities on Amazon and eBay. A March 2017 search for Furlock on Amazon, for example, offered the bear for £44.95 on the U.K. site, five pounds higher than its U.K. convention price; the description noted that only eleven bears were still available (with an exclamation mark alerting potential buyers to the fact that the item may sell out) (Sherlock). On eBay, the buy-it-now price was £39.99, but the March 2017 "trending" price based on prices during the past ninety days was £41.86. The eBay seller, like the one on Amazon U.K., must have bought Furlock in bulk; the listing noted that five bears had been sold but ten more were available (incognitocomics). Despite the erosion of Furlock's exclusivity to one fan convention, the bear still is limited in availability and is far from being a mass-produced product available through dozens of online outlets.

Association with Cast and the Producer

In addition to the exclusivity and quality of the product, Sherlocked the Event used the power of celebrity to entice potential fan-buyers to want Furlock. This may have been a move toward establishing an authentic and ostensibly meaningful connection to *Sherlock* in order to entice fans to make a purchase. After the initial announcement, a follow-up Facebook notice reported that "We took Furlock on set this year when [the cast was] filming the series and Benedict and Martin really loved him.... Mark and Sue also told us they had to have one." This notice points out that the Massive Events staff putting together the convention are *Sherlock* insiders. They are on a first-name basis with actors Cumberbatch, Freeman, and Gatiss and producer Vertue. Furthermore, if these television powerhouses (who are adults not perceived as prone to bear buying) "love" Furlock and "have to have" him, then fans may buy into the idea that they should love and want Furlock, too. Getting the "approval" of their favorite actors— even if Cumberbatch, Freeman, or Gatiss do not know them personally— or thinking like these actors may help some fans feel kinship with the stars.

During the convention, however, this announcement about Furlock love seemed in error or, as some fans tweeted, Cumberbatch was unaware of the announcement and did not follow the official script regarding Furlock. Fans attending a panel session tweeted that Cumberbatch did not love Furlock, in contrast to his reported feelings from meeting the bear on set. The following tweets illustrate the common thread among fans noting this dissonance:

> IAmSherlocked: Heard #BenedictCumberbatch wasn't too impressed with #Furlock at UK convention.
> Sophie: Benedict hates Furlock. "It just seems sooo wrong!"
> Lisa_L: Way to follow the party line.

As might be expected, use of the #Furlock tag in these and similar messages alerted fans interested in *Sherlock* (who would recognize the bear's name or might be following a #Furlock thread) that if they are simply buying the product because Cumberbatch likes it, they might want to consider his reaction. Other fans, already critical of Furlock, might feel these tweets justify their reluctance to buy the product and be pleased upon finding out that Cumberbatch agrees with them. Aligning themselves with Cumberbatch may give some fans a feeling of superiority over other fans or an excuse to shun the expensive bear.

Especially because the initial marketing announcement played up the resemblance between Cumberbatch and Furlock and the later Facebook notice furthered that connection, these fan posts are notable for going against the marketing strategy and attempting to make other fans aware of Cumberbatch's true feelings—as stated in a public forum—about Furlock.

Despite this dissonance between marketing and "reality," some fans were not dissuaded from liking or buying Furlock. (By the time of the convention, the pre-ordered Furlocks already had been united with their eager buyers.) Representative of those who relied on their interest in the product and not Cumberbatch's approval of their purchase, EmmaBadame tweeted that "Benedict Cumberbatch might think ... #Furlock is ridiculous (and he'd be right) but I have zero regrets." Even if buyers recognize that they are being manipulated by marketing strategies or peer pressure, some simply like the bear and would have bought Furlock because they find him cute. Adults who purchase Furlock for themselves may agree, as Emma-Badame seems to imply, that such a purchase may be a "want" instead of a "need" and could even be a guilty-pleasure purchase. Nevertheless, they bought Furlock and enjoyed owning him.

Furlock as a Character in His Own Right

By 2017, Furlock had a life of his own, although he still is connected to Sherlock and *Sherlock* in the minds of fans. He has become the star of his own adventures, as shared on Twitter. Using the #Furlock tag, Furlock's friends have shared photographs or news of the bear who, like Sherlock, solves cases and travels. He even attended a cinematic screening of "The Final Problem." Through tweets, fans show their creativity in providing a new context for Furlock beyond being an item to be purchased as an impulse buy and shelved as part of a collection. He has his own searchable tag within Archive of Our Own's fan fiction database. Furlock has become a companion to some and a separate character fulfilling the promise of that first announcement touting him as if he were a human guest and the equivalent of one of the series' actors. This and the aforementioned shifting attitudes toward Furlock illustrate the ways in which fan merchandise can change significance and meaning over time and in different circumstances. Fans ascribe and even make meaning through their criticism, praise, and creative "play." In this case, fan play has led to the evolution from stuffed toy to character in its own right.

Unofficial Merchandise

On Etsy, Café Press, Amazon, eBay, and independently owned websites, fans showcase and often sell the *Sherlock*-themed products they make by hand. Usually these products emphasize an aspect of a favorite character or a theme that may resonate far more with highly invested fans than with casual viewers. An example of the latter is a Sherlock-and-Bluebell polymer clay miniature sculpture that exalts the glow-in-the-dark rabbit featured in "The Hounds of Baskerville." The one-of-a-kind artwork might seem an obscure subject to people who enjoy *Sherlock* episodes but likely will not remember a rabbit's name. Bluebell's role in this episode, however, makes her memorable to ardent fans who may want the sculpture not only for its choice of subject matter but the bonus that this Bluebell also glows once the lights are out (KinkoWhiteArt), just as she does in "The Hounds of Baskerville."

Whereas many fan-created products are G-rated in tone or content, erotica and explicitly depicted homosexual relationships also are popular. These items particularly appeal to that segment of *Sherlock* fandom who read sexual intimacy primarily into the Sherlock-John friendship. A Johnlock-themed t-shirt pictures John and Sherlock about to kiss. Much more explicitly, a print captures the pair nude in post-coital cuddling in bed. Nude Sherlock is the subject of other drawings, one which illustrates him stretched out in bed with his robe discreetly draped over his penis. As these examples indicate, the range of *Sherlock* merchandise created by fans for fans is more context specific than official or mass-produced items.

A search of *Sherlock*-themed, fan-produced items results in lists of lower-priced prints, t-shirts, coffee mugs, jewelry, and refrigerator magnets that may cost less to make or be able to be reproduced easily, as well as higher-priced unique paintings or sculptures, knitted or crocheted dolls, and cosplay wardrobe items (such as a knockoff of Sherlock's Belstaff coat). Whereas many of these types of items—especially t-shirts, jewelry, coffee mugs, refrigerator magnets, buttons, and bookmarks—are commonly produced by fans in almost every fandom, the re-creation of Sherlock's coat (Fanrek), a pill bottle necklace inspired by the cabbie killer's modus operandi in "A Study in Pink" (KearaCreations), and a cookie cutter shaped like the door to 221B (BoeTechLLC) are specific to *Sherlock* fandom and require fans to know the details that will appeal to other fans.

Through the display of merchandise they have created, fans not only can make money but, perhaps just as important, increase their credibility and status within the fandom. They make others aware of their creativity, talent, and skills, as well as their vast knowledge of details about the characters, plots, and settings. Although they may not consciously develop strategies to market themselves or their creations as official producers or purveyors of *Sherlock* merchandise do, they, nonetheless, understand what fans like and want because they are part of the target audience.

Although *Sherlock* has been an official cash cow since it became a television hit, it has inspired within fandom a wealth of creative expression. Certainly fans are an important market for official merchandise and events; they can be analyzed as a group for mass marketing or as a subset of fans with disposable income and the desire to buy exclusive, high-end experiences and goods. Yet fan-created items are often a labor of love more than a commercial endeavor; they provide a way of sharing what fans find most appealing about *Sherlock* and enrich fandom.

6

Sexuality in
the World of *Sherlock*

Throughout thirteen movie-length episodes allowing a great deal of character development, *Sherlock*'s main and recurring characters are most often non-heteronormative in lifestyle or sexual orientation. All characters have at least a few quirks that mark them as "other" from peers in their profession or generation. Although Sherlock Holmes is often the focus of discussions about sexuality and multiple ways to read the character's sexual orientation, other characters within the world of *Sherlock* also are far less heteronormative, according to many fan interpretations, than is typical within most television series. The following table illustrates the range of sexual relationships that have been hinted (perhaps baited) and, in most cases, the lack of heteronormativity across four seasons. Because Sherlock will be discussed in great detail later in this chapter, he is not included in the following table. Although several examples across episodes are listed in Table 1, they are not the only ones; additional examples are included throughout the chapter. Not all behaviors (e.g., Mrs. Hudson's) are sexual in the "non-heteronormative" category but are atypical characteristics of the way heteronormative characters are portrayed on television or, more specifically, in Sherlock Holmes canon or adaptations.

Table 1. Non-heteronormative Relationships within Sherlock

Character	Textual evidence of a heteronormative reading of a character's sexual orientation	Evidence allowing multiple non-heteronormative readings of the text
John Watson	Sherlock lists John's recent string of girlfriends, and one girlfriend is shown on screen before she breaks up with John ("A Scandal in Belgravia").	After John has ditched yet another date to assist Sherlock, his girlfriend tells John he is a wonderful boyfriend. When he preens, she adds "for Sherlock

Character	Textual evidence of a heteronormative reading of a character's sexual orientation	Evidence allowing multiple non-heteronormative readings of the text
		Holmes." "A Scandal in Belgravia": possible reading of John as bisexual
	John marries Mary Morstan ("The Sign of Three") and has a daughter with her ("The Six Thatchers").	On her wedding day, Mary sees Sherlock jealously watching John's reunion with his former commander, Major James Sholto (Alistair Petrie). She reminds Sherlock that "neither of us was his first," alluding to a possible sexual and/or love relationship. "The Sign of Three": possible reading of John as bisexual
Mycroft Holmes	At Buckingham Palace, Sherlock and John wait to learn why they have been summoned to the Queen's residence. When someone approaches, Sherlock tells John that it is the Queen, but Mycroft enters the room, encouraging John and Sherlock to snicker like children ("A Scandal in Belgravia"). Some viewers interpret this scene only as sibling rivalry and Sherlock's juvenile attempt to needle Mycroft.	Another possible reading of this scene is that Mycroft is gay. Sherlock's reference to him as a "queen" in dialogue and later by playing "God Save the Queen" when Mycroft must provide his sovereign or the government with an update about the Irene Adler (Lara Pulver) case is still juvenile but based in fact that Mycroft is homosexual. "A Scandal in Belgravia": possible reading of Mycroft as homosexual
	Mycroft is interested in the welfare of Lady Elizabeth Smallwood (Lindsay Duncan), whose husband was apparently forced into suicide after being blackmailed by Charles Augustus Magnussen (Lars Mikkelsen; "His Last Vow"). In a brief scene at the end of "The Lying Detective," Lady Smallwood tells Mycroft she is going away for the weekend and gives him her private phone number, in case he ever wants to have a drink with her. Although hesitant and unsure how to respond, Mycroft nonetheless takes the card.	Mycroft's hesitance in this scene can be read as his reluctance to reject an old friend and co-worker, rather than his sexual interest in meeting her privately. "The Lying Detective": possible reading of Mycroft as homosexual
	When Moriarty is summoned by Mycroft to Sherrinford ("The	This scene can be interpreted as Moriarty being aware of

Character	Textual evidence of a heteronormative reading of a character's sexual orientation	Evidence allowing multiple non-heteronormative readings of the text
	Final Problem"), he learns he is to be a Christmas present. Moriarty asks Mycroft, "How do you want me?" Mycroft then explains that Eurus wishes to talk with him privately. Mycroft does not react to Moriarty's innuendo.	Mycroft's sexual orientation and assuming the powerful Holmes brother is interested in asserting authority over the then-minor criminal mastermind. "The Final Problem": Mycroft's and Moriarty's possible homosexuality
	In "The Final Problem," Mycroft references a dramatic performance in school as Lady Bracknell in *The Importance of Being Earnest* and considers going in disguise as this character when he infiltrates Sherrinford. It is likely that Mycroft attended an all-boys school, where males played female or male roles on stage.	Mycroft's considering dressing as Lady Bracknell again, added to his pleasure that Sherlock thinks he did well in the role at school, may be perceived as an interest in dressing as a woman and seeking an excuse to do so when he goes undercover. "The Final Problem": Mycroft as someone who enjoys wearing women's clothes
Jim Moriarty	Upon being introduced to Sherlock as Molly's boyfriend, "Jim from IT," Moriarty slips Sherlock his card and, when the consulting criminal meets the consulting detective at the pool to discuss their possible business future, asks if Sherlock likes the way he "played gay" to get his attention ("The Great Game").	Another reading, one that fans have embraced, is that Moriarty really is gay and tries to use his dress and mannerisms to "play gay" in order to get Sherlock's attention. Although he may not be sexually interested in Sherlock, he enjoys flirting with him. Moriarty is only interested in meeting Sherlock and uses Molly toward that objective. "The Great Game": Moriarty's possible homosexuality
	In "The Final Problem," Moriarty arrives via helicopter to Sherrinford and blatantly comments on his male bodyguards'/employees' sexual stamina, insinuating a sexual relationship with more than one man. However, Moriarty is never shown in a sexual situation throughout the series and uses his sexuality to manipulate both men and women. He seems sexually attracted to Eurus in a	Moriarty's specifically sexual dialogue regarding the men accompanying him to Sherrinford and his nonchalance at discussing their sexual encounters can be read as an admission of Moriarty's preference for men. Although he flirts with women or even dates Molly (according to her dialogue but not shown on screen), his most intense relationship is his infatuation

Character	Textual evidence of a heteronormative reading of a character's sexual orientation	Evidence allowing multiple non-heteronormative readings of the text
	later scene but also baits Mycroft about wanting a sexual liaison with him.	with Sherlock. "The Final Problem" and other episodes, including "The Great Game": Moriarty's possible homosexuality
Irene Adler	Adler is introduced as a dominatrix, and for her first meeting with Sherlock, she is nude ("A Scandal in Belgravia"). She seductively asks him for "dinner" on several occasions and says she would have him begging for mercy on the kitchen table. Her profession is non-heteronormative; on the job Adler has sex with men as well as women.	In addition to having sex with women for pay, Adler self-identifies as lesbian and is shown sharing her home with Kate, her partner. In her dealings with Sherlock, with whom she seems to be fascinated because of his intellect as well as the challenge of his being uninterested in her sexually, she beats him with a whip and drugs him, not typical "court-ing" behaviors for heteronor-mative couples. "A Scandal in Belgravia": Irene Adler's homosexuality and non-heteronormative lifestyle
Charles Augustus Magnussen	In "His Last Vow," villain Charles Augustus Magnussen is not shown with a partner and seems content to be a lone powerhouse. He manipulates the lives of men and women by threatening them with blackmail. He enjoys physically hurting them (e.g., flicking John's eye) to prove his control. Magnussen uses Sherlock's pressure point— John—in hopes of manipulating "the British government" (Mycroft), whose pressure point is Sherlock. Although Magnussen is not a nice man, he seems to adhere to heteronormative sexual standards, a determination made simply because not much is provided about his personal life.	In a deleted scene from "His Last Vow" that has been included as a DVD/Blu-ray extra, Magnussen is shown in Sherlock's hospital room as the consulting detective is recovering from a gunshot wound. Sherlock appears to be unconscious or sleeping; he does not react to Magnussen's presence. Magnussen cradles Sherlock's hand and comments on it being "womanly." He fondles Sherlock's hand and arm and tells Sherlock that he soon will get used to his touch. The implication is that Magnussen is sexually interested in Sherlock, perhaps as a power play only. "His Last Vow": Magnussen's possible homosexuality or bisexuality, or at least his willingness to use sex to control Sherlock

Character	Textual evidence of a heteronormative reading of a character's sexual orientation	Evidence allowing multiple non-heteronormative readings of the text
Mr. and Mrs. Holmes	As introduced in "The Empty Hearse" and developed in "His Last Vow" and "The Final Problem," Mr. and Mrs. Holmes (Timothy Carlton and Wanda Ventham) have been happily married for years and are apparently faithful to each other. Mr. Holmes still thinks his partner is "hot" after all these years ("His Last Vow").	Although the couple is heteronormatively faithful to each other, Mrs. Holmes was a renowned mathematician and author who (hetero-normatively) gave up her career for marriage and family. Yet the idea that the Holmes' siblings get their intelligence from their mother, not their sweet but dotty father, can be perceived as an atypical portrayal of "traditional" television parents ("His Last Vow").
Greg Lestrade	In "A Scandal in Belgravia," Lestrade is happy that he and his estranged wife are reconciling for Christmas.	In this episode, Sherlock tells Lestrade that his wife is having an affair, and the relationship apparently dissolves off screen after this point. "A Scandal in Belgravia": marital infidelity
	Greg Lestrade and Mycroft Holmes seem to have developed an interpersonal relationship by the time of "The Hounds of Baskerville." Although Lestrade is on vacation, he checks up on Sherlock and John at Baskerville for Mycroft. Evidence to the contrary, he tells Sherlock "I don't do what your brother tells me to do."	By the end of "The Final Problem," when Lestrade makes a brief appearance at the clean-up of the Eurus debacle, Sherlock requests Greg—using his first name correctly for the first time—to look after Mycroft. This is an odd request if Lestrade only knows Mycroft because of Sherlock and has a working relationship with him—per-haps as a minder by proxy for Sherlock. However, when Lestrade says he will look after Mycroft, many fans' assump-tion is that theirs is now a per-sonal relationship or possibly a sexual one. "The Final Prob-lem": Lestrade's possible bisex-uality, Mycroft's possible homosexuality
Mrs. Hudson	Mrs. Hudson was married and lived in Florida with her husband ("A Study in Pink" and others). As his widow, she lives	Sherlock ensured that Mrs. Hudson's drug dealer husband was legally executed in Florida ("A Study in Pink"). She had

Character	Textual evidence of a heteronormative reading of a character's sexual orientation	Evidence allowing multiple non-heteronormative readings of the text
	in London on her inheritance ("The Lying Detective").	worked as a typist in her husband's drug cartel and then became an exotic dancer ("His Last Vow"). She enjoys marijuana, what she calls "herbal soothers" ("A Study in Pink"). Her inheritance likely is based on her husband's illegal gains as a drug lord: Mrs. Hudson drives a red Aston Martin and makes John realize that she has enough money to own property in central London. All these behaviors are atypical for the way senior women are portrayed on television or, specifically, the way Mrs. Hudson was written in canon and portrayed in other adaptations.

Sherlock's fans enjoy playing detective and figuring out clues not only to plots but to the lives of characters when they are off screen. After all, if Steven Moffat's and Mark Gatiss' television canon explains that, for example, Mrs. Hudson worked (in a clerical capacity only) for the drug-dealer husband Sherlock helped to have executed in Florida, was once an exotic dancer, and was able to buy property in central London and a flashy Aston Martin from her late husband's business profits, then fans' interpretations of other characters, often based on snippets of dialogue, cannot really be any more unexpected. Even if Moffat or Gatiss do not share fans' reading of characters, other fans are highly supportive of these alternate interpretations, especially when they increase the series' diversity.

Making Sherlock Sexy

During Season One, a Byronesque Sherlock sports longer, curling locks and an aloof expression, wears form-fitting shirts beneath his billowing Belstaff coat, and reflects light off his sharp cheekbones. As John Watson notes in Season Two's "The Hound of the Baskervilles," Sherlock frequently flips up his collar to look more "mysterious." Perhaps if Sherlock had not been what Gatiss terms the "first sexy Holmes" (Denham), fandom—

digital or otherwise—might not have become so deeply invested in this specific incarnation of the Great Detective. Between 2010 and 2017, when the series' four seasons and a special Victorian-themed episode were broadcast worldwide, *Sherlock* faced competition from the Guy Ritchie-directed *Sherlock Holmes* films (*Sherlock Holmes* [2009], *Sherlock Holmes: A Game of Shadows* [2011]) and CBS's *Elementary* (2012–present, shown on Sky in the U.K.). Whereas Benedict Cumberbatch and Martin Freeman are an attractive duo as Holmes and Watson, so, too, are Robert Downey, Jr., and Jude Law on film or Jonny Lee Miller and Lucy Liu on U.S. television.

The "sexiness" of the BBC's Sherlock Holmes cannot simply be attributed to the physical attractiveness of actor Cumberbatch, who has frequently questioned his looks as the basis of his apparent sex appeal and, early in his stardom, often joked that he has a "weird face" that is "something between an otter and something people find vaguely attractive" (Rich). Nor can sexiness be merely a matter of talent. Although Cumberbatch has racked up an Emmy for *Sherlock* and an Academy Award nomination for a film role, he is far from alone in this group of highly talented, award-winning actors. Freeman also received an Emmy for *Sherlock*, as well as a BAFTA. Miller shared with Cumberbatch an Olivier award for the theatrical *Frankenstein*, Liu has a Critics Choice Award for another television role, Law has been awarded a BAFTA for his film work, and Downey, Jr., like Cumberbatch, earned an Oscar nomination but also has more nominations and awards for television and film than the other actors in this list. In short, the actors portraying Holmes or Watson during the resurging interest in Sherlock Holmes in the 2010s are a highly talented, attractive group. The ability to portray a character memorably does not distinguish one production from another, and every film or series involves its characters, at least, in innuendo-laden scenes (most notably and heavy-handedly in service of the *Sherlock Holmes* films' Holmes-Watson bromance) and, at times, more explicit sexual situations.

Even other areas of innovation in adaptation—like bringing Holmes to the 21st century and making him a contemporary to viewers—is not enough to account for *Sherlock*'s unique popularity and "sexiness." Like *Sherlock*, *Elementary* modernizes and modifies canonical characters, but the two series take decidedly different approaches. (*Elementary*'s differences beyond setting may be attributed, in part at least, to Hartswood Studios' refusal to give permission for an American remake of its British hit [Gardner].) In *Elementary*, Watson is a female character, but there is no romantic tension between her and Sherlock Holmes—she does, however, have a fling with Mycroft (Rhys Ifans). Making the modern characters far more sexual than their Victorian canon counterparts is just one more commonality between the series.

Elementary also sexualizes the lead characters as part of their modernization, yet this series has not been deemed as "sexy" as *Sherlock*. In particular, from the opening moments of the pilot episode, Holmes has been graphically shown and discussed as a man with sexual appetites and urges, as well as a great capacity for romance. His conquests (e.g., having sex with his brother's fiancée several times to prove that she does not love Mycroft—a rather strange way of "protecting" his big brother) are legendary. However, the acknowledgment of a character's sexuality has not been enough for *Elementary* to generate the kind of sustained interest and advocacy exhibited by *Sherlock* fans.

What makes Sherlock and *Sherlock* "sexy" and separates it from its competitors is, as Table 1 illustrates, the number of characters hinting, discussing, or implying information about their sexual orientation or sexual practices in each episode. Every main and recurring character (with the possible exception of Mr. or Mrs. Holmes) has piqued fans' interest and provoked continuing online debate, including confrontation with actors or showrunners, about the way a character can or should be interpreted and why that reading can be empowering. Sherlock is sexy not just because of his long Belstaff coat swirling about him or his "mysterious" demeanor. Sherlock—and in many respects most main cast members—is "other" from societal norms. However, no matter how different Sherlock is in other respects to social norms (e.g., creating his job and job title to be the only consulting detective in the world, initially but erroneously claiming to be a high-functioning sociopath), fans especially have latched onto Sherlock's "otherness" regarding sexual orientation or, at least, a clearcut sexual identification. Numerous fan works and online discussions support often controversial and certainly varied readings of Sherlock's and other characters' sexual orientation and heteronormative or, more frequently, non-heteronormative philosophies and activities.

In *Sherlock*, "sexy" goes beyond physical attractiveness, talent, or actor/character chemistry. It reflects a wide array of heteronormative and non-heteronormative characters and relationships that are enmeshed in the fabric of the series. Throughout four seasons' episodes, plots increasingly focus on Sherlock's emotional and social development rather than on solving mysteries or assisting New Scotland Yard or the British government on cases, a lengthy process that allows viewers to develop a deeper understanding of him. Even when Sherlock is being "socialized" over time to accept and show emotion as often as intellect (i.e., to become "normal"), he is still very much sexually "other" and has become a role model of sorts for many fans seeking validation of their identity. Such an integral focus on character development and the expanding definitions of *partner, family, relationship,* and *love* invites fans to become more emotionally attached to characters and to identify with them. As discussed in Chapter 7, this close identification can, in turn, lead at least some fans toward greater advocacy for sexual equality on television or greater understanding of a range of sexual orientations in mainstream culture.

From the Beginning, a Perceived Partnership in Every Way

Since the pilot episode, the world created by this television show espouses heteronormative ideals regarding sexual partnerships and marriage, which are constantly called into question. Most specifically, Sherlock Holmes and John Watson are often perceived, in the most favorable of ways, as a couple by other characters in the show who seem either delighted or incredulous that Sherlock has finally paired up with someone. Not coincidentally, the constant recognition of the possibility that Sherlock and John are intimately involved also stokes the flames of some very popular fan theories and fan fiction in which Sherlock and John are lovers.

Modern Sherlock still lives in London at 221 Baker Street, in the upstairs flat (B) rented from Mrs. Hudson (Una Stubbs). During the first two seasons' episodes, he shares 221B with John, a soldier-doctor who is home after being wounded in Afghanistan (just as the original Watson was wounded in a much earlier Afghan War). Within twenty-four hours of their introduction by mutual friend Mike Stamford (David Nellist), Sherlock invites John to look at the flat on Baker Street with him, and they agree to move in together ("A Study in Pink").

The instant friendship between Sherlock and John is necessary to have the pair immediately involved in stopping a serial killer, thus hooking the audience into the first episode's plot. Dialogue and the usage of first names, however, insinuate that their close friendship may be more than "like" at first sight. Unlike customary references to the main characters as Holmes and Watson, *Sherlock* showrunners and frequent scriptwriters Moffat and Gatiss insist on modern informality by referring to the characters as Sherlock and John. In addition to indicating that Sherlock and

John are immediately comfortable with each other, this first-name basis makes the characters more accessible to audiences, who more easily view them as contemporaries or even "friends."

Becoming "friends" with Sherlock and John also helps establish the foundations for the series' little "family" of characters its audiences soon come to know. Modernized canon characters include Mycroft Holmes (portrayed as "the British Government" and played by Gatiss), New Scotland Yard Inspector Greg Lestrade (Rupert Graves), and Mrs. Hudson, but the series also introduces new characters created for this series: St. Bartholomew Hospital pathologist Molly Hooper (Louise Brealey), New Scotland Yard detectives Philip Anderson (Jonathan Aris) and Sally Donovan (Vinette Robinson), parents Mr. and Mrs. Holmes (Timothy Carlton and Wanda Ventham, who are Cumberbatch's parents), Holmes sibling Eurus (Sian Brooke), and the Watson's baby Rosamund, who is nicknamed Rosie. Modern Sherlock has developed relationships with the people outside his biological family through his work as a consulting detective who accepts private clients but also works with New Scotland Yard, at their request, on their most difficult cases. Just as the series expands its plots and changes its focus from cases to an exploration of Sherlock's emotional and psychological well-being, so does Sherlock's chosen family expand and become intertwined in a way that makes the consulting detective's work life nearly indistinguishable from his personal life. In the pilot episode, Sherlock tells John that he is "married to his work," indicating that he has no time for personal relationships. However, by "The Final Problem," Sherlock's choice of cases and his sometimes questionable decisions in the way to eliminate villains increasingly become personal. Sherlock, it turns out, will do anything in his attempt to protect his chosen family, even more than his biological family—although they, too, become more important to him by the end of Season Four.

The BBC's adaptation increasingly strays from Arthur Conan Doyle's plot lines and characterizations, especially in Seasons Three and Four, but some elements of the canon remain a fundamental part of *Sherlock*. Two key aspects of the modern television series—the close friendship between Sherlock and John and Sherlock's occupation as a consulting detective, complete with the required familiarity with current technology and forensics procedures to allow him to deduce crime scenes more expertly than anyone else—are consistent with Conan Doyle's original stories. In particular, the Sherlock-John relationship has encouraged literary scholars to study the correlation between the original texts and the current television series. For example, Rebecca L. McLaughlin's thesis research into the BBC television series and its characterizations of Sherlock Holmes and John Watson early on asserts that

> *Sherlock* writers Steven Moffat and Mark Gatiss fully understand the relationship between Holmes and Watson in the original texts, and place emphasis on the characterization and development of this homosocial relationship within the show. Although it is set in contemporary British society, the show draws from and relies on the original representation of the relationship between these two men. Throughout *Sherlock*, Moffat and Gatiss explore the reasons for this male friendship, often incorporating, within the diegesis, elements of literary criticism about the original texts [2].

The Victorian–like male friendship described in Conan Doyle's stories reflects the social expectations of the author's time. Unmarried men who shared lodgings for financial and collegial reasons were not perceived as "gay." In fact, because homosexuality was criminalized in Britain until the mid-twentieth century, the original Holmes and Watson would have been in legal peril if anyone suspected that their friendship had become sexual. Close male friendships, however, were encouraged by a society in which men's sphere of influence was very different from women's. Men of the upper middle classes often attended university together and developed close friendships with their classmates. Watson not only had been educated as a physician but served with the Fifth Northumberland Fusiliers, where he lived and worked closely with his brothers in arms. That two young men, Holmes and Watson, would share a home as well as adventures until the time that Watson is married was not considered strange or sexually suggestive in the original stories' setting. Moffat and Gatiss are true to the characters' original portrayal when they immediately set up the situation by which Sherlock and John become flatmates and close friends. However, the close male friendship depicted in canon takes on a different meaning for viewers, especially when Moffat and Gatiss use audience expectations regarding a homosocial relationship to create sexual tension throughout the series. This "teasing" of Sherlock's or John's sexual orientation and the "true" nature of their relationship beyond the eye of the camera has become a hallmark of the series, beginning with the first episode.

When Mrs. Hudson shows the flat to Sherlock and John, she mentions the availability of a second bedroom upstairs, "if you'll be needing one." Perplexed, John replies that they need two bedrooms, one for each flatmate. Apparently Mrs. Hudson, like many people who grew up in Western culture during the 1940s and 1950s, has a heteronormative view of romantic relationships, although she is also aware of changing social attitudes toward homosexual relationships. For Mrs. Hudson, everyone should be paired with an intimate partner. She has known Sherlock for several years, ever since he ensured her troublesome husband's execution in Florida, and she is surprised when he brings a potential roommate to see the flat she is going to rent to him. Throughout the first episode, viewers are presented with plenty of evidence that Sherlock Holmes is a loner. Mycroft, for example, tells John that Sherlock has no friends; the closest relationship he has is with his "enemy," Mycroft (who, John later learns, is Sherlock's brother). New Scotland Yard's Sergeant Donovan is surprised that Sherlock brings a "colleague" to a crime scene, an unheard-of occasion; Detective Inspector Lestrade, who has known Sherlock for five years, also questions Sherlock about John's presence at the crime scene. No one, it seems, is accustomed to Sherlock having a friend. Thus, when Mrs. Hudson sees Sherlock bring "home" John as a potential roommate, she is pleased that he seems to be following an expected social construct: "pairing up." This "pairing up" is antithetical to Sherlock, who, according to evidence throughout the series, is not interested in a female romantic partner, may be attractive to men and women but is not sexually interested in them, and is emotionally closest to John, who consistently proclaims his heterosexuality throughout the series and, by Season Four, is considered "family" by Sherlock. Sherlock might always want to "pair up" with John for casework or friendship, but the majority of evidence about Sherlock's sexual orientation is that he may be an aromantic asexual—one who is not interested in romance or sex with a partner but may have meaningful platonic relationships.

Although John repeatedly indicates that he is only a roommate, in the first episode and even, two seasons later, when John confides in Mrs. Hudson that he is to be married, Mrs. Hudson is undeterred in assuming Sherlock has been in a (likely sexual) relationship with John and shocked that John is marrying a woman ("The Empty Hearse"). When she first shows 221B to Sherlock and John, she whispers that the next door landlady, Mrs. Turner, "has married ones" and indicates that she is not averse to renting rooms to a homosexual couple ("A Study in Pink"). In this way, Mrs. Hudson seems more open-minded than many of her generation. In fact, she takes on a competitive glee in assuming that she will have her very own "married" ones living together. Because marriage equality has gained traction, it is no wonder that Mrs. Hudson can make the leap to accepting a potential homosexual relationship, but she (and many others in the series) cannot seem to let go of the idea that Sherlock must be paired up romantically with someone, rather than considering that he may be asexual and uninterested in the traditional trappings of intimate partnerships. This lack of consideration of an asexual identity reveals an inherent heteronormative bias. The series' recognition of this bias continues throughout the seasons and in many different contexts, allowing viewers to pick up on this perspective. After John has moved into 221B and gone to his first crime scene with Sherlock, a mysterious man "encourages" John to enter a dark car and be driven to an interrogation in an empty garage, where John is asked about his relationship with Sherlock. Because Sherlock apparently has no friends and John, according to his therapist, does not easily trust people, the mysterious man, who turns out to be Mycroft, wonders why John has so quickly become involved with Sherlock. "Might we expect a happy announcement by the end of the week?" he asks, implying that the only reason the pair would move in together so quickly is if they have an intimate relationship.

Everyone, gay and straight alike, is subject to the shaping force of heteronormative instantiations of social and cultural practices. Ultimately, *Sherlock*'s depiction of a character that can be read as asexual, Sherlock, has no interest in such social/cultural precepts. He thus enables the audience to acknowledge the power that heteronormative constructs have to shape perceptions of how intimate relationships can and/or should be structured, especially when it comes to the expectation that one should seek intimate partnerships that lead to sex and marriage. Currently that pressure might extend to marriages between gay couples, as well; theorists have dubbed this "homonormativity" (a concept first introduced by New York University Professor Lisa Duggan, in 2003) to signify the myriad ways in which some of the gay community, despite the trappings of queer culture, may be perceived, perceive themselves, or want to be perceived as just like heteronormative people. The characters in *Sherlock* certainly seem to be progressive in their perception of lesbian and gay characters as "just like heteronormative people," though less progressive when it comes to perceptions regarding alternatives to traditional notions about partnerships and intimacy. While Sherlock eschews marriage and kinship in favor of "work," viewers can sense how heteronormative expectations function like a gravitational pull for most people who, unlike Sherlock, cannot easily dismiss them in favor of "work." In the episodes comprising Seasons Three and Four, Sherlock—who still has problems with the institution of marriage but nonetheless becomes John's best man when John marries Mary Morstan (Amanda Abbington; "The Sign of Three")—feels the gravitational pull of kinship and love and uses his deductive prowess to help protect those he loves. Yet Sherlock, and *Sherlock*, never seeks to meet heteronormative expectations. The Watsons' marriage and Sherlock's place within it simply become another way to subvert heteronormative expectations while, on the surface, allowing John and Mary to "conform" to such expectations (e.g., get married, create a home, have a baby, choose godparents, christen the child).

The expectation for intimate relationships to be sexual and implications regarding the expected "pairings" continues to mount as the season progresses, even Sherlock (the show's genius, "out of the box" thinker) is constrained by underlying heteronormative expectations that limit one's perspective regarding the possible range of relationships for humans. Dialogue, such as that in a restaurant scene in "A Study in Pink," implies that Sherlock, who can correctly deduce most facts about anyone he meets, thinks that John is at least bisexual and interested in him, despite John's constant protestations that he is heterosexual. During a stakeout, Sherlock takes John to an Italian restaurant operated by Angelo (Stanley Townsend), a man Sherlock once proved was not responsible for a serious crime. From the restaurant's window, Sherlock can watch for the suspected serial killer (the plot or case element of this episode). Not realizing that Sherlock is working, Angelo is thrilled that Sherlock has a date. Despite John's protest that he is not Sherlock's date, Angelo insists on placing a candle on their table because it is more romantic. During dinner, John asks Sherlock if he is romantically involved with anyone. Sherlock explains that women are "really not my area." John assumes that Sherlock has a boyfriend, "which is all right, by the way," but Sherlock replies that he does not have a boyfriend, either. Instead, Sherlock tells John that he is flattered by his attention but is "married" to his work. Flustered, John explains that he is not coming on to Sherlock. He reaffirms that Sherlock is single, just like he is. John's inability to even consider that Sherlock may be asexual is indicative of the lack of recognition in popular culture for this identity, despite such clear reference to asexual identity markers, which continue to build as the show progresses.

Sherlock, as one of very few television characters that fans identify as asexual, does not self-identify as any orientation, nor do the actors or showrunners corroborate the interpretation that way. For Sherlock, sexual interest is theoretical—how passion may lead to violent crime, for example, or, on a more personal level, how John's marriage may affect the amount of time Sherlock and John can spend together. Sherlock contrasts with the rare character that openly identifies as asexual, such as Voodoo Dunacci (Kelly O'Sullivan) on short-lived USA Network series *Sirens* (2014–2015). Whereas a self-identified asexual may be more common on a cable network television series with limited distribution, the more ambiguously identified asexual like Sherlock is more common on mainstream television series. *Sherlock* is one of BBC Worldwide's most popular global exports. That this series, reaching mainstream audiences who may not be familiar with asexuality, does not specifically label its lead character as asexual is not all that surprising. Furthermore, Moffat refers to Conan Doyle's text to reiterate that Sherlock is heterosexual but simply too preoccupied with work to consider sexual relationships, a rationale that Cumberbatch also has given during interviews to subvert alternate fan readings of the text.

Instead, Sherlock couches his self-identity in ambiguous terms that allow viewers to interpret the dialogue to support the reading they prefer. In the previously discussed restaurant scene in "A Study in Pink," Sherlock resists John's questions about personal relationships and explains that he is married to his work. The dialogue could be interpreted as Sherlock being asexual (in his case, not interested in intimate, non-sexual relationships with anyone) or celibate (choosing not to have sexual relationships). Throughout the series, Sherlock is hinted as being a virgin and possibly "alarmed" by sex ("A Scandal in Belgravia") and uninterested in finding a sexual partner. At John's wedding, maid of honor Janine (Yasmine Akram) attempts to hook up with Sherlock, but he dodges her advances and deduces possible partners for her. Janine's comment, "I wish you weren't ... whatever you are" can be read as Sherlock's ambiguous (to her) orientation or her lack of understanding his asexuality ("The Sign of Three").

The special episode "The Abominable Bride" is perhaps the most revealing, because it takes place within Sherlock's mind—he subconsciously determines what the "Sherlock" and "John" solving a crime in his Mind Palace will say or do. Once again, John expresses concern that Sherlock is alone and alludes to "experiences" that he assumes Sherlock has had. Visibly uncomfortable, Sherlock tries to steer the conversation in other directions. Finally, John asks "What made you like this?" The implication, from the married man's worldview that everyone must pair up, is that Sherlock must have had a previous relationship that scarred him emotionally and left him unwilling to risk becoming involved again. Sherlock, however, proudly proclaims, "Nothing made me. *I* [actor's emphasis] made me." Viewers may read this dialogue as indicating that no one or prior experience has made Sherlock, the lone consulting detective, more content with his work than with a sexual partner. However, it also may indicate that, without a vocabulary to express his sexual orientation—or, indeed, a definition that the public can understand or accept as valid—Sherlock "made" himself and feels unique among his circle of family, friend John, and work acquaintances. As with many areas of his life, Sherlock prides himself on being unique, from his choice of profession to the way he thinks to the independent way he lives. Being asexual may be read as part of Sherlock's uniqueness or "otherness."

Fans gather "evidence" such as the previous examples from the show that Sherlock could be perceived as asexual so that they may co-opt this character as a possible representation of asexual identity in popular culture. This group is so in need of representation that they act as detectives themselves, building a case for the possibility that they may be on the cusp of representation. While this is certainly a worthwhile endeavor, as it draws attention to the plight of asexuals, Sherlock, as representative of asexual identity, is not as compelling a representation as it would be if the character were to self-identify, validating *asexual* as an identity, rather than marking the presence of asexual behavior.

Furthermore, Sherlock's asexual behavior may be used to pathologize his asexuality in such a way that it adds to the misperception that asexual behavior is always a sign of dysfunction, rather than entertaining the possibility that it may be part of one's identity. In the first episode, Sherlock proclaims himself to be a "high-functioning sociopath," a claim reiterated after he kills Charles Augustus Magnussen (Lars Mikkelsen) many episodes later ("His Last Vow"). Nevertheless, as many scholars (e.g., Dondero and Pippin) have noted, Sherlock is not, by medical definition or character development, truly a sociopath. He may claim sociopathy so that he does not need to be socially acceptable to those he deems his intellectual inferiors or to mask his emotions, but Sherlock increasingly shows that he is capable of love, particularly when it comes to John. Sherlock is "other" from the social norm, but his potential asexuality is not the only reason why he is so different from the rest of the characters in *Sherlock* or on U.S. or U.K. television. His behavior regarding sex or sexuality is merely another factor—like (incorrectly) self-identifying as a sociopath, being able to deduce facts from observation, choosing not to eat or sleep during a case— that is outside the norm and may initially seem to pathologize asexuality and has been troubling to fans who are also asexuality advocates. Because viewers learn nothing specific about Sherlock's relationship history other than that he has not really had any, they receive no trite or convenient explanation for his remaining unattached. At least until "The Final Problem" (the episode that explains Sherlock has sublimated troubling emotions and been traumatized since childhood because of his sister's murderous cruelty), they have no reason to believe that his ideology stems from pain or dysfunction, which allows savvy viewers to perceive his "lifestyle" as not a reaction to something but as a queer identity.

Just because Sherlock may be perceived as asexual does not mean that he is incapable of feeling or demonstrating great love. This aspect of his identity has been championed by advocates who emphasize that sex does not have to equal love, or that love does not require sexual attraction. Throughout the series, Sherlock increasingly sacrifices himself to save John—most notably, faking his death in order to save John from Moriarty's hired assassin and leaving behind his friends and livelihood in order to finish the job of dismantling Moriarty's criminal network ("The Reichenbach Fall") and, a few episodes later, murdering a publishing magnate who blackmails John's wife and threatens John physically ("His Last Vow"). Sherlock even returns to drug addiction and, in his words, is "off my tits for weeks" in an attempt to get John to save him from himself and thus force a reconciliation following the death of John's wife ("The Lying Detective"). During "The Final Problem," Sherlock's solution to choosing to kill either John or Mycroft is to threaten suicide, and Sherlock later saves John from drowning in a well. However, Sherlock does more than physically or emotionally save John's life on several occasions. Despite the many traumas John suffers because of his friendship with Sherlock (e.g., being kidnapped more than once, believing Sherlock is dead for several years, discovering his wife shot Sherlock, seeing his wife sacrifice herself in order to save Sherlock), the consulting detective ultimately gives John purpose and becomes, according to John, his best friend ("The Sign of Three"). Sherlock considers John his only friend ("The Hounds of Baskerville") and, during the best man's speech at John's wedding, proclaims that he and Mary are the two people who love John most ("The Sign of Three"). By "The Final Problem," Sherlock tells Mycroft that he considers John part of their family and allows John to hear long-buried family secrets. As a result, Sherlock's obvious emotional reliance on John's well-being has become the focal point of many types of fan readings of the Sherlock-John relationship and the subject of much online discussion and fan works.

The amount of sexually suggestive dialogue, especially within the pilot episode, establishes what Carlen Lavigne describes as Sherlock's amorphous sexuality: "he is assuredly queer, in the most generic, non-heteronormative sense of the word, and he *could be* [original emphasis] gay, straight, bisexual, asexual, or pansexual. He does not commit himself in any way" (18). In subsequent episodes, Sherlock only seems interested in keeping John's attention, ensuring that John remains (or, after Mary's death, returns as) his flatmate, or protecting John. Even when tempted by

Irene Adler (Lara Pulver, "A Scandal in Belgravia"), Sherlock resists her less-than-subtle seduction attempts; Adler eventually tells John that she is attracted to Sherlock, but that John and Sherlock are the ones in a relationship. Sherlock's sexual experience, however, is also questioned in this episode, indicating that he may feel emotionally close to John but has not entered a sexual relationship with anyone.

Early in "A Scandal in Belgravia," Sherlock and John are summoned to Buckingham Palace, where Mycroft introduces Sherlock to a representative of his royal client. The men explain that Adler is blackmailing a member of the royal family and show Sherlock a series of sexually suggestive photographs that Adler is using to prove she can ruin the royal's reputation. Mycroft warns Sherlock not be alarmed, even though the case "has to do with sex." Sherlock quickly assures his brother, "Sex doesn't alarm me," to which Mycroft replies, "How would you know?" Although the banter may merely reflect sibling rivalry, more specific dialogue near the episode's end reinforces the visual evidence (i.e., Sherlock avoiding Adler's advances at two points in this episode). Adler tells Mycroft that criminal mastermind Moriarty refers to Mycroft as the "Iceman," but Sherlock is called the "Virgin." With the number of insinuations about Sherlock's lack of sexual experience given throughout this episode, the character's sexual identity seems especially fluid and leads many viewers to think of Sherlock as asexual rather than gay or bisexual. The view of asexuals as virgins is a common misperception, as asexual people may have varying degrees of interest in certain types of sexual activities.

During the third season, Sherlock (who has returned to London after faking his death and working to dismantle Moriarty's criminal network) strives to repair his friendship with John, who has mourned Sherlock and is horrified that Sherlock cruelly deceived him. However, Sherlock also becomes friends with Mary Morstan. He seems comfortable with his asexual role in this three-way friendship. Whereas John tries to compartmentalize his post-marriage relationships (Mary = spouse, Sherlock = best friend), he nonetheless keeps returning to Sherlock, and the John-Sherlock relationship remains the foundation on which the series continues to be built.

In addition to Sherlock's continuing emotional investment in his relationship with John, he continues to provide evidence that he may be asexual. When he shams an engagement to a woman to gather information for a case, his fiancée Janine is affectionate and continually tries to place him in provocative situations. She moves into 221B and makes herself at home, rearranging furniture and wearing Sherlock's shirt. However, later in the episode, when she realizes that she has been used, she tells Sherlock that she wishes they had consummated the relationship: "Just once would've been nice." Sherlock drolly explains that he is saving himself for marriage. Despite Janine saving face by reporting to London's tabloids that Sherlock is an insatiable lover, viewers understand that, according to Sherlock, he is still not interested in sex with a woman, whether it be professional seductress Irene Adler or wholesome fiancée Janine ("His Last Vow").

Sherlock does not bother to eschew insinuations about his sex life, like John does, and intimations that he has had sex with a man can be ruled as a joke shared between Molly and Sherlock. In "The Empty Hearse," John is so angry that Sherlock faked his death, leaving John to grieve for years while Mycroft and Molly know of the deception, that he abandons Sherlock. When Sherlock seeks an assistant on a case, he enlists Molly, who realizes that she is merely a stand-in for John. While Molly and Sherlock are working together, he asks her out for chips and explains that he always receives extra portions because he helped the proprietor "put up some shelves." Sherlock smirks at the slang reference to gay sex, and Molly seems to be in on the joke. Although some fans read this reference as proof of Sherlock's homosexuality, others perceive it more as an insider joke shared between friends who understand Sherlock is not interested in having sex with anyone. In any case, throughout four seasons and a special episode, Sherlock is not shown in a sexual relationship or professing any interest in a sexual relationship with men or women.

The Ideal Sherlock: *A Variety of Polyamorous, Homosocial and Homosexual Possibilities in Season Four*

As John D'Emilio explains, the nuclear family's original significance was primarily as an economic unit. When it no longer had to serve only this purpose, a wider range of interfamilial relationships became possible and, indeed, socially acceptable, and the family unit became a place for emotional nurturance and support. During Season Four's final episode, "The Final Problem," *Sherlock* seems to return to this philosophy of the significance of a nuclear family—but, as might be expected of a series that does not embrace most heteronormative situations—Sherlock's depiction of "family" as both an economic unit and a means of emotional and psychological support is ever shifting and pragmatic while feeding into fans' expectations and multiple possible readings of the text.

Although Season Four has been criticized for deviating the most from case-solving plots and for introducing confusing, convoluted plot or character elements that defy logic (especially in the controversial "The Final Problem"), scenes within the episodes posit further possible non-heteronormative futures for Sherlock and multiple new ways to read the character's relationships and their reflection on his sexual orientation.

Before Mary Watson gives birth, she, John, and Sherlock are shown working on cases together ("The Six Thatchers"). In fact, the trio is so involved in their mutual work that, when Mary announces she must go to the hospital, she is brushed off until John and Sherlock realize that she is indeed in the late stages of labor. Of course, for comedic value, Mary and Sherlock share the backseat while John drives to the hospital. Baby Watson cannot wait, and, to Sherlock's horror, Mary delivers her daughter in the car. However, this scene also serves to establish that, from the moment of her birth, Rosamund (Rosie) Watson will be raised unconventionally. Later scenes establish that she will be guided not just by her parents but by godparents Sherlock, Molly, and Mrs. Hudson, and during much of her babyhood Sherlock is a familiar influence.

After Rosie's birth, Sherlock, John, and Mary continue to work together on cases. At times, Sherlock seeks Mary's assistance rather than John's, leaving John with childcare duties. When the three adults go together into the field, John is shown wearing a bjorn carrying Rosie. However, Sherlock also shares childcare duties. In another scene played for comedy, he talks to "Watson" as if she were an adult and explains the logical outcome of her throwing a toy multiple times only so that Sherlock can retrieve it ("The Six Thatchers").

What might be perceived as a polyamorous relationship by some fans (who have written fiction in which these three adults love each other as sexual as well as work partners) is portrayed as a chaste polyamorous love on screen, the culmination of Sherlock's many sacrifices to keep the Watsons together and out of harm's way and John's willingness to help keep Sherlock sober. Sherlock sacrifices himself to protect Mary (and thus John and their unborn child) by killing Charles Augustus Magnussen, who has the potential to blackmail and manipulate the trio ("His Last Vow"). When Sherlock overdoses at the start of his aborted government-instigated suicide mission to Serbia, John agrees to take over Mycroft's protective oversight of Sherlock and "look after him" ("The Abominable Bride"). These episodes lead into "The Six Thatchers," in which the working relationship among Sherlock, John, and Mary seems to be balanced with their shared childcare duties. Although John and Mary live separately from Sherlock, the married couple and, later, Rosie are shown just as often visiting Baker Street.

Yet this polyamorous work-love (platonic or otherwise) relationship becomes fractured by the end of "The Six Thatchers." Mary's past as an assassin returns to haunt her. While she attempts to lead her would-be murderer away from her family, John and Sherlock apparently are left behind to take care of Rosie (again, the topic for fan fiction speculation). When they leave to find and confront Mary, the likely village helping to care for Rosie includes her godmothers Molly and Mrs. Hudson. In an attempt to bring his chosen family back together, Sherlock promises John and Mary that he will protect her if she returns to London. When the person who hired the assassins and led to Mary's being hunted by one of her former colleagues is revealed, Sherlock misjudges the situation and faces death after confronting Mary's former boss. In a room full of witnesses, including Mycroft, Lestrade, and a late-arriving John (a set-up convenient to establish the resulting estrangement between Sherlock and John), Mary leaps (in slow motion on screen, no less) between Sherlock and the bullet and dies a hero. This action, however, shatters not only the familial triumvirate of Mary, John, and Sherlock but the longer-standing John-Sherlock relationship. Ironically, by the end of "The Final Problem," Mary succeeds in bringing Sherlock and John together in a closer homosocial (but what some fans return to reading as a homosexual) relationship.

A series of DVD messages that turn up after Mary's death illustrates that not only was the former assassin aware that she may not live long in marital (or polyamorous) bliss but that the series' true pairing is always Sherlock and John. Mary's instructions to Sherlock encourage him to nearly kill himself by returning to drug addiction so that John can save him and presumably get over his anger/grief at Mary's death ("The Lying Detective"). After a convoluted plot in "The Final Problem" forces Mycroft, Sherlock, and John to join forces in order to survive the destructive machinations of the previously unmentioned Holmes' sibling Eurus, John and Sherlock are shown rebuilding the destroyed 221B. The symbolism is obvious; not only are they reconstructing the home they once shared, but they are also rebuilding the foundation of their friendship. Both Sherlock and John play with Rosie while they all are within the restored 221B. The final freeze-frame of Season Four shows John and Sherlock, side by side, running into action as they embark on yet another case. The status quo has, in large measure, been re-established, and the homosocial relationship introduced in "A Study in Pink" is again intact. However, Rosie introduces a key change to this homosocial relationship. Instead of merely being two bachelor-friends sharing living space, John and Sherlock are strongly hinted to be sharing childrearing duties. Although Molly makes a brief appearance (about a second of screen time showing her enter 221B) and Mrs. Hudson still lives downstairs, the emphasis is on "my Baker Street boys," as Mary calls them in her posthumous voiceover. The final moments of the episode indicate at least a homosocial relationship that has become far more permanent and familial since the first episode. As explicitly stated in dialogue and heavily implied by the closing montage, John and Sherlock have formed a non-heteronormative family.

For many fans, the evidence of a homosexual reading of the Sherlock-John relationship indicates far more than the homosocial relationship depicted on screen. A scene in "The Lying Detective" concludes with John breaking down in tears about being an unfaithful husband (if only via text messages with another woman), in addition to his grief over losing Mary. Sherlock comforts John by gingerly placing his arms around him and oh-so-briefly pressing his cheek to the shorter man's head. Sherlock seems awkward, as if this is the first time he has dared touch John this intimately; similarly, John has never been so vulnerable or accepted comfort from Sherlock. Fans who long for a within-text homosexual pairing of Sherlock and John have perceived this scene as implying a future sexual relationship between the two.

In contrast, Sherlolly (Sherlock + Molly) fans use one scene in "The Final Problem" as evidence of a potential heterosexual, heteronormative relationship, although other fans can read this scene only as proof of Sherlock's determination to save yet another friend from peril without that determination indicating sexual interest. When Eurus threatens to blow up Molly's home unless Sherlock convinces her by phone to declare her love for him, Molly first forces Sherlock to say that he loves her. Of course, the friendship between Molly and Sherlock has been expanded throughout the series, and Molly's unrequited love for the consulting detective has led to him allowing her to accompany him on a case ("The Empty Hearse") and to face her wrath ("His Last Vow") and agony ("The Lying Detective") regarding his drug abuse. Undoubtedly Sherlock does feel love for ever-devoted Molly, but he has never expressed a sexual interest in her. Despite the context of the exchanged "I love you"s, fans who want to read a het-eronormative romance into this scene have done so via fan fiction and discussion on Tumblr forums, whereas fans who prefer a heterosexual or an asexual reading prefer interpreting this scene as evidence of Sherlock's capacity for platonic love and his increased awareness of and ability to express his emotions for those in his chosen family.

By the conclusion of Season Four, almost everyone—Mrs. Hudson, Mycroft, John, Moriarty, Irene Adler, Eurus—has made assumptions about Sherlock's sexual orientation and his sexual activities (or need for them). Unlike most television texts, this ambiguity has not been resolved by the time of a possible series' finale or the "reset" before years of hiatus before another new *Sherlock* episode. (In 2017, the BBC had not canceled *Sherlock* but also had not approved a fifth season, and the showrunners and actors discussed in interviews that it might be a long time before any new stories are told.) Whereas most television characters' stories resolve the sexual tension by such a watershed mark as "The Final Problem," Sherlock may be read as heterosexual but celibate, homosexual, or asexual, depending on the evidence that fans choose to emphasize and their determination of what is truth or jest, baiting or fact. Although other characters are non-heteronormative, either sexually or with their lifestyle choices, Sherlock is most often the topic of online discussion and the object of fan fascination. As such, he has become the focus of online advocacy and confrontation between fans and showrunners/actors about the "correct" interpretation of characters. *Sherlock*'s global popularity and fan attraction to Sherlock as an "other" character in many respects has encouraged, more than most television series, a discussion of asexuality and prompted at least some fans to become more actively involved in advocacy.

7

Toward an Ethos
of Advocacy for Asexuality

While discourse regarding LGBTQ people has largely evolved in subtle but important ways, and a movement toward the inclusion of other marginalized groups is evident in the more inclusive moniker LGBTQIA+ (adding intersex and asexual, as well as "+" to represent the myriad gender and sexual identities to which people ascribe that are not represented by a letter in the current acronym), neither representation nor discourse regarding asexuality has significantly expanded into popular culture. For example, in many personal accounts of asexuals coming to terms with and attempting to understand their identity, as is the case with homosexual "coming out stories" of the 1970s, they most often lack a cultural referent and the language to describe their sexual identity because there is no popular culture referent or common language to express it. For example, Cathy, a 20-year-old asexual woman who participated in a The Asexuality Story Project, a website in which asexuals discuss their experiences, describes hearing the word *asexual* for the first time on her first day of college. After researching asexuality, Cathy "couldn't believe how much it sounded like me. My life suddenly made sense. I never knew there were other people like me [*sic*] I thought I was all alone." This sentiment of lacking the language and understanding to identify one's sexuality is continuously repeated in the narratives of asexuals.

While this sentiment likely rings true for gay men and women coping with the discovery of their sexuality forty or fifty years ago, the attention being paid to LGBTQ issues and identities in our current culture has profoundly affected young people identifying as gay, lesbian, trans, or queer. They are likely to be aware of both discourse and representations to which they may relate when they attempt to navigate a burgeoning sexual identity outside the heteronormative ideals. In contrast, asexual identity exists under erasure. Because the definition of asexuality is the absence of sexual attraction, and, according to the Asexual Visibility and Education Network (AVEN), there is not one singular experience for all asexual people, AVEN provides the following definitions:

> DEMISEXUAL: Someone who can only experience sexual attraction after an emotional bond has been formed. This bond does not have to be romantic.
>
> GRAY-ASEXUAL (GRAY-A) OR GRAY-SEXUAL: Someone who identifies with the area between asexuality and sexuality, for example, because they experience sexual attraction very rarely, only under specific circumstances, or of an intensity so low that it is ignorable.
>
> AESTHETIC ATTRACTION: Attraction to someone's appearance, without it being romantic or sexual.
>
> ROMANTIC ATTRACTION: Desire of being romantically involved with another person.
>
> SENSUAL ATTRACTION: Desire to have physical, non-sexual contact with someone else, like affectionate touching.

Because there is no singular type of expression for asexual identity and because asexuals are not always read as "other," asexuals may "pass" as heteronormative in the same way that bisexuals may be perceived, at times, as straight. This misperception has the potential to disempower both bisexuals and asexuals because it leads others to question why they need representation and advocacy.

This erasure is evident, in a commonplace example; as of the writing of this book, Microsoft Word's autocorrect continuously corrects the spelling of "asexuals" (a plural noun akin to homosexuals) to "asexual" (an adjective) or, without autocorrect, highlights "asexual" as a word not matching any recognized term. This lack of representation in popular discourse reduces asexuals to a description of their lack of sexual behavior, at best, and to a type of single-celled organism and plant reproduction, at worst, rather than validating asexuality as an identity, as who people are, rather than what they do or, in the case of asexuality, what they do not do.

As a result of the many examples described in the previous chapter, twenty-first-century Sherlock has become caught in the crossfire of a heated online debate about his sexuality. The lead character's asexual behavior has shed some light on and given a voice to those fans or audience members who identify as asexual. The series also actively promotes online discussion regarding a multiplicity of sexual orientations and societal interest in or response to *Sherlock*'s character revelations and development. Fan engagement with these issues leads to many thoughtful online discussions, not only about the series but also about concepts of sexuality in a broader scope.

The series' character development and evolving plot lines allow viewers, and more specifically fans, to create safe spaces online for communities in which they can discuss both their and the characters' sexuality and perceptions regarding both traditional and non-traditional relationships. The value of a show that pushes the typical heteronormative boundaries and represents alternative sex/love relationships cannot be overstated. These main characters heavily imply a world in which characters of any sexual orientation are normal, and the "atypical" relationship between Sherlock and John cannot easily fit preconceived definitions of *family*, *couple*, or even the concept of *love*.

Exploring the content of these digital communities and the ways in which they and the technology that makes them possible function and contribute to a modern understanding of identity, community, and even advocacy online are tantamount to understanding what it means to be a contemporary citizen in the digital age. Thus, in a digital age, authentic representation of non-normative expressions of both sexuality and gender becomes increasingly important. In order for authenticity to be established, there needs to be a "witness" to these subjectivities, first to instantiate their existence and then to think about how these queer subjectivities affect and are affected by the dominant discourse.

Donna Haraway, in her book *Modest_Witness@Second_Millenium. FemaleMan Meets Oncomouse*, explores the concept of the traditional "modest witness." This classic modest witness claims to be "the legitimate and authorized ventriloquist for the object world, adding nothing from his mere opinions, from his biasing embodiment" (24). The classic modest witness is always a male of some social standing, which reveals the way in which heteronormativity shapes social and political consciousness in that it is the default "culture of no culture" that Susan Traweek first describes and Haraway inscribes as part of her rhetoric. This "culture of no culture" presupposes that the classic and outmoded modest witness' identity and, consequently, his or her documentation of the witnessed events magically transcend any subjectivity that might otherwise be present. In this way, those whose voices are a privileged part of that "culture of no culture," which presupposes heteronormative-embodied maleness, are also those who exercise socio-political power over marginalized identities.

Sites for advocacy online can be said to host a new generation of "witnesses" who contribute narratives about their personal experiences and advice based on their opinions and experiences, and their "biasing embodiment" is at the forefront of their claims. By allowing people who contribute/create texts to speak their truths in their own words, advocacy websites like the Asexual Story Project provide an authentic representation of the asexual community and reliable information about the community's needs. This site accomplishes two things: first, it instantiates their existence, and second, it provides an opportunity for those both in and out of the asexual community to think about how the very existence of these queer subjectivities affects and is affected by the dominant discourses. These sites do a good job of putting contributors in the position to make claims of situated knowledge, especially because they offer diverse claims from diverse people about asexual experience.

Haraway asserts that, in order "to enable compelling belief and collective action" (which is the mission of any social action movement), society must find a new modest witness who, "while eschewing the additive narcotic of transcendental foundations" (22) like those that guarantee objective representation of a universal truth, must be "in the action, be finite and dirty, not transcendent and clean" (36). In other words, the public needs to see and hear the voices of those who lack recognition within the framework of traditional society if there is to be a better understanding of the way that the "real world" produces knowledge, because "nothing comes without its world, so trying to know those worlds is crucial" (37).

Acknowledging subjectivity is crucial when considering objectivity. The most objective and, consequently, useful "witnesses" document their observations about the world through the lens of their own situated knowledge and who practices "critical reflexivity"—a witness who is aware of and attempts to make others aware of a distinctive subject position. This "critical reflexivity," especially when espoused by a witness who identifies with a marginalized subculture, makes room for new ways of producing and reconfiguring knowledge, which is necessary for an understanding of the representation and rights of those groups that fall outside of the traditional "norms" that dictate the limits of a community's and/or society's perceptions. The value inherent in working in a social media environment is that accomplishing this production and reconfiguration of knowledge requires a minimum of time and effort and allows participation from contributors all over the world from different social standings and cultural backgrounds.

Those fans and advocates who share their stories and perceptions online are the new modest witnesses, and their ability to have an impact on culture is directly related to the post-human condition and online environment that enables their texts to be consumed and even to be understood in a way that would not be possible without the affordances of digital technology, digital culture, and digital literacy. Whereas this platform has much promise for advocacy, it is also limited in some profound ways. For example, in the opening to her talk at the University of Central Florida on October 19, 2012, seasoned activist and feminist icon Gloria Steinem began her talk by addressing the audience directly:

> I especially appreciate your coming together in one room in the age of twitter and pressing send and so on. I just want to remind us that, as miraculous as the electronic age is, something can happen in a room like this that can't happen anywhere else. We have to be together in order to truly understand each other. If we don't have all five of our senses connecting, the chemicals in our brain that allow us to empathize with each other don't get triggered. You can't raise a baby on the Internet. So, I hope that this feels as special to you as it does to me.

Steinem's take on the issue of embodied face-to-face communication and computer-mediated digital communication has profound implications for how some people may perceive activism in an online environment. Her comments speak to the tension between digital and face-to-face interactions. Being a part of the audience and hearing Steinem speak in person, as well as responding to the reactions of other audience members, is a unique experience. Reading a transcript of the speech does not create the same experience or invoke the same emotions as being part of a group and feeding into the in-person interaction between the speaker and audience or among audience members. Cultural critic Walter Benjamin makes sense of this phenomenon when he claims that with even "the most perfect reproduction" (filmic reproduction being as "perfect" as it gets), a mechanically reproduced text "is lacking in one element: its presence in time and space, its unique existence at the place where it happens to be." This removal from its original, temporal moment changes something about the text and how a viewer perceives it. Benjamin identifies that which is changed through mechanical reproduction as "the aura" of the text:

> The concept of aura ... may usefully be illustrated with reference to the aura of natural ones. We define the aura of the latter as the unique phenomenon of a distance, however close it may be. If, while resting on a summer afternoon, you follow with your eyes a mountain range on the horizon or a branch which casts its shadow over you, you experience the aura of those mountains, of that branch. This image makes it easy to comprehend the social bases of the contemporary decay of the aura. It rests on two circumstances, both of which are related to the increasing significance of the masses in contemporary life. Namely, the desire of contemporary masses to bring things "closer" spatially and humanly, which is just as ardent as their bent toward overcoming the uniqueness of every reality by accepting its reproduction.

Benjamin's observations help to interpret the current media culture that strives to, as Marshall McLuhan notes, expand "our central nervous system in a global embrace, abolishing both space and time as far as our planet is concerned" (3). As people attempt to "bring things 'closer,'" they may be diminishing "the aura" of a text, rendering it less authentic and thereby alienating it from the possibility for the authentic "closeness" that actual temporal and physical presence renders.

Benjamin asserts that "to pry an object from its shell, to destroy its aura, is the mark of a perception whose 'sense of the universal equality of things' has increased to such a degree that it extracts it even from a unique object by means of reproduction." This contemporary misperception by audiences about the authenticity and quality of digital texts, those texts removed from the "human life world," marks the tension created when activism and advocacy are performed through new media. However, considering a new understanding of the potential for digital media to invoke a subjective and affective experience, as well as Benjamin's argument, opens up opportunities to create new ways to navigate and facilitate understanding of ourselves and others. In Steinem's talk, she does not diminish the value of digital media; she cautions listeners to be aware of the difference. Looking at those differences and analyzing existing participation in activist media online, such as through this analysis of television texts and fan works, helps to facilitate an understanding of the current circumstances of advocacy through new media and the potential for new kinds of advocacy experiences to emerge.

These face-to-face and computer-mediated platforms have implications for how activism works for different audiences and in different circumstances. Previously, one would have to attend a rally or other social forum in order to feel the impact of these messages; now, people can be influenced in increasingly profound and engaging ways through new media that have the potential to make the mechanisms for social activism more efficient rather than diminish the activity itself. An important consideration is that, whereas more than two hundred people attended Steinem's talk and shared that unique experience; many more could share and discuss the video of her talk via modern technology. The importance of proliferation of a message to the success of a social action campaign is imperative, and the digital and face-to-face "talk" that this video has inspired has an "aura" of its own, one that is unique and participatory. It is this model of online advocacy that is enacted by *Sherlock* fans in service of the asexual community.

Fan-generated texts and fan-maintained communities, as Matt Hills explains in "Virtually Out There," "support and sustain a community of the imagination," rather than the often referred to "imagined community," in which theorists tend to focus on the "pleasure" derived from fan activities rather than the affective attachments (147). *Affect* refers to emotion, and fans' highly affective attachment to the objects of their affection and their devotion to them are key elements in understanding why and how fans and fan communities are particularly well suited for advocacy work. These affective attachments, when cultivated in online affective spaces, lead to fans/advocates who are passionate and well versed. Hills explains that virtual communities are "unlike fan conventions, which are restricted to specific times and places, and which therefore function as ritually bounded spaces separated off from fans' everyday lives" (148). While this embodied contact remains significant and important to many fans (and advocates like Steinem), it is not central to their lived experiences in the same way virtual communities are. While this may seem, at first, challenging to apprehend because what is being asserted is that the embodied experience is more separated from everyday life than the disembodied-virtual experience, Hills adds that virtual communities break down the barriers that fans face as they go through their everyday lives with others who are not likely to share their values or acknowledge/understand their fan identity/culture. Virtual communities allow "fan expression and identity to leak out into, and potentially permeate, the fan's everyday life" because their community is accessible through digital technology all the time, unlike those embodied fan experiences like conventions (149). The access and the distribution power of online media prove important for both the affective fan experiences and cultural identity and advocacy. Unlike the very limited distribution of print texts, like fanzines, the texts distributed online are accessible by anyone with an Internet connection and interest in either a particular fandom or a particular cause.

Sherlock *and the Fan Community: Enacting Asexual Advocacy Online*

Just as the "official" word about Sherlock's sexuality, espoused by Steven Moffat and Benedict Cumberbatch in media interviews, often contradicts fans' definition of *asexual,* so do their comments reflect a very different understanding of asexuality as a sexual orientation rather than a lifestyle choice. In an interview with *Indie Wire* in 2012, during the television season when dominatrix Irene Adler attempts to sexually tempt

Sherlock and reveals that Moriarty's code name for the consulting detective is "The Virgin" ("A Scandal in Belgravia"), Cumberbatch describes his character's sex drive in terms that led to dissenting discussions in asexuality forums. The actor replies to a question about Adler influencing Sherlock's sexuality and his apparent "non-existent sex drive" during the first (pre–Adler) season:

> Well, I see no reason at all why he shouldn't be sexual. Everyone recruited him to their perspective, their interpretation. I've had asexuals come up to me and thank me for representing asexuals. I don't know how that came about. I mean, the man's too busy to have sex.... Like a lot of things in his life where he's purposely dehumanized himself, it's to do with not wanting the stuff that is time wasting, that's messy [N. Smith].

This quotation indicates that Cumberbatch does not seem offended or distressed when asexuals thank him for his character giving visibility on television to asexuality, but he consistently chooses to describe Sherlock as preferring celibacy as a lifestyle. His understanding of asexuality, at least as expressed during interviews, is that asexuals have no sex drive. What is more troubling to the asexual community is that the actor who, through Sherlock, may represent them on television also describes Sherlock's decision to avoid sex as "dehumanizing," as if an integral part of the definition of *human* is someone who is sexually active or at least does something about his or her sex drive beyond suppressing it.

During an *Elle* interview more than two years later (in October 2014), in response to a question about Sherlock's sexual prowess, Cumberbatch again mentions asexuality: "He's asexual for a purpose. Not because he doesn't have a sex drive, but because it's suppressed to do his work. Cold showers, looking at a lot of dead bodies ... that'll do it for you" (Brog). Cumberbatch further speculates that Sherlock has hot sex off camera with Adler after he saves her from a beheading. To many fans, these types of comments seem designed to make Sherlock more of a heterosexual sex symbol and less of a poster man for asexuality. Perhaps not so coincidentally, during fall 2014 Cumberbatch was in the middle of an Oscar campaign for his role as Alan Turing (*The Imitation Game*), whose homosexuality became as much of a discussion topic as his brilliance as a World War II code breaker and the father of the computer. During the film's promotion, the actor was often perceived as trying to establish himself as a Hollywood leading man. Making his best-known character Sherlock seem determinedly heterosexual may have been part of Cumberbatch's campaign to steer clear of being primarily identified with homosexual or asexual characters, as they are not typically Hollywood leading-man roles. Nonetheless, as Cumberbatch notes in the 2012 *Indie Wire* interview, he realizes that fans often perceive the character differently than he does and co-opt Sherlock for different purposes.

What showrunner Moffat says about Sherlock's sexuality is frequently quoted within asexuality forums as the starting point for a (sometimes angry) discussion about Sherlock's sexuality and the ways that Moffat's comments seem contradictory to the aims of the asexual community. Not only does Moffat rely on canon as his proof that Sherlock Holmes, in the Victorian or modern eras, is celibate, not asexual, but he notes that asexuality is an atypical choice for a television character. Within a *Guardian* article published in January 2012, shortly after the Adler episode "A Scandal in Belgravia" was broadcast, Moffat is quoted as saying that "If he was asexual, there would be no tension in that, no fun in that—it's someone who abstains who's interesting" (Jeffries).

To some asexuals posting on Tumblr blogs or asexuality forums, Moffat's use of "no fun" is translated as "boring," as in the title of an Asexual Education Tumblr site: "A Lovely Interview About Sherlock Wherein Steven Moffat Says That Asexuality is 'Boring,' That Sherlock is Definitively Not Gay, and That Sherlock Wouldn't Be Living With a Man If Men Were Interesting." The discussion garnered nearly 2,000 notes by July 2017 (some recently added to the ongoing discussion), including comments that illustrate the type of response Moffat's seemingly innocuous interview comments commonly generate. missyankovic asserted that "Asexuals can be fun." raonddx more vehemently disagreed with Moffat, noting that the Conan Doyle canon Moffat is so fond of citing also does not have the language to describe sexual orientation. This fan explains that, because everyone was assumed to be heterosexual in Conan Doyle's time, there was not language to describe heterosexuality until there was a concept of homosexuality. (Presumably this person could make the same argument for asexuality, which also is not a term used or a concept publicly discussed during the Victorian era of the canon stories and is only just becoming part of popular culture in the 21st century.) raonddx concludes that, if Moffat's definitions are limited to language available during the Victorian era, he will not find references to asexuality. flynnsarcade took an active approach to educating Moffat about asexuality, as well as the impact of his comments on many asexuals. He tweeted Moffat that if "he researched asexuality he would find it anything but boring, told him that he had likely hurt the feelings of many fans, and linked him to a glossary of the different facets of asexuality."

Such comments not only indicate the type of discourse resulting from what the asexual community and asexuality advocates view as disturbing misinformation provided by the series' official spokespeople (in this case, Moffat), but the desire by those who, like flynnsarcade, host forums representing asexuality communities to educate the misinformed, whether Moffat or the mainstream *Sherlock* television audience. As noted on the home page, AsexualityEducation.Tumblr.org "was created for the purposes of educating, helping & supporting other asexual spectrum people and questioning asexual spectrum people." However, the educational focus also has been extended to *Sherlock*'s official media voices, like Moffat, who may inadvertently offend asexuals and provide inaccurate information about asexuality to fans who follow media interviews with the cast and crew. These "conversations," which are inspired by fans' dedication, are only possible because of the online environment in which they thrive. The immediacy of the comments and the access to an audience is unparalleled outside of the online environment.

However, making these processes overly efficient might reduce what Steinem perceives to be special about face-to-face communication. While this participatory medium is certainly a positive, some drawbacks exist as well in terms of these types of texts actually functioning as part of a social justice movement. One's commitment to challenging and potentially dangerous tasks is mitigated when participating in an online dialogue. One would not face the same consequence (e.g., physical violence, incarceration) as would be possible in face-to-face activism (e.g., sit-ins, riots), though online attacks, as mentioned in Chapter 3, can be quite damaging; the level of commitment for lending one's support is notably lower, despite the potential of "outing" oneself online by posting assenting remarks/materials. Still, Janet Murray describes "agency" as "the satisfying power to take meaningful action and see the results of our decisions and choices" (*Hamlet on the Holodeck,* 126). She claims that agency is achievable in digital environments because those environments can provide immediate and even evocative feedback for actions. Lynnette Porter explains in an article for *PopMatters,* "The bonus features [in The Abominable Bride] conclude with the 'Sherlockology Q & A,' in which actors Amanda Abbington, David Nellist, Una Stubbs, producer Sue Vertue, and showrunner/ writer Moffat answer questions submitted to premier fan site Sherlockology. Although fan access to the *Sherlock* cast and crew is carefully controlled through this Q & A—questions are posed to cast members without the fans asking in person." This indicates how Moffat and Mark Gatiss attempt to reach out to heavily invested fans but, by the same token, may be contributing to creating the illusion that fans have access to these celebrities in ways that they do not because celebrity participation in fan activities is so calculated and coordinated in *Sherlock* fandom. While it is certainly democratizing to see fan commentary replicated in mainstream media alongside comments made by celebrities and fans elevated to a status in which their questions are deemed important enough to be entertained by the celebrities they like and though a more unfettered contact is possible when facilitated online, it is rarely utilized.

Nevertheless, sites like AsexualityEducation.Tumblr.org obviously reach hundreds, if not thousands, of *Sherlock* fans with carefully crafted and archived content, and the "encyclopedic" nature of digital texts, as Murray describes, does much for both accessibility and staying power. Tumblr sites are often used for sharing information or images instead of promoting education. On the non–Tumblr side of the Internet, websites like AVEN have an even more serious reputation as an educational forum with the potential for greater advocacy. Following the publication of the *Guardian*'s early 2012 Moffat interview, forum members posted their often-emotional reactions to the article. After reblogging the paragraph that includes Moffat's quotation about "no fun" in Sherlock's characterization if he were asexual, sherlockhasthetardis questioned whether Moffat's statement means that Sherlock is heterosexual and celibate. That interpretation would make the fan "very unhappy." TheGreatWTF was even more incensed by Moffat's interview and explains that this type of commentary by Moffat results in "ignoring anything that man does that doesn't involve Time Lords" (a reference to Moffat's role as then-showrunner of *Doctor Who*). Anything that Moffat says about *Sherlock* simply irritates this fan, often because the showrunner's statements discuss Sherlock's sexual or romantic depiction. More explicitly, JangoFett termed Moffat a "douche" for the implication that asexuals are not fun and cannot be the subject of worthwhile television viewing. Instead of anger, Bat feels sad that people think asexuals are not fun or entertaining as television characters, and that the "[b]est stories are ruined that way." Other commenters, such as Sinisterporpoise, found Moffat's lack of understanding of asexuality unfortunate, at least, especially when Sherlock could be and has been used as a way for asexuals (including, according to his post, TheGreatWTF) to educate their friends about asexuality. Nogitsune sarcastically wonders if the "powerful majority" of asexual viewers prompted Moffat to feel that he had to comment on asexuality. This fan further stood up for asexual fans who read Sherlock as ace by writing that, despite what Moffat thinks, fans should determine for themselves what they find meaningful or entertaining about a television character. Such a range of responses illustrates how seriously fans take Moffat's words and in how many ways Sherlock has been used to represent one or more concerns or aspects of the asexual community.

Several other posts provide similar information about being upset or angry that Moffat does not seem to understand asexuality. Whether Sherlock is indeed an asexual character is not as important in this thread as the fact that someone in a position of power, such as Moffat has within BBC entertainment as the co-creator/showrunner of *Sherlock*, either does not know or care to learn about asexuality and does not realize or ignores the impact that his comments have on asexual fans. Whereas about a third of the posts note that Sherlock has not self-identified as asexual and Moffat's reading of the character's sexuality is just as valid as anyone else's (including asexuals'), the most pertinent comments to this chapter indicate the need for additional public education about asexuality and derision or disappointment that someone as influential in television entertainment as Moffat continues to make statements that asexuals believe misrepresent their community.

This thread also illustrates how asexual community forums function; they allow a multifaceted discussion of a hot topic—such as Moffat's article in the first days following its publication—and, months or years later, as a way for readers to read what others have expressed as concerns or attempts to set the record straight about asexuality. Most readers of this forum are likely to identify as asexual or to seek such a site to learn more about asexuality. In this regard, the forum not only provides members with an outlet to express themselves, but it also creates an increasingly large archive of information from the asexual community that may be helpful to readers who seek out opinions about topics of concern to the asexual community. In addition, *Sherlock* fans Googling a topic like "asexual Sherlock" or "Moffat interview, asexuality" may incidentally encounter the AVEN discussion. Such threads as those previously noted may indirectly promote advocacy within the larger community of *Sherlock* fans.

Long after the initial discussion about Moffat's comments died down, another AVEN discussion picked up the thread of Moffat not understanding asexuality before Season Four episodes were broadcast. A mainstream media article touting spoilers for Season Four includes information from Moffat that Sherlock would not have a love interest in the upcoming episodes. Furthermore, the article reports that, according to Moffat, "the detective's love life is non-existent because he is not interested in women—but that doesn't mean he is gay" (Massabrook). In response, AVEN members asked whether that cryptic comment means that Sherlock is celibate or asexual, and a few even found it amusing that Moffat's latest comments suggesting a possibly asexual Sherlock had been published in the *International Business News,* as if asexuality had suddenly become a business-themed topic because of Moffat. More importantly, Warrigan listed the fallacies about asexuals found in previous published interviews with Moffat and concluded that "it's great (for visibility) that there's someone [Sherlock] who doesn't get involved in sexual/romantic relationships but the characterization is built upon pretty huge misconceptions." At least within this forum, members discuss incorrect information or misperceptions about asexuality being given the public through mainstream media and present asexuals' experiences or other sources to counter these claims. Moffat and *Sherlock* are far from being a one-time discussion on forums like AVEN.

Whereas specialized forums within the asexual community serve several functions that can be tapped for advocacy or education, blogs produced by fans who, as part of their career (e.g., as academics, fiction writers, journalists), write professionally but post under pseudonyms to protect their anonymity often provide longer texts. Some texts, such as those posted within the Archive of Our Own (AO3) fan fiction collection, are considered meta and designed to reach *Sherlock* fans who also read fan fiction. These essays may provide in-depth insights into the ways that fans interpret *Sherlock* characters and respond to developments within episodes. Other essays/blogs posted to personal Tumblr sites usually respond to a "hot topic"—such as an interview with Moffat—and represent a thoughtfully written response that may serve to educate other fans about asexuality. Both types of longer texts illustrate the seriousness with which fans consider and respond to comments made by the series' showrunners or actors. That these texts also may educate a wider public than "Sherlock fans who are asexuals or are curious about asexuality" is an important consideration in light of advocacy, but such advocacy may not be the specific impetus that compels these fan/authors to write and post their responses to *Sherlock* or articles published as part of the series' promotion within mainstream media.

When Dreamwidth was more frequently used by fan fiction writers in the early 2010s (before its resurgence in light of changes to LiveJournal in 2017), a meta article in 2010 about Sherlock's asexuality generated a lot of reading interest within the fan fiction community. scienceofdeduction posted "Ace + Fandom = Awesome" in the subcommunity of Dreamwidth entitled asexual_fandom. Although this meta is now outdated because it only deals with Season One *Sherlock* episodes broadcast in 2010, scienceofdeduction's conclusion is still timely: "*Sherlock* brings asexuality to the table in discussing sexual orientation like never before. Countless young (and old) people are joining the Asexual Visibility and Educational Network (AVEN for short) with either questions about or understanding that they, too, may be asexual." The blogger recalls an AVEN discussion about Sherlock possibly being homoromantic, "for it is obvious that if Sherlock has any kind of emotions for anyone, it is highly likely to be John Watson, the person who becomes his closest companion." Although scienceofdeduction adds that not much has been written about the possibility of Sherlock being an aromantic asexual, there is room to explore this reading. As is typical of meta posts, this one includes episode summaries providing evidence of an asexual reading. However, this early exploration of Sherlock's sexuality within the series also opens the discussion into a new direction: types of asexuals.

Categorizing Sherlock as a type of asexual runs the gamut from technically accurate terminology to less formal descriptive language often found in blogs or online fan discussions. A 2016 blog debunking "Five Common Myths About Asexuality" identifies early-series Sherlock as a prime example of the first myth: The Robotic Asexual. This depiction fits with canon John Watson describing scientific Holmes as being akin to Babbage's calculating machine (Conan Doyle, *A Study in Scarlet*), a line that lent itself to "The Reichenbach Fall" when John, angry that Sherlock refuses to visit a possibly dying Mrs. Hudson, classifies his flatmate as "You machine!" "Robotic Sherlock" comes from the mistaken notion that "not having a sex drive [is] indicative of there being something wrong. Clearly not feeling sexual urges means that you can't possibly be human, or even have a pulse" ("Five Common Myths"). The blog further notes Moffat's invoking of this stereotype in *Sherlock* yet saying that Sherlock is not an asexual character. The controversy and confusion about asexuals, the blogger implies, are a result of these myths that are often supported when someone like Moffat deems asexuals "robotic or uninteresting." Particularly because this blog is tagged not only by categories of asexuality (e.g., demisexuality, greysexuality) but for Ace and Aro Awareness Week, the concluding statement is meant to empower asexuals and account for variety in the asexual experience, as evidenced by Sherlock: "Asexuality is just another part of the book of humanity—a book we're finally finding all the pages to after spending centuries trying to hide them."

By Season Four, some viewers even perceived Mycroft as "classically asexual and disinterested in passion" (Keene). Outwardly at least, Mycroft seems emotionally contained and far from passionate about anything, but it is interesting as the series progresses that critics and fans see even more evidence of asexuality within the Holmes family. That Mycroft would be possibly paired with Lady Smallwood, who intimates that having a drink with her could lead to something more ("The Lying Detective"), seems odd to this critic—as well as to many fans. Because Sherlock is and perhaps Mycroft may be read as asexual by so many fans makes them wonder why the scriptwriters have such difficulty seeing what they see as evidence not only of asexuality but of Sherlock, in particular, being a specific category of asexual.

Particularly in fan fiction, the exploration of Sherlock as, for example, aromantic or homoromantic continues the discussion within the scope of Johnlock, which is also one of AO3's most popular meta categories, with 125 articles by July 2017 delineating the sexual possibilities within the Johnlock relationship. scienceofdeduction's post anticipated these later explorations. As this post demonstrates, another purpose behind a meta-analysis of characterization is to provide readers with evidence not only from episodes but from other sources. Thus, a single meta citing sources to previous posts on other forums helps direct even more online traffic to additional information about asexuality that has been posted on a variety of sites, from fan fiction to blogs to organizational sites and forums to mainstream media.

Whereas a meta article most often analyzes a fine point within an episode or a theme across several episodes, blogs provide personal insights into a wider treatment of a topic. They also seem to appeal to a wider audience, for example, asexuals in addition to asexual *Sherlock* fans. A widely read blog was published by Cuddlytogas on the author's Tumblr site, although the content was originally intended for a queer issue of *Honi Soit*, a weekly student newspaper produced by the Students' Representative Council at the University of Sydney. The writer is likely a student who felt the need to analyze "Queer Identities in *Sherlock*: A Study in Embarrassing Failures" for a mainstream campus audience but later revised the article for *Sherlock* fans. The article/blog covers what the author views as queerbaiting in many forms: character dialogue and portrayal (e.g., the way a character is dressed), the handling of the John-Sherlock relationship that focuses on love or infatuation but not sex, and, finally, asexuality. When discussing this latter topic, Cuddlytogas complains that "Sherlock and Moffat have a history of outrageously bad handling of asexuality. It has not been made a secret that many fans—particularly asexual-identifying fans in search of fictional representation—read Sherlock Holmes as asexual. The writers have proven themselves not to be ignorant of the phenomenon. However, Moffat's handling of the issue has left much to be desired." Cuddlytogas references the much-quoted scene from first episode "A Study in Pink" in which John questions Sherlock about his relationships. The blogger explains that "Understandably, many a fan interpreted this scene as an implicit admission of asexuality. Whether Sherlock knows the term or not, he makes it clear that he is not interested in relationships, regardless of gender. At the time, the brief exchange was even praised as the closest anyone had come to making a Holmes explicitly asexual." Despite what Cuddlytogas terms as a "promising start," Moffat then disappoints the author by publicly stating in interviews that Sherlock is not asexual (or gay) and dismisses this reading.

Cuddlytogas states the problem that many asexual fans have with the showrunner's stance, which goes beyond some asexual fans' complaint that Moffat's reading of Sherlock does not match their own. Instead, Cuddlytogas explains, Moffat's stance is much more demeaning to asexuals: "He deliberately restrains the interpretation of Sherlock's sexuality to comply with his own, and with his own ignorant ideas about sexual minorities. His faux-educated statements about asexuality are downright offensive." When this blogger brings up Moffat's statement from the previously discussed *Guardian* article, the tone shifts toward condemnation of a showrunner in such a position of power, as the co-creator/writer of a globally successful television show. Cuddlytogas concludes that "If Steven Moffat thinks asexuality is a choice, then he has misunderstood the concept entirely, and really has no authority to be talking or writing about the issue. If he thinks asexual people are boring, I can name one asexual at least who would like to exchange with him a few interesting words." The argument that sexual orientation is a choice harkens to advocacy issues from the past several decades, when homosexuality was also considered a lifestyle choice. Asexual advocates are currently fighting the same battle—to convince mainstream audiences (i.e., the public) that asexuality is a real orientation, not a choice. With this blog, Cuddlytogas not only illustrates a personal response to *Sherlock* and to Moffat's interview, but to the way asexuals are portrayed on television and discussed in the media.

Given the popularity of this blog (nearly 1,400 notes posted by July 2017, with more than 100 added in the past year, but undoubtedly many more hits than notes), Cuddlytogas has reached an audience of *Sherlock* fans. However, it is also read by those who click the article's link because it comes up in the Google search results. In particular, this article may be an indicator of the author's "seriousness" in discussing the series and asexuality; the blog concludes with a bibliography of seven sources, including mainstream media articles and books about Sherlock Holmes. Such an academic approach and connection with the University of Sydney may give this blog additional weight because readers may think of a bibliography or academic affiliation as adding greater legitimacy to a fan blog.

Perhaps the most eloquent blogged discussion of *Sherlock* has been posted by Amphiboly on Tumblr in February 2013, about a year after the previously discussed Moffat interview became a hot topic within the asexual community. The introduction indicates a compelling, non-judgmental tone that explains the source of the conflict between those discussing Sherlock's "official" sexual orientation in the BBC series and those reading Sherlock as asexual.

The essay defines *asexuals* for readers unfamiliar with the range of sexual expression included with this definition. Asexuals, as described by Amphiboly, "have little or no inherent inclination to engage in sexual activity—not because they're celibate, but because they don't experience sexual attraction on a significant level." Nonetheless, asexuals may feel romantic or sexual attraction and even have a sex drive. Despite more information about sexualities and orientations becoming available to the public, asexuals are still marginalized. To explore what might be another way to make asexuality more "mainstream," Amphiboly then explains "there is convincing evidence that one of literature's most prized creations, Sherlock Holmes, is in today's terms an asexual." Even more important is Sherlock's contribution to a greater societal understanding of asexuals and asexuality; "Sherlock has arguably begun contributing to the validity of the identity in the mainstream."

Amphiboly does not only discuss the reasons why Sherlock Holmes in canon (viewed through a modern lens in a culture that has a vocabulary to discuss asexual behavior) and the BBC's adaptation can easily be read as asexual, although Cumberbatch and Moffat do not intend to portray the character this way. The author also summarizes the power of an asexual reading of Sherlock within a fan community that uses the tag ace!Sherlock to denote fiction featuring asexual Sherlock, who is sometimes in an aromantic or a homoromantic relationship with John. Perhaps more important for advocacy, Amphiboly notes that S.E. Smith posted both a blog entitled "Sense and Sensibility on *Sherlock*" to the Think Progress website and a more mainstream article entitled "Asexuality Always Existed, You Just Didn't Notice It" in *The Guardian*. (The *Guardian* article generated 596 comments from the public, many, as might be expected, criticizing the author or asexuals in general. However, at least some who posted comments created a thoughtful dialogue about what it means to be asexual; some posts were several paragraphs long.) As Amphiboly notes through this blog and by referencing blogs written by other fans, the asexual community, because of *Sherlock*, has more opportunities to educate other fans and the public through online blogs, posts, and articles. Not every *Guardian* reader, for example, may understand all the issues associated with asexuality (e.g., claiming that asexuality is a convenient "excuse" for not having sex with people they want to turn down or that asexuals cannot face discrimination because no one can tell their sexual orientation by looking at them). Nevertheless, asexuals are using the popularity of *Sherlock* to gain an online audience for their blogs and articles in order to define asexuality within a public forum.

In the conclusion to this blog, Amphiboly summarizes what many fans believe about Sherlock as portrayed in the BBC series and the controversy surrounding an asexual reading of this character. Not only do *Sherlock* and Sherlock provide asexuals with a perceived representation on television, but the possibility of such a reading further opens the likelihood of additional alternate readings of canon Holmes. Amphiboly asks, "Would Holmes have considered himself in such terms, living as he did in Victorian-era England? Of course not. But in today's society, as we increasingly recognize and accept different identities, the discussion is one worth having." Allowing the possibility of alternate readings and inviting *Sherlock* fans to interpret the title character in a way that is meaningful to them is a positive step toward a broader understanding of asexuality and the increasing possibility that openly asexual characters will join the casts of popular television series.

As evidenced by these example posts, blogs, and articles, the asexual *Sherlock* fan community is invested in having such a discussion within the asexual community, but, more important, in taking that discussion to Moffat (via Tweets) and the public (through mainstream media articles and comments in response to articles). In this way, the asexual community helps to educate individuals and the public at large and to advocate for greater understanding of asexuality and the social issues surrounding it.

Stories Advocating Greater Awareness of Asexuality

Just as the BBC's and producer Hartswood Films' official *Sherlock* texts—the episodes—provide a wealth of critical readings that may form the foundation of social advocacy, so does the series' online fan community. Although these artifacts are primarily used for fans' entertainment, they can also be used for the community's education or advocacy. Fan fiction encourages more than a passive experience for many readers; the comments section following a story often facilitates a conversation among readers and with the author and illustrates the "uses" of fan fiction that go beyond mere entertainment. This response is particularly true of stories in which Sherlock says that he is asexual or is perceived as asexual. Stories written in honor of Asexuality Awareness Week specifically refer and provide links to the Asexuality Visibility and Education Network (AVEN), an advocacy site that provides discussion forums and information about sexuality.

The *Sherlock* fans who participate in online communities may be perceived as privileged to engage in this type of communication, and many young fans in countries that do not highly regulate Internet usage or ban sites having anything to do with sex may benefit from participating in digital culture. Young digital natives who do not feel comfortable discussing their orientation or asking questions face to face, perhaps because of fear of censure or ostracism, can discuss sexuality freely online, where they can use the name Anonymous or a creative pseudo identity that allows them privacy. (Although discovering a real person's identity is possible through hacking or tracking IP addresses, for example, online advocacy communities and fan fiction archives have strict rules about the appropriate use of sites and can ban, at the least, users who threaten others.) The participatory culture evident in online communities, in particular, sets the scene for advocacy work in which new knowledge is foregrounded in the form of the entertainment inherent in fan fiction and the mentoring/connection that members of the community share.

As might be expected, fan fiction communities are united in their passion for the source text, in this case *Sherlock*. This "affective attachment," as Hills explains, is a powerful motivating force, and community members take their contributions and those of others very seriously, despite the "playful" nature of most popular, web-based fan sites. According to Roberta Pearson, in *It's Always 1895: Sherlock Holmes in Cyber Space*, "ideological appropriation of popular heroes" is a hallmark of fan culture, and a "virtual community may be the perfect forum for such an appropriation" (45) because "those seeking community in cyber space have the desire to control exposure and create security and order" (54). This feat is most often accomplished because the digital environment allows "play." Henry Jenkins, in *Confronting the Challenges of Participatory Culture*, defines "play" as the "the ability to experiment with one's surroundings as a form of problem solving" (xiv) and because "appropriation" is such a part of participatory culture, the type of play that fans enact should prove unsurprising, because their attachment to source materials is the impetus for their works. What may be surprising is the extent to which this "play" has the capacity to create alternate epistemologies within fan communities, to create an ethos of advocacy. Linden and Linden explain the "the highest goal for a fan is not necessarily to be seen as 'normal' in the eyes of the general public ... especially when normative ideals represent the polar opposite to what the fan (or the object of fandom) represents (in terms of values)" (74). Generally, fans embrace the notion that they are perceived as outsiders by society at large, but they are most often only comfortable as being identified as outsiders when they are part of an anonymous fan community. If they are personally called out as being "strange" because of their fan work or activities, they may want to be disassociated with their fandom or may resent the "outsider" label. The previously discussed incident in which Moran called out a fan for her fan fiction and publicly embarrassed her is a practical example of the difference between fans maintaining an anonymous identification as part of a large fandom and being publicly, and often negatively, identified as a fan.

Fan fiction stories often elevate Sherlock to asexual poster child/hero status, despite the showrunners' and Cumberbatch's insistence that Sherlock is just too focused on his work to consider intimate relationships, rather than leaving open the possibility that the natural expression of Sherlock's sexual identity is asexuality. The "head canon" created and maintained by fan fiction communities is evidence of these groups' ability to upend traditional authority (showrunners), in favor of adding alternatives to AO3's discourse, not just about Sherlock, but about asexuality.

By July 2017, more than 920 English-language stories resulted from an AO3 search of "asexual Sherlock." The earliest stories were published in September 2010, within about a month of *Sherlock* debuting on the BBC in late July and months before PBS brought the series to the U.S. Authors writing about the series in 2010 would have seen the first-season episode "A Study in Pink," in which Sherlock tells John that he does not have a girlfriend or boyfriend and is married to his work; "The Blind Banker," in which John tells Sherlock he has a date and defines it for him— "It's where two people who like each other go out and have fun"—to which Sherlock explains that is what he was suggesting he and John do as part of a case; and "The Great Game," in which Sherlock realizes that John is the "heart" that archenemy Moriarty hopes to burn out of him, and John offers to sacrifice his life for Sherlock. Although the evidence used by fans can support a sexual Johnlock reading, it also can indicate that Sherlock feels emotion (e.g., love) for John that he feels for no one else, but that he is not usually interested in a "typical" heterosexual or homosexual relationship. Because of scenes such as that in "The Blind Banker" when John feels he must define dating for Sherlock (and admits he hopes Sherlock is not suggesting that they are dating when they go out on cases together) and Sherlock shows up during John's date, fan fiction authors often interpret Sherlock's actions as an atypical but very Sherlockian way to "court" John. Early fan fiction featuring Sherlock as asexual emphasizes these themes.

The plots of *Sherlock*-based stories often end up with John and Sherlock in a committed relationship, although Sherlock is not interested in sex. Authors' interest in pairing Sherlock and John does not diminish throughout the series' four seasons and special episode, even when the television-canon plots indicate such a development is increasingly less likely on television (especially when John weds Mary Morstan and they have baby Rosamund together, although Mary's death in "The Six Thatchers" makes John potentially "available" to Sherlock again). Whether John and Sherlock have sex is not so much the point of these stories as John and Sherlock having a long-term, most often loving partnership in which each supports and understands the other.

During the second season, Irene Adler is introduced as a potential love interest for Sherlock, but he rebuffs her advances ("A Scandal in Belgravia"). Although he displays emotion for Adler, especially when he thinks she has been killed, he does not seem interested in any sexual activity with the professional dominatrix. Nevertheless, he is intellectually attracted to her, and she to him; she coins the phrase "brainy is the new sexy" in honor of Sherlock. What is perhaps most pertinent to this episode regarding Sherlock's sexual orientation, however, takes place during a discussion between John and Adler after she returns to London after faking her death. She kidnaps John, who demands that she tell Sherlock she is alive. Adler forces John to reconsider his relationship with Sherlock. She asks if John is jealous of her relationship with Sherlock, and he replies that he and Sherlock are not a couple. "Yes, you are," Adler counters. John vehemently denies this statement and protests that he is "actually not gay," although "who the hell knows about Sherlock Holmes." Adler replies, "Well, I am [gay]. Look at us both" ("A Scandal in Belgravia"). The relationship dynamic between Adler and Sherlock, as well as Sherlock and John, is not bounded by heteronormative standards. Although Adler self-identifies as lesbian but is bisexual in her roles as a dominatrix with her clients, she is infatuated with Sherlock, despite his lack of sexual interest in her.

Similarly, whereas John may enjoy a homosocial relationship with Sherlock, he, in canon, does not consider himself part of a couple, although he, too, acts jealous throughout this episode. This first episode of the second season allowed many fan fiction authors the opportunity to expand the ways that Johnlock could be read, and asexual Sherlock in a relationship with John withstood the test of The Woman (as Arthur Conan Doyle first dubbed her and Moffat continued) coming between Sherlock and John—especially within the realm of fan fiction.

The stories that speak most to advocacy, albeit a much smaller subset of this collection of fiction, involve Sherlock "coming out" as asexual or dealing with others' preconceptions of asexuality. In this way, authors can perhaps project their own experiences through Sherlock and receive (mostly) supportive feedback from the community.

The following stories illustrate the way that fan fiction can provide a potentially cathartic or educational experience for writers and offer readers entertainment that may inform or educate them about asexuality. These examples were selected because of their plots and the number of comments regarding asexuality, but they are admittedly a very small sample of the types of stories involving some aspect of asexuality found within *Sherlock*. "Unusual Symmetry" and "Inflammable" involve Sherlock and John in an intimate partnership. Only Sherlock is asexual, and his relationship with John varies, depending upon the author's perspective on asexuality. These stories are illustrative of fan fiction written primarily for entertainment, although readers often take away more than a few minutes' reading enjoyment.

Uploaded in September 2010, mresundance's "Unusual Symmetry" deals with asexual Sherlock in a long-term partnership with John, who sometimes masturbates in front of Sherlock as part of their intimate relationship. By July 2017, this story had received more than 20,000 hits and 450 kudos, as well as 82 comments. Furthermore, this story has become so popular that it also has been recorded as a podcast.

The writer notes before the fiction begins that this is the first time he (a gender designation based on the author's profile photo) is writing about asexuality. The urge to write "Unusual Symmetry" is the result of mresundance's reading of two asexuality blogs (which are linked to this story). He indicates that Sherlock's experience is not his own and asks readers to let him know if he got it "horribly, completely wrong." Apparently the writer's story has resonated with many readers, who either deem that mresundance got it right or, like the author, had no first-hand experience with asexuality but were intrigued by the Sherlock-John relationship. The comments are all positive and generated comments specifically about asexuality.

Prentice notes "Oh, this is lovely. You've done an excellent job of making it clear that what they have is every bit as meaningful as what others have, it's just a bit different. The bits with Sherlock thrilling in John's mental growth are delightful." Other readers posted even more personal responses to this story and its depiction of a mutually satisfying relationship in which one partner is asexual. mustbehavingfun used this story as a form of advocacy—to explain to others what asexuality is and what an asexual character does: "Thank you so much for writing this! I've shown it to a friend in an attempt to explain my own asexuality, and I think she understands, thanks to it."

By the time the next season of *Sherlock* episodes arrived in early 2012, stories tagged "asexuality" were not as often based on specific television-canon scenes but expanded the universe created by the television episodes. dreamlittleyo's "Inflammable" was published on AO3 as part of the "Combustion" series of related stories. "Inflammable" is notable for the way the story portrays asexual Sherlock and the number of comments (27) applauding this realistic, but different from early 2010, depiction.

"Inflammable" describes Sherlock's attempt to sexually seduce a confused John. Sherlock already sees them in a committed relationship, but John believes they are still friends with the one-time benefit of Sherlock bringing him to orgasm with his hand. John believes that Sherlock is not interested in sex and is perplexed when Sherlock not only seems interested in not only bringing him to orgasm again but in playfully kissing and petting, which he sees as part of an established relationship. Thus, a frustrated Sherlock must illuminate John about the true nature of their relationship and Sherlock's asexuality.

John asks Sherlock a series of questions: Why would he want to initiate a sexual encounter if he does not want to participate in sex? Is Sherlock sexually attracted to John? Does Sherlock expect to have penetrative intercourse? Sherlock finds John's questions tedious. "Of course, I'm attracted to you," Sherlock explains, although John wants to verify that Sherlock is sexually attracted to him. "Why does that matter?" Sherlock replies, truly perplexed. John verifies that Sherlock is not interested in sex but is interested in him. Sherlock insists that "I *do* want this. What difference does it make whether or not you '*turn me on*,' as you so quaintly put it?" After a particularly pleasurable sexual experience for John, he asks Sherlock if he ever masturbates, because he seems particularly adept at getting John off. The writer provides a thoroughly Sherlockian response akin to what his television counterpart would say: "'Boring,' Sherlock mutters dismissively. 'Much more interesting to do it to you.'" The fact that Sherlock is an active participant in their intimate relationship and enjoys bringing John to orgasm, although he is not interested in meeting that objective himself, is only part of this story's appeal to many readers. Sherlock also knows what he wants, articulates it clearly, and enjoys being with John sexually.

For many self-identified asexuals who wrote comments regarding this story, Sherlock's demeanor is familiar but a seldom-addressed component of fan fiction about asexual Sherlock: he can enjoy being with John sexually, although he is not interested in achieving orgasm and, in fact, prefers that John not reciprocate. Among the 27 comments posted by readers, veronamay enthusiastically approves of this story: "Oh, yay! An ace!Sherlock/John fic where Sherlock really, really isn't interested in sex for himself and John is *okay with that*. These are rarer than you'd think. Loved it!" Writer dreamlittleyo replies almost immediately with a comment suggesting that a character within a story responds much the way that many real-world potential partners would when faced with someone presumed to be completely uninterested in sex: "Getting John to UNDERSTAND (at least enough to be okay with the arrangement—I think that even at the end of this fic he doesn't understand completely) was a fun challenge." Perhaps the challenge is not nearly as much "fun" for real-world partners negotiating what, to many non-asexuals, may seem a one-sided relationship. However, this negotiation also reflects a real-world situation with which at least some asexual readers could identify. In this way, it can be considered a form of advocacy, in which a story meant primarily for entertainment engenders a conversation about real—not fictionalized—asexuality and possibly educates those readers who read the story and the comments attached to it. The verification of personal experience also can make such a story as "Inflammable" seem more legitimate to readers, as well as provide positive feedback to the writer, who may decide to write further stories about asexual Sherlock.

Whereas many stories describing Johnlock have incorporated elements of television canon, such as John's marriage, into the number of options authors may consider when they write a story primarily about John and Sherlock, the fan fiction about asexual Sherlock listed in the advocacy category does not appreciably change in reaction to television canon. Instead, the plot in each places Sherlock in a situation where he is misunderstood and must explain his sexual orientation, usually to a familiar character (e.g., John, Molly Hooper, someone in Sherlock's family).

These stories form a small but persistent core of asexual Sherlock stories in the archive that can help educate readers about the nature of asexuality and provide a supportive space in which authors may "come out" themselves or help others to do so.

One of the most respected writers in the Sherlock TV fandom is flawedamythyst, who has written more than 120 stories about *Sherlock*, many receiving more than 200 kudos. Such is the case with "It's All Fine," a story flawedamythyst wrote for Asexual Awareness Week in February 2011. In this story, Sherlock and John are investigating a crime scene alongside New Scotland Yard's Sergeant Donovan, a character known primarily in fandom for calling Sherlock a "freak" and warning John away from him during the first episode ("A Study in Pink"). In this story, Donovan again calls Sherlock a "freak" when he makes comments about his lack of interest in sex. (The crime scene includes two dead bodies found entwined in bed.) After Donovan says that "Everyone does it" (i.e., has sex), Sherlock replies, "I don't 'do' it." The resulting conversation revolves around Donovan's conviction that Sherlock is abnormal and Sherlock breaking down her assumptions, first, that he has not had sex because no one wants to be his partner and then that someone without a sex life is freakish. Sherlock explains that "I've had plenty of offers, but absolutely no desire to take any of them up. Sex is of no interest to me at all." Only when John, in his role as a physician, supports Sherlock by telling Donovan that someone having no interest in sex is not only in the range of normality but more common than most people would think, does Donovan back off (after also terming John "a freak" who probably has a kinky sex life). Once again, John is supportive of Sherlock and, as he does in "A Study in Pink" after Sherlock explains that he does not have a girlfriend or a boyfriend, concludes that "It's all fine." flawedamythyst underscores her familiarity with television canon and fidelity to it by using John's line from "A Study in Pink"; this stylistic choice bolsters her credibility with *Sherlock* fans and, by extension, may make some readers assume that this writer is equally familiar with asexuality (i.e., is a "legitimate" source of information about asexuality).

Throughout the many years in which flawedamythyst has been writing *Sherlock* fan fiction, she has built up a reservoir of social capital within the AO3 community. Readers familiar with her work or those who read a story just because she is the author have, through "It's All Fine," been introduced to flawedamythyst's interpretation of asexual Sherlock and to Asexual Awareness Week. Thus, this story, in particular, has the potential to reach a larger readership than stories by other authors who are not as well known within the *Sherlock* fan fiction community.

This story generated seven comments. However, several are specific to asexuality. Kephiso, who does not self-identify a sexual identity in this message, offers constructive criticism: "I would have found it nice, to read a bit more about Sherlock's doubts—I doubt he's always been so comfortable with being asexual with everyone around him being sexually active." BookGirlFan, in contrast, begins the post with "As an asexual" and expresses her displeasure with Donovan expecting everyone to enjoy sex. Because flawedamythyst also tagged this story as being written for Asexual Awareness Week, asexuality is also highlighted in this forum. "It's All Fine" links this fan fiction community with the larger Internet community and organizations related to asexuality. Such a bridge between communities can help readers learn more about asexuality in the "real world."

The range of stories involving asexuality and characters within the *Sherlock* universe suggests that the AO3 *Sherlock* community provides a safe space in which readers may learn more about asexuality, identify with Sherlock as both "other" and asexual, share information about asexuality, and portray a world in which asexuality may not be as well understood or accepted as other sexual orientations but in which everyone has at least someone (e.g., John) in whom an asexual (e.g., Sherlock) can confide and find acceptance. However, the *Sherlock* fandom has an important difference from most other fandoms; it revolves around a lead character that many readers and writers read as asexual. Its fan fiction can uniquely represent a world in which asexuality is as well defined and internationally understood as homosexuality or heterosexuality. Although many stories reflect the reality that not everyone can believe that asexuality is real or acceptable, they still portray a character (usually Sherlock) who, in almost every plot, has a happy ending with someone who understands and accepts him for who he is. What he is or is not willing to do sexually is not part of the reason why Sherlock is valued or loved. That message can be powerful, especially to teenage readers who are questioning their sexual orientation.

Pridelolly Fan Fiction

Sherlolly fandom pairs Sherlock Holmes and Molly Hooper, which may seem an odd combination for a celebration of LGBTQIA+. Most often, stories involving a character's sexual orientation or identity involve Johnlock and may describe heterosexual, homosexual, bisexual, or asexual relationships. However, many fans read both Sherlock and Molly individually as queer, and the #Pridelolly hashtag has been used to share coming-out stories and thoughts about being LGBTQIA+. As the Pridelolly 2016 Tumblr site explains, the types of stories have significantly expanded since fans first began to use the #Pridelolly hashtag: "The original purpose of Pridelolly was ... to promote the creation of fan works showcasing lgbtqia+ Sherlock and/or Molly—but it seems also to have morphed into a way for lgbtqia+ fans to communicate with and support each other." As with asexuality advocacy through fan fiction on AO3, Pridelolly stories educate and entertain; they may help fans learn about a range of sexual identities. In addition, Three Patch Podcast and other fan sites have promoted Pridelolly fan fiction. A Pridelolly 2016 fan fiction challenge asked authors to submit their stories and art for an Archive of Our Own (AO3) collection. The stories also were cross-posted to other fan fiction archives and collection, giving *Sherlock*-themed LGBTQIA+ stories a much larger potential audience.

An example typical of Sherlolly fan fiction: In Iwantthatcoat's "Slow Chemistry," Sherlock is tagged as asexual and panromantic; Molly is identified as asexual and biromantic. The story picks up where "The Empty Hearse" leaves off regarding the Sherlolly relationship. Newly engaged John is no longer speaking to Sherlock, who has recently returned from faking his death and traveling far from home to destroy Moriarty's criminal network. Whereas the television episode shows Molly often humorously filling in for John as Sherlock's partner in solving crime, "Slow Chemistry" takes their deepening friendship more seriously and allows it to grow into an intimate relationship. The story is notable for allowing Sherlock and Molly to explain their experiences and assumptions about sex.

When Sherlock considers a sexual relationship, he looks closely at his feelings about sex and his sexuality:

> He could do sex. Everything certainly functioned properly. And while it wasn't a goal, it wasn't anything he was averse to, as such. It just never quite made sense. To be clear, it made a great deal of biological sense, but it was much more something one does, or is expected to do, rather than something he ever *wanted* to do.

Sherlock even questions whether he is a virgin, because, he reasons, that depends on one's definition of virginity. Sex just seemed "a bit foreign and purposeless. But it wouldn't be purposeless to someone else. For them, it would be essential—to feel desired—and ... that was fine." He reasons that altruistically having sex with someone who values sexual validation would be a compromise he could make. He rationalizes that he would not even have to fake desire, because it would simply be a different type of desire. Desire, like virginity, could be dependent on the person defining it.

Throughout this story, Sherlock expresses his changing feelings toward Molly as a friend who becomes a confidante and love interest. His asexuality is described in a way not found in Johnlock stories, and both Sherlock and Molly negotiate compromises so that they can please each other while being true to themselves. This story is highly atypical of the traditional heteronormative romance stories under the #Sherlolly tag.

In contrast to Sherlock's virginity, Molly has had "lots of sex" with boyfriend Tom, but she is not satisfied with their relationship. She explains to Sherlock that, after not feeling sexual desire, she decided to try sex "the way normal people do. Lots of people used to say that you weren't supposed to like sex much anyway, right? ... That it is something to put up with, even though everyone I saw really wasn't just putting up with it. They were rather enjoying themselves. So I tried again, with Tom.... Sex isn't that bad. It's a bit like doing a chore you don't really like—like doing the dishes." With Sherlock, Molly can explore a sexual relationship in which she is valued for who she is, and if neither she nor Sherlock enjoys intercourse, they can focus on activities they both like, such as cuddling.

Throughout the story, Molly and Sherlock are honest with each other about their sexual drive—or lack of desire—and their preferences. They do not want anyone to feel the need to "fix" them, because they know that they are fine as they are and deserve a partner who can understand, accept, and enjoy them.

Despite the popularity of and within-fandom promotion for Pridelolly, not all readers can accept a queer interpretation of either Sherlock or Molly if they end up in a happily-ever-after relationship that seems to mimic a heterosexual pairing. The Sherlolly writing challenge specifies that authors must bring Sherlock and Molly together in a relationship by the happy ending. To some readers, that qualification nullifies these stories as Pride fan fiction because they seem to force a non-heteronormative relationship into expected societal parameters instead of truly embracing the characters' queer individuality.

Among the 34 comments following "Slow Chemistry" are important mini-conversations with the author about the right of non-asexual authors to write asexual characters, accurate definitions of *bisexual* and *pansexual*, and the separation of companionship and sex. Unlike many stories that prompt short, usually positive responses, "Slow Chemistry" has instigated longer conversations that allow the writer and readers to explain in greater detail their perspectives on the characters' sexual experiences and societal "norms."

Unlike an event like Asexuality Awareness Week, which transcends a fandom, Pridelolly is a *Sherlock* fan-created writing challenge that lacks a reference to an official organization's site, such as AVEN. Instead, *Sherlock* fans who ship Sherlolly or read Molly and Sherlock as queer characters have created their own within-fandom event. They do not direct fans to sites about asexuality, for example, but authors and readers use the comments section to ask questions, debate different perspectives about sexual identities, and highlight dialogue or actions within the story that mimic real-world situations with which authors or readers have experience. Although advocacy may most often be perceived as fan action or support on behalf of an established organization (e.g., Asexuality.org) or network (e.g., AVEN), Pridelolly illustrates how *Sherlock* fans create their own events or celebrations to encourage creative works such as fan fiction or art and conversations about larger issues than a story or a character. Such continuing, open communication seems more likely to occur within the safe space afforded by fan sites like AO3.

Fan Philanthropy for Advocacy Organizations

As a result of many fandoms' concerns about the social changes being proposed during the 2016 U.S. presidential campaign and the hateful rhetoric espoused by candidates vying for election from the presidential level down to the smallest local election, fans began a campaign of their own— Fandom Trumps Hate—to host an auction "to benefit charities in the wake of the US Presidential election" (Fandom Trumps Hate). All types of fan works were auctioned: fiction, digital art, videos, podfics, and fan labor including betaing (i.e., reading and editing) or translating stories. The winning bidder selected the charity from among the site's list and donated the winning amount to that charity. The fan whose work was purchased at auction received a receipt showing the winning bid had been donated as promised. Only digital fan works, not physical items, could be auctioned, making this philanthropic event created by and for fans truly the work of digital fandoms. Among the charities receiving donations were the American Civil Liberties Union, the Anti-Defamation League, and Planned Parenthood—organizations designed to help people of color, women, the LGBTQIA+ community, and others deemed threatened by the rhetoric and actions taking place during the election campaign ("FAQ"). Charitable contributions as a result of the auction totaled $32,002.85 ("Auction Total"). Stories archived on AO3 that were written for the auction can be found using the #FandomTrumpsHate tag, and the *Sherlock* fandom contributed 32 AO3 stories to the auction.

New Media Performing Advocacy

Fan-generated media is a good *first* step for asexuality advocates, especially in the beginning stages of their social justice movement. It collects evidence that there is indeed a problem and provides compelling accounts that certainly encourage empathetic responses, and these online texts have the potential to reach people in power positions. New media has been cited as foundational to many current movements. Though new media has the potential to inspire agency and become "transformative and immersive," to use Murray's terms, it is rarely used that way outside of fine art or video gaming.

What the types of online texts mentioned in this chapter do accomplish is embedded in an understanding of identity as discursively formed and maintained (e.g., Van Djiik, Fairclough). Fans know who they are, not simply because of some innate ability to apprehend their identity, but because they see themselves reflected in others and either rejected or reinforced through those discursive interactions. As Ann Frances Wysocki explains in "Drawn Together: Possibilities for Bodies in Words and Pictures," identity is constantly being constructed in and through the texts we create. As Wysocki explains a concept introduced by cultural theorist Stuart Hall, she notes the following:

> It is not that we find our selves in our work because there was a unified self that preceded the work and that only needed being made present somehow in the work; it is rather what the work is—its status as a shaped object in front of us—makes visible to us 'what we are' ... the [subject] position has had to be constructed—produced—before it can be judged [26].

This "judgment" to which Wysocki refers explains the way in which we "see ourselves in what we produce," and this judgment also provides the opportunity to ask "Is that who I (at least in part) am? Is that who I want to be? Is that the position through which I want to be seen?" (26). The ways in which identities are embedded in the texts that are produced have profound implications for advocacy work online. Being able to judge who we are and who we might want to become by navigating and negotiating the texts we produce and the texts of others, we are able to make those "judgments," and that opens a space for change. There is nothing more important to advocacy work than that.

8

New Directions
for *Sherlock* Fandom
and TPTB

Although digital culture has been mired in criticism regarding the extent to which users have become passive consumers of filtered knowledge, as per writers like Nicholas Carr, or anti-social, as per writers like Sherry Turkle and Neil Postman, *Sherlock* fan works illustrate the extent to which the affordances of digital media and certain contexts (e.g., #SherlockLive) make possible empowering opportunities to deepen self-knowledge and to build community. Fan communities have the ability to shape the perceptions of those who passively observe or actively participate in a forum, but they can also shape the popular culture texts to which they are responding, making fans both producers and consumers. Such has been the case with *Sherlock;* the series' content has been influenced by fans who take to the Internet in a variety of ways to creatively and/or critically express their varied views of the show and its characters. The following sections illustrate activities that may or should be incorporated into the interactions between and among The Powers That Be (TPTB) and fans, academics and fans, and the many digital subcommunities within *Sherlock* fandom. Encouragement for additional activities and a few warnings about potential perils to digital communities summarize what may be future directions for *Sherlock* fandom.

#SherlockLive and the Potential for Interactive Games

Although not all Twitter interactions between TPTB and *Sherlock* fans have been positive, one forum in which fans and showrunners successfully and innovatively interacted in real time was the one-time #SherlockLive Twitter event. It took place on 10 January 2017, between the second and third episodes of the fourth season—a prime time to generate more fan and media interest in the upcoming season finale, "The Final Problem."

The official BBC Sherlock *Twitter* account was hijacked by Sherlock (in a way reminiscent of the way that #Setlock fans "took over" filming locations and directed a collective fan experience by sharing photos, videos, and tweets). The first video message showed Sherlock, who is "bored, so tonight I'm taking over your Twitter feed." Just as Sherlock signs his texts in the series, the tweet is signed SH. The BBC One account (@BBCOne) posted this message with their own claim: "We have received a text from someone claiming to be Sherlock Holmes. We won't let this happen. #SherlockLive." With this tweet, the game was on. This message, at 7:12 a.m. on the day of the Twitter event, was reposted by 2,567 people and liked (using the heart icon) by 7,222. Throughout the day BBC One posted more messages from Sherlock, along with a video or photo, and the announcement "Tonight! 8pm #SherlockLive." After a final pronouncement that the BBC One account would not be taken over by Sherlock, promptly at 8 p.m. London time, the red-and-white BBC One logo was replaced by the wallpaper pattern from Sherlock's flat and 22-One-B. Sherlock wrote "Too late. I'm already here. I'm bored and angry and I need a distraction. So this is me, Sherlock, taking over the BBC. #Sherlock Live." The consulting detective then provided video, photos (sometimes with evidence circled in red when Sherlock thought everyone was being slow), case notes, and Lestrade's notes about the murder of Daniel Collard.

The game lasted only 30 minutes, as Sherlock pointed out in an early message: "In about half an hour I'll be bored of you but let's see who can do this. I'd solved it before I even realised it was a case. #SherlockLive." Participants were asked questions, with the understanding that Sherlock would comment on the first response received. They also voted in polls about who they thought had committed the murder or whether a piece of evidence is key to solving the case.

Sherlock questioned, commented, chided, and guided participants with frequent tweets, and his voice unsurprisingly sounded as sarcastic or arrogant as he would toward Anderson or Donovan on television. When he received a perceptive insight from a player, he commented "Hm. Interesting." Although participants may not have known it at the time, Mark Gatiss and Steven Moffat took turns tweeting as Sherlock, ensuring that his textual voice "sounded" just the way it does in the series. As well, veteran BBC scriptwriter Joe Lidster (*Doctor Who, The Sarah Jane Chronicles*) created the case so that the game would have a manageable number of suspects and amount of evidence that could easily be presented in formats familiar to Twitter users: photos, videos, text, and polls. Those playing the game not only interacted with "Sherlock" but each other, and others who only wanted to follow the event as it happened could read the stream of #SherlockLive tweets. Although #SherlockLive was designed only as entertainment, its innovative design and popularity among participants signal the potential for much wider applications.

Online gaming has the potential to take virtual social action to another level, to induce people to come up with implementable solutions to real-world problems by creating an immersive environment in which to participate—in which to "virtually" live. Taking advantage of the culture of computer-mediated communication, online games, particularly Alternate Reality Games (ARG) like #SherlockLive, have the potential to work within the context of generative modes of meaning making and collective action. ARGs are not role-playing games. In these games, players participate as themselves in an alternate reality, in which they must meet the challenges of this new but reality-based gaming world. An ARG that addresses LGBTQIA+ issues, for example, might take place in an alternate reality, like the Sherlockverse, where players can gain points by engaging in productive dialogue about asexuality. The design possibilities are virtually endless and can all help participants consider ways to positively address social change.

Jane McGonigal, online ARG designer and author of *Reality is Broken: Why Games Make Us Better and How They Can Change the World*, makes some sweeping claims about the value of gameplay:

> Game developers know better than anyone else how to inspire extreme effort and reward hard work. They know how to facilitate cooperation and collaboration at previously unimagined scales. And they are continually innovating new ways to motivate players to stick with harder challenges for longer and in much bigger groups. These crucial twenty-first century skills can help all of us find new ways to make a deep and lasting impact on the world around us.... Gameplay isn't just a pastime. It's a twenty-first century way of working together to accomplish real change.

These claims illustrate the *potential* for gaming to benefit social action movements, although little formal study of them has been done. The success that McGonigal claims she has had with ARGs, which tackle real-world issues through a transmedia approach and generate global user responses, could be considered models for such an endeavor, even though there are not yet any ARGs that address LGBTQIA+ issues.

To signal the end of #SherlockLive after 30 minutes, Sherlock concluded "Bored of reading your nonsense now. Tweet a video or pic of you telling me who the killer was. #SherlockLive." Sherlock also suggested that those unable to deduce the murderer should delete their Twitter account. The resulting photos or videos showed selfies of individuals as well as parents and children playing the game together. Of course, several photos of Moriarty also were posted along with "his" deductions about the murderer. The BBC did not strand players who did not solve the murder; the solution was revealed in a video message posted by BBC One.

Jo Pearce, the Creative Digital Director at BBC Wales, told the *Telegraph* that she had been waiting for the right opportunity to launch an interactive game, and the *Sherlock* fandom's use of digital media and the nature of Sherlock Holmes storytelling provided the ideal combination. "What could be better than bringing together sheer genius and testing Sherlock against the rest of the world? Sherlock Holmes' unique style of deduction offers a fascinating format to play with, and social media means anything is possible" (Molloy). The live event proved successful with fans and official personnel and, a few months later, garnered a Webby Awards nomination in the Social Events category as one of only five nominees, where it was up against CNN Election Night 2016, 24 Hours of Le Forza, Meeting the Moment (Real Madrid soccer), and 2015–16 NBA All-Star Week. When award winners were announced in late April 2017, #SherlockLive won the People's Voice award in that category, receiving the greatest number of votes from the public. (CNN Election Night 2016 received the award as the best event within that category.) Considering that #SherlockLive was promoted only within two days of the event (a tease at the end of a *Sherlock* episode, but only in the U.K.), it is based on a television series instead of a sport or a national event like an election, and it lasted only 30 minutes, the creativity of the event, its level of interactivity, and the positive attention it generated among the media and fans increases its newsworthiness.

Fans who participated tweeted their praise to BBC One:

I want more #SherlockLive please do more of this, it'[s] amazing. (Ingrid)

The #SherlockLive takeover tonight was amazing. [hands clapping emoticon] (Luke)

brilliant. genius. incredibly fun. (pet)

Others commented on the personal fan experience:

I can't believe I've been told to delete my Twitter cause I'm so stupid by Sherlock Holmes himself. I feel so blessed. (Sonja)

Missing my mums birthday for this but I just can't put my phone down. (Em is Okay)

Although the majority of players seemed to be located in the U.K., at least theoretically, the experience was free and available to anyone who knew about it and could be online at the time the event took place. The time zone difference may have provided a barrier to those in, for example, the U.S. who might be at work on that Tuesday afternoon and unable to play, unlike someone at home at 8 p.m. in the U.K. As well, the event was teased only on U.K. television, not in the *Sherlock* episode broadcast hours later on PBS in the U.S. However, anyone searching for #Sherlock or, more specifically #SherlockLive, or fans who follow @BBCOne or other *Sherlock* Twitter accounts would have been able to learn of the event or to follow it live or archived.

The event was enjoyable for fans and, as a promotional and positive public relations vehicle both when the event took place and when it was nominated for a Webby, was valuable to the BBC and *Sherlock*. However, #SherlockLive illustrates the type of controlled interaction between official personnel (e.g., Moffat, Gatiss) and fans with which showrunners are most comfortable. During this event, they could hide behind the guise of Sherlock, a beloved character, and use his characterization to make the event more realistic for participants. Fans could tweet "Sherlock," and many were likely to get an immediate response. The context of the game also helped to preclude trolling—the information about the case kept the game on track and the pace speedy so that, unlike Sherlock, participants would not be bored. Those fans who may have a gripe against the showrunners did not find out until after the event that Moffat and Gatiss were online, and few fans would be likely to send negative messages directly to Sherlock, especially because of his caustic replies. The event took place in a controlled online space that "protected" the showrunners and likely encouraged them to participate, especially when the event could gain them and the show positive publicity in mainstream media before and after the event. Fans could participate in realistic role play in which Sherlock entered the real world to share a case. Members of the digital community could read each other's tweets and share insights about "who done it" and could discuss the game—as well as share photos, videos, and comments about their personal experiences. In this interaction between the showrunners and fans, the showrunners and creative personnel who developed the media and scripted the case have all the "power" in what is presented online, just as they do with the television series. However, #Sherlock Live needed players in order to be successful, and, according to the number of retweets and likes to BBC One/Sherlock tweets during the game, thousands of people participated either directly or by following the tweets in real time. #SherlockLive would not have been successful if no one had attended the virtual event. At the conclusion of the event, Sherlock encouraged players to post their own content, which not only verified that they played the game but, if they successfully identified the murderer, gave them online credibility for being like Sherlock. Although the BBC, Moffat, or Gatiss could not control the amount or type of content fans posted at the conclusion of the event, they directed "acceptable" content through Sherlock's final tweet. Fans had to interact with Sherlock and each other in order for the event to be successful, but the series' official voices effectively managed the content through carefully scripted messages and clues and a short response time.

As one blogger noted, "BBC One showed us how to appeal to the online generation and successfully integrate a popular TV series with an online fandom via social media with #SherlockLive.... The opportunity for fans to be recognised by the man himself made sure that people weren't just sitting back and watching all the action happen, but were furiously tweeting BBC One trying to solve the murder and get noticed by Sherlock" (Thomas). While fans were enjoying the game, the BBC was building credibility with a generation interested in gaming and adding a new layer of interactivity to its television series. The BBC's Twitter account also received a boost in popularity during the event, a trend that was noticed by others on Twitter who were not playing along.

Perhaps this type of event provides the "solution" to the problems with interacting via Twitter that *Sherlock*'s official personnel—such as Amanda Abbington, Moffat, and Gatiss—have sometimes faced. It provides what many fans crave: instant recognition by a celebrity they admire. It also capitalizes on the fan-detective characteristics of this particular fandom. Although in this case the "celebrity" is a fictional character and the person behind the keyboard was unmasked only after the event, the fact that "Sherlock" responded to what they had tweeted was a very satisfying interaction for fans because of the fidelity of the #SherlockLive experience regardless of whether it was connected to the celebrity actors or not. This is particularly promising for future interactions, since fan relationships with celebrities, as discussed previously, have been quite fraught. This official connection to the character of Sherlock supersedes much of the challenges associated with TPTB connecting to fans.

An event like #SherlockLive works best in an environment provided by the digital *Sherlock* fandom: participants who can be easily reached by social media and choose to "play" on social media, the potential for international access, a game that fits within the inherent nature of the television series' storytelling (i.e., a murder mystery for Sherlock and his temporary colleagues to solve), and fans who enjoy and appreciate the context of the game. *Sherlock* fans, as indicated especially through #Setlock, like to seek clues and try to deduce what is happening (in the case of episodes being filmed for future broadcast) or what has happened (in the case of a murder mystery role-playing game). Although such an event will not be appropriate for every television series or every series' fandom, the combination of Sherlock and the digital community worked exceptionally well to create innovative, award-winning entertainment. As blogger Sian Thomas pondered, "is this BBC One throwing down the gauntlet and recognis[ing] that social media for the younger generation TV viewers shouldn't be ignored? Is this the beginning of a new era of connecting what we see on screen and off screen by linking into social media?" As an experiment or perfect opportunity for BBC Wales' Creative Digital Director to introduce hybrid programming, #SherlockLive is a success. However, the test of its viability will be whether a major television entity like the BBC chooses to allocate resources for free social media entertainment to keep fans hooked between new television episodes or how a more traditional television-centered company can compete with the creativity of the digital community it seeks to court. It represents a conscious effort on the part of TBTB to work with fans to create content, because the contributions by fan detectives were as much a part of #SherlockLive as were the contributions from TPTB.

Although the TPTB, in the case of *Sherlock* or any television series, are likely only interested in keeping their fan base engaged to generate ratings, the potential for involving fans in elaborate games designed to intrigue but also to educate would likely bring together people of disparate age, gender, and/or nationality in unique ways. Because of the talent and dedication of fans and fan-advocates, it is possible that such a game might be developed without the knowledge or consent of official sources.

Although Sherlock: The Game Is On is a Role Playing Game (RPG), not an ARG like #SherlockLive, it illustrates the potential for creative fans to develop games without the input of TPTB (including their funding). An RPG invites players to enter a fictional world and act as a character within it, instead of interacting as oneself in a game, as in #SherlockLive.

RPGs are popular within Sherlock Holmes fandom, but interactive video games are usually developed and released by for-profit companies. "Baker Street: Roleplaying the World of Sherlock Holmes," for example, was developed by Fearlight, with the blessing of the Arthur Conan Doyle Estate; its $20 price tag makes it affordable for most fans to play. Although fans certainly have the creativity to make their own RPGs, even a group of fan volunteers has a limited amount of time and money to spend on game development. Thus, the reality is that the creation of an RPG like Sherlock: The Game Is On may take years. Fan interest from potential players as well as game developers has not waned since this crime-solving puzzle game was announced in 2013, but in the years since this announcement, Improbable Studios' game site most often has provided programming updates, illustrations of the animation process, and audio clips from the soundtrack. However, work on the game continues, and writer Melissa Wilkinson helped generate more interest in it during Sherlocked USA, where she had a table in the vendors' room to explain the game and hand out promotional stickers. Although the reality of creating a game makes the process especially lengthy for fan volunteers, the potential exists for additional RPGs or ARGs created by and for fans.

Censorship of Fan Communities and Danger to Future Advocacy

Pitfalls associated with the digital nature of fan-based activities have the potential to threaten the work that is done in cyberspace, which is where most fans produce and consume "for us, by us" kind of content. U.S. or U.K. members of digital communities have grown accustomed to freedom in posting almost anything they want. Of course, companies hosting the servers on which digital content is stored and on whose site users upload and share content post Terms of Service (ToS) or rules to which participants must adhere or likely face the elimination of their account. Whether on Twitter or another content-hosting service like LiveJournal (LJ), most account holders—whether representing individuals or a group— must agree to the server/host's rules and the laws regulating the account where the server/host is located. Twitter, for example, provides individual English-language ToS directed to those who live in the U.S. or those who live in the European Union or otherwise outside the U.S. Although Twitter has been frequently bashed for not effectively banning trolls, especially those who threaten harm to or encourage self-harm by other users, it has standards and strives to make Twitter a safer digital space. In addition to the ToS, the Twitter Rules state "In order to ensure that people feel safe expressing diverse opinions and beliefs, we do not tolerate behavior that crosses the line into abuse, including behavior that harasses, intimidates, or uses fear to silence another user's voice. Any accounts and related accounts engaging in the activities specified ... may be temporarily locked and/or subject to permanent suspension." The list includes violent threats, harassment, multiple account abuse (to evade having one account blocked and allow abusive behavior to continue via another account), the posting of private information (commonly known as doxxing), impersonation, and self-harm. Of course, as anyone who keeps up with Twitter news quickly realizes, policing accounts is time consuming, and content that violates the Twitter rules often is viewed hundreds or thousands of times before being removed by Twitter or the account owner. For the most part, members of the digital *Sherlock* fandom who live in a country with relatively few constraints on Internet use (e.g., no posts suggesting terrorism, illegal activities, hate speech) are most familiar with individuals' accounts being locked or deleted after the owner commits a specific offense. Effectively banning an entire community, such as a fanfiction community publishing LGBTQ stories, is rare.

However, in April 2017, a change in the ToS of LiveJournal, a popular place for *Sherlock* (and other fandoms') writers to post fiction and readers to comment on it, increased the likelihood that LGBTQ content posted in an account would result in that account being deleted. Although Russian company SUP Media bought LJ in 2007, its servers were housed in the U.S., and fanfiction communities felt safe because of U.S. legal protections for their content. When the company moved its servers to Russia in December 2016, content posted to LJ accounts became subject to Russian laws and stricter censorship. Nothing seemed to change legally for community members until a new, unannounced ToS was implemented in April. Before existing account owners could access their accounts, they had to agree to the new ToS. For non–Russian speakers, the Russian language ToS was the only legally binding version; an English version was described on the site as possibly not legally binding if any differences were found between the official Russian and unofficial translated-into-English versions. Yet the most troublesome part of the ToS for *Sherlock* communities was the prohibition to "post advertising and/or political solicitation materials unless otherwise directly specified in a separate agreement between User and the Administration" or "perform any other actions contradictory to the laws of the Russian Federation" (Elderkin). Although most non–

Russian LJ account holders likely have no idea what the laws of the Russian Federation might be, they quickly came to understand through online posts and articles that any content deemed potentially harmful to Russian children would violate the law. As an *io9* article explained, "the new agreement is designed to put the site in compliance with Russia's Internet laws, which are subject to extreme censorship under the guise of protecting children" (Elderkin).

Part of this protection is the ban against "gay propaganda," and fanfiction presenting a positive portrayal of LGBTQ characters or discussions of characters' sexuality can fall under this category. Because thousands of *Sherlock* stories involve themes or invite discussions of sex, sexuality, or sexual orientation, communities like the SherlockBBC and the 221B Recs LJ fanfiction communities quickly discussed online whether to risk having all stories deleted without prior notice—thus not only destroying the community but years of archived comments and stories—or to migrate the files to another site. Ironically, the change in the LJ ToS brought many users back to Dreamwidth. Both LJ and Dreamwidth lost popularity with the advent of other social media sites, including Instagram and Tumblr, as a place to post fan works and comments, but because Dreamwidth offers an interface similar enough to LJ's to make migration less complicated, it became the primary choice of communities seeking a new home in a less censored environment.

The fact that many communities had held an LJ account for years and individual writers' cross-posts between a personal account and the community's often went back more than a decade made the possible loss of information potentially devastating. *Sherlock* communities may go back to 2010, during the series' first season, and even communities that have dwindled over time provide a wealth of information about early *Sherlock* fandom that is accessed years later by fans coming late to *Sherlock* or researchers like academics seeking documentation of fan activities. Advocacy links and information also are embedded in fanfiction archives and within discussion threads about specific stories or community announcements; fans looking for information about Sherlock's sexual orientation or explanations of asexuality, for example, may search archives years after a story, link, or comment was first posted. The possibility of losing this information without advance warning frightened enough individual and community account holders into relocating their backlogs and immediately ending new posts to LJ sites.

The LJ ToS also noted that accounts inactive for six months would be automatically deleted. Therefore, account moderators or individual users who posted the new address of archived stories would only be able to direct fans to the new site for a few months. Anyone who much later discovers an LJ link to a writer's or a community's account or a story will be unable, at least through LJ, to find any trace of the old account or indication where or if the former site had been moved. Unovis, the community account owner/moderator of 221B Recs, discussed this problem during one of the last posts to LJ: "Some worries about the move are a loss of community members and readership; a loss of reccers [those who recommend stories and post introductions to or synopses of them]; a loss of coverage in newsletters and links to the comm. I hope networking and publicity can help somewhat." The decision to leave LJ, a host with which many long-time users had grown familiar and where communities had established long-term homes, was not easy but, as users frequently posted in early April 2017, necessary.

One longtime LJ user succinctly summarized the response of many leaving the site as a result of the revised ToS: "I have made the decision to leave LJ, because of their new Terms of Service." Among the reasons for crazyscot's displeasure with the ToS are "being coerced" into agreeing to it, no prior notice that a change to the ToS was going to be made, references to Russian law, and lack of definition of terms like *political solicitation* (especially within the context of Russian law). crazyscot, like many LJ users living outside Russia, has no real way of knowing "what Russian law says about appropriateness for children, how the norms and mores might differ from where I live." Beyond these pragmatic problems with continuing as an LJ user, crazyscot, like many members of the LJ community protesting the change, is concerned what the new ToS means for the LGBTQ+ community. crazyscot describes the Russian government's stance toward this community as "unconscionable for me." As a final point, the former LJ user worries about the Russians' acquisition and use of information from LJ subscribers—a security threat that seems impossible to determine but likely to exist.

As *io9* also mentioned, the potential for the Russian government's security agencies to spy on users becomes much easier with the new ToS. Other posters requested that anyone using LJ refrain from discussing sexuality or directing comments to a specific user or responding to a post about a sexual topic so that the Russian government would not be able to compile lists of users who are at the least interested in "gay propaganda" and can be targeted as homosexual. Keeping all community members safe, especially regarding their sexuality, has become an increasingly significant topic given the global political climate from 2016 onward.

After engaging the SherlockBBC LJ community in a discussion of what the group should do as a result of the new ToS, the moderators posted a final message to thank fans for their discussion leading to a decision about the community's future. The group decided to move to Dreamwidth, even though the shift likely would mean some community members would not make the move or would not like or would not want to learn to work with the Dreamwidth-style forum. Similarly, 221B Recs provided a rationale for moving to Dreamwidth: concerns about free speech and solidarity with "LGBTQ and other identities." The 221B Recs community also determined that the risk of their site being deleted by LJ authorities had increased to an unacceptable level, and they wanted to preserve the creative works that had been created and were being enjoyed. Moving the community to a new home seemed a prudent move, as well as an appropriate political one.

A problem for communities like SherlockBBC and 221B Recs is the way that LJ could consider the legality of posting anything at all to do with LGBTQ topics and the possibility that non–Russian users could potentially be brought to court in violation of the "gay propaganda" law. Another troubling section of the LJ ToS states that if "more than three thousand Internet users access [a] Blog within 24 hours," LJ can ban "disseminating ... extremist materials and also the materials propagating pornography" as well as "materials containing obscene language" (Valens). User accounts having such an influx of traffic also become considered as "media outlets" and face the restrictions placed on such larger-scale information outlets. Although most fan sites do not generate this many hits within 24 hours, the possibility exists, and a site's "pornographic" or "obscene" content could lead to the deletion of the account, as well as legal sanctions. Whether readers deem slash fiction or explicit heterosexual fiction as pornography or art, obscenity or realistic use of language, a great deal of *Sherlock* fanfiction could be deemed illegal under Russian law. One Tumblr user further enlightened non–Russian LJ account holders: "Short version, as I see it: nothing obscene by Russian legal standards (in Putin's Russia LGBTA discussions could fall within that, much less actual smut), and even if you're squeaky clean and hetro-vanilla, any and everything you say is subject to their (legal) judgment" (Valens).

In a presumably safer Dreamwidth blog, telophase commented on the aspect of the ToS scaring fanfiction communities the most: "[G]iven the anti-gay sentiment in Russia right now, I don't know how they're going to view slash and pro-gay content on LJ in the future." In response, solarbird elaborated that "Any mention of LGBT people at all—at least, that isn't explicitly condemnational—where anyone under 19 could see/hear/read it is a violation of Russian law.... By including this, LJ's ToS is not explicitly anti–LGBT." In addition, both telophase and solarbird wrote they are considering changing their user names to protect themselves or possibly making any future accounts private so that only those they know and approve can view their posts. Although, in a climate of fear, such reactions are understandable for personal protection, they signal a potential end to a truly global *Sherlock* digital fandom—or any fandom that frequently features posts and fosters discussions of sexuality or sexual orientation. One factor that has made *Sherlock* fandom especially robust and beneficial to asexual advocacy in particular may also make it politically or legally hazardous to members, depending on where they live or to which server host they subscribe. When LJ's servers moved from the U.S. to Russia, Anton Nossik, a former advisor to SUP Media, made a Russian-language post that has been translated and reported by Global Voices Advocacy as this: "LJ's servers have moved 'closer' not to its authors and readers, but to those who want to monitor them" ("LiveJournal, Now Based in Russia").

To illustrate how the change to LJ's ToS might affect *Sherlock* fan communities with accounts still listed on LJ as of April 18, 2017, Table 2 tracks, as only a sample of communities, those listed as "journal" communities with posts, announcements, activities, or stories related to *Sherlock*. Other LJ categories not included in this sample are "challenge" communities providing writing prompts or challenges to fan fiction writers, "actor" communities (primarily devoted to Benedict Cumberbatch or Andrew Scott), or pairing-specific fan fiction communities.

Table 2. *Sherlock* Journal Communities on LiveJournal

Community's Name	Year Founded	Description	Number of Journal Entries	Number of Comments	Number of Members	Status on April 18, 2017
SherlockBBC	2010	Fan fiction community, slash allowed	25,165	152,095	11,466	Moved the archive to Sherlock-bbc.dreamwidth.org
BBCSherlock	2010	Fan fiction community, slash allowed	4,621	5,721	3,120	Voted to remain on LJ but maintain a backup

Community's Name	Year Founded	Description	Number of Journal Entries	Number of Comments	Number of Members	Status on April 18, 2017
						archive on Dreamwidth
221B_Slash	2010	Slash fan fiction community	1,804	938	1,300	Very active in 2016 but minimal activity in early 2017; no notice of leaving LJ
Sherlock_Search	2010	Community to help fans find stories	1,633	5,081	1,327	Active in 2017; no notice of leaving LJ
SherlockIcons	2010	Community to create and share icons and graphics	568	102	852	Active in 2017; no notice of leaving LJ
Asexy_Sherlock	2010	Community for fan fiction involving any asexual *Sherlock* character but mainly focused on asexual Sherlock	280	811	514	Periodic posts through 2016; no notice of leaving LJ
DailySherlock	2010	Private account to post news or an image of Sherlock daily	319	370	1 (but initially posted so anyone could see the entries)	Active through 2011; closed
Sherlock_Stamps	2010	A stamping community	189	1,438	95	Active into early 2012; no notice of leaving LJ
IHazABlanket	2010	Community to create macros	124	1,005	322	Active through 2013; no notice of leaving LJ
Sherlock2010	2010	Community for Sherlock Holmes and John Watson diaries	120	34	253	Active through 2014; no notice of leaving LJ
ShBBC_QuickFix	2010	Community of writers of short, often	99	19	113	Active through 2013; no notice of

Community's Name	Year Founded	Description	Number of Journal Entries	Number of Comments	Number of Members	Status on April 18, 2017
		quickly written fan fiction (e.g., drabbles, flashfic)				leaving LJ
SherlockBBC-Fic	2014	Fan fiction community, slash allowed	82	431	9	Moved to Dreamwidth in 2015 because of technical problems on LJ
ImSoChangeable	2010	Moriarty-themed fan fiction community, slash allowed	55	95	108	Active through 2013; no notice of leaving LJ
Sherlock_Rant	2012	Community in which to rant about *Sherlock*	50	426,838	5	Active until early 2015; no notice of leaving LJ
SherlockRPF	2010	Community with stories about real person fiction	29	267	646	Active into 2014; no notice of leaving LJ
Sherlock-RPF	2012	Community with stories about real person fiction	4	192	36	Short-lived community with no activity since 2012; no notice of leaving LJ

Among the many *Sherlock*-themed LJ communities founded in 2010, the year the series began, only a few are active through the series' fourth season. The gradual dwindling in interest, particularly after Seasons Two or Three, is understandable. Many fans drift away from a series after the initial "honeymoon" phase of entertainment media frenzy and immediate fan love for something new and popular. Especially because *Sherlock* forced fans to wait two or more years between seasons and only provided twelve movie-length episodes and a special episode within four seasons, less-than-diehard fans may have lost interest or moved onto another fandom while waiting for new episodes. As well, as LJ became less popular in recent years, fan fiction of every type flourished on other sites, such as

Archive of Our Own, perhaps indicating that, although a specific community may flounder or a platform lose members, *Sherlock* fan fiction continues to thrive.

Communities in danger of disappearing from LJ without being backed up elsewhere signal not only the loss of parts of the *Sherlock* fandom's history but its advocacy of non-heteronormative characters. LJ communities like Asexy_Sherlock receive new comments months or years after stories were posted, and they are one of the few archives of stories about asexual *Sherlock* characters. Losing this archive would mean one less site where fans looking for information about or a positive portrayal of asexual characters could find information; yet, if it is left inactive on LJ, under the ToS it will be deleted within six months, even if the subject matter does not result in deletion even sooner. Many communities apparently left to languish on LJ in recent years will vanish.

Given how often *Sherlock* fans continue to discuss blogs, stories, interviews, or posts years after their publication, as well as the many years' of information about sexuality and advocacy embedded within an archive or a community, the LJ ToS serves as a warning to communities hosting information about LGBTQ characters, themes, or discussions. At the very least, individuals and communities must be pragmatic and store the history of their discussions, as well as their texts, in multiple locations, in case one online site is destroyed. Fans must band together to share information again once it is not available on one server and find new ways to share information electronically. Advocacy is likely to face the most dire impact of censorship and possible persecution of individuals posting to a discussion or providing information about topics being censored. Fans participating in communities must realize the negative aspects of global interconnectedness that can categorize fan works as illegal or harmful under restrictive laws governing sites and servers that may be established in one country but whose national law is being applied to all community members.

In the week following the new ToS, LJ subscribers were encouraged to delete their accounts after migrating content elsewhere. Twitter lit up with angry comments about the ToS and the social standards being imposed legally on users. Mainstream media posted articles about LJ users leaving in droves, and individual users urging others to leave LiveJournal ended final posts with lines like "Will the last person turn out the lights?" British site We the Unicorns summarized what many saw to be the end of LJ: "While LiveJournal hasn't been especially popular in the U.K. for many years thanks to social media developments such as Facebook, Instagram and Snapchat, it still has a thriving community. But these new rules look set to end that platform once and for all" (Brooks).

Although digital communities like SherlockBBC and 221B Recs responded to LJ by moving to a presumably safer online space, the issues that the LJ ToS brings up are likely to be faced again on another service or server. However, the speed with which individuals and communities— many of them posting LGBTQ content—migrated to a less restrictive (i.e., far less censored or legally threatening) site indicates that these communities remain conscientious regarding the digital platform and want to remain online to freely post content. As Marshall McLuhan is famous for saying, "the medium in the massage." Choices regarding the platform or the content impact what can be said, to whom, and how it might be proliferated by others.

Merging Academic and Fan Scholarship

The Organization for Transformative Works supports fan fiction haven Archive of Our Own and, more important for academics wanting to publish research about fandom, publishes the journal *Transformative Works and Cultures (TWC)*. The online journal, published twice a year, features articles about popular media, fan communities, and, of course, transformative works. Like traditional academic journals, *TWC* uses a blind-review process involving at least two peer reviewers, three if there is a split decision about an article's suitability for publication. Reviewers are "scholars in media studies, fan studies, English, communication, and related fields," and an article is evaluated for "appropriateness of theoretical application, relevance for *TWC*'s audience, and importance of the contribution to the field" (*TWC*, "Peer Review Process").

In 2017, *TWC* published a special issue devoted to Sherlock Holmes studies, which included discussions of early Holmes fandom, pastiches, copyright, and early Sherlockian scholarship. Especially interesting to *Sherlock* fan-scholars and "traditional" academics is an article analyzing the tensions between fans preferring fan practices and traditional frameworks for expressing fandom (e.g., those prior to the 21st century) and fans preferring transmedial frameworks.

Even more specifically is a study of female *Sherlock* fans over 50, or "the florals," as they are known within the fandom. The term comes from an *OUT* magazine interview with Cumberbatch in 2014. During a lunch meeting with the interviewer, the actor noticed two middle-aged female fans, wearing floral dresses, watching him. He cursed and said, "Oh lord, here we go, here we go…. The florals over there…. They're giving a bit of a head-turning—it's begun" (Hicklin). When the article came out, fans of all ages were upset at Cumberbatch's apparent insensitivity, although some chose to make the term *florals* their own, and "the florals" has become an age-related but not ageist label used in online fan discussions. This article discussing "the florals" and, more generally, aging in fandom is as rigorous as any article published in non-fan-related academic journals. To those who understand the rigor with which researchers conduct research and analyze data within fan studies, the high quality of work in a journal devoted to this subject is not surprising. Its research methodology is sound (and explained in detail for those who might replicate the study), its analysis logical, and its conclusions important to a deeper understanding of aging within fandom (Petersen). Because *Sherlock* fandom spans a wide range of ages, it is an especially appropriate fandom to study. Yet in many academic departments, fan studies often is not deemed as "real" or rigorous an area of research, as if professionals with PhDs in media studies, digital communication, anthropology, linguistics, popular culture, and other areas should not apply their theory and praxis toward fandom—an area in which they likely participate on some level.

Perhaps interviews in which Cumberbatch, Moffat, Gatiss, or Abbington complain about a subset of fans within the whole fandom and seem to ridicule fandom in general have sensitized all *Sherlock* fans—academics as well as non-academics—to the way they are perceived by the public, as well as the series' showrunners and cast. To be further scrutinized as a subject of anthropological study by academics who are perceived as outside fandom thus should be avoided, especially within the supposedly safe space of a fan convention. Over time, the gap between academics and fans might be alleviated if more scholar-fans publicly "come out," both in academia and at fan events. Making fans aware of more positive or insightful depictions of fandom might help mitigate the fear or anger about journalistic reports that have ridiculed fans in the past. The notion that one can be a fan or an academic—but not at the same time or in the same place—needs to be debunked.

The Future of Sherlock *Studies*

Despite biases that may in some respects hamper the study of *Sherlock* as a text or the *Sherlock* fandom, there has been a great deal of academic scholarship since shortly after the series' first season. Although the number of academic books, articles, conference papers, and reviews about *Sherlock* or university courses studying the series is fewer than those for fan favorites such as *Buffy the Vampire Slayer*, there is no reason why *Sherlock* studies (within the much broader realm of Sherlock Holmes studies) should not be as viable as *Buffy* studies (within the much broader realm of Joss Whedon studies). In fact, because *Sherlock* is based on Arthur Conan Doyle's literature that is and has been for decades an acceptable area of academic study, *Sherlock* studies is even more likely to become a "respectable" area of study. Given the robust nature of *Sherlock* fandom, *Sherlock* studies could help academics better see the value of fan studies in relation to their academic works in related fields. For example, individually or jointly, we have taught a *Sherlock*-themed humanities course three times, written five chapters and edited books of essays, published four episode or disc reviews, presented seven conference papers, and written a PhD dissertation about *Sherlock* fandom. Such activities should be common within *Sherlock* studies. On a smaller scale (because of fewer episodes to be studied as texts), *Sherlock* studies may (or should) follow in the footsteps of now-well-known *Buffy* studies.

Father of *Buffy* studies David Lavery co-founded, with Rhonda Wilcox, the Whedon Studies Association; it published the journal *Slayage* from 2001–2009, when the title was changed to *The Journal of the Whedon Studies Association*. The Association held six conferences between 2006 and 2016. In a 2015 *Atlantic* interview about the prominence of *Buffy* studies, Lavery lauded Whedon for the "complexity, intertextuality, [and] authenticity of his stories that make them so rich for study" (Schwab). Although some fans, fan-scholars, or scholar-fans may argue that Moffat's and Gatiss' later *Sherlock* episodes have become too complex for many viewers, certainly Lavery's description of Whedon's work can be applied to *Sherlock*. It is a rich text that has generated a wealth of articles, chapters, or presentations about narrative structure, the concept of the Mind Palace, religion, mythology, fairy tales, the series' place within Holmes adaptations, virtual tourism, technology, addiction, modernism, acting styles, special visual effects, fandom, feminism, and sexuality, to list only a few topics.

To date, *Sherlock* does not have its own journal, although articles or chapters about the series and its fandom have been published in several academic publications. The premier journal for Sherlock Holmes studies, *The Baker Street Journal*, invites scholarly works that promote "a world where it is always 1895," which precludes *Sherlock* scholarship. The Sherlock

Holmes Society of London publishes a journal that is mostly for members, although some articles are available online. The site describes the journal as "home to the most erudite scholarship, publishing learned articles from Holmesians world-wide who have something to say on any aspect of Sherlock Holmes and his world." In theory, *Sherlock* scholarship fits within this definition, but no articles specifically about the series have been published in this journal.

The content of these and other Sherlock Holmes journals and newsletters seems biased toward an exploration of the canon. Thus, *Sherlock* is less likely to be the subject of scholarly research in these publications than in journals analyzing fandom or fandom-published journals, such as *Transformative Works and Cultures*. For *Sherlock*-specific scholarship to become well established within the wide range of scholarly works published by academic institutions or fan-based organizations, it must overcome a perceived bias within Sherlock Holmes fandom that an adaptation may not be as "real" or as worthy of study as the original Arthur Conan Doyle canon.

Final Words About Fandom

Fandom, in general, engages in detective-type work, but the emulation of and regard for sleuth-like activity is certainly a primary focus of *Sherlock* fandom and is instrumental in making this fandom particularly suited to creative, critical, and advocacy work. Participants in *Sherlock* fan culture are positively affected by the opportunities for community building and free self-expression that exist in unique ways in online environments.

However, even greater support within a fan community for members with a similar interpretation of a series' texts (e.g., Sherlock as asexual) is necessary for further growth of the digital community. After "The Final Problem" was broadcast, several fans immediately tweeted the BBC, Gatiss, and Sue Vertue to express their shock and displeasure with aspects of this episode that, to them, seemed to negate any but a heterosexual reading of Sherlock. Yet, as discussed in previous chapters, even this episode can be interpreted in many ways, some which still support a fan reading of Sherlock as asexual or homosexual. When fans fall prey to the notion that only the showrunners' or actors' interpretation of a series' meaning or a character's identity is an appropriate reading, they may feel betrayed and disempowered—especially when they have followed *Sherlock* for several years and found clues in previous episodes to support a non-heteronormative reading. With a more vocal and even more supportive community of, for example, fans who provide evidence of a valid reading of Sherlock as asexual, the fans who tweeted TPTB might have better been able to assimilate "The Final Problem" into their personally-important reading of Sherlock.

Sherlock fans might also do well to remember that not every official voice may agree with the showrunners' interpretation of characters. In an *Entertainment Weekly* interview after "The Final Problem," Moffat waves off concerns about Molly Hooper (Louise Brealey) and her relationship with Sherlock. During this episode, Sherlock forces Molly to confess her love for him; she thinks him cruel but does not realize that he believes his sister will blow up Molly's home if he does not get his friend to say "I love you." Many fans dislike the dismissive way that Molly's emotions are treated in this episode, and Moffat stirred up even more controversy about Molly's treatment by saying "She gets over it! Surely at a certain point you have to figure out that after Sherlock escapes [he] tells her, 'I'm really sorry about that, it was a code, I thought your flat was about to blow up.' And she says, 'Oh well that's okay then, you bastard.' And then they go back to normal, that's what people do. I can't see why you'd have to play that out" (Hibberd). Not only many fans, but Brealey disagree. She had been besieged by fans on Twitter who accused her (not the scriptwriters or her character) of being anti-feminist and regressing the character to the Sherlock-fawning Season One depiction. In response, Brealey took on Moffat by publicly disagreeing with his "She gets over it!" comment. Her first tweet refutes fans' displeasure directed to her that Molly is far from feminist: "Loving someone after years is not reductive, retrograde, antifeminist or weak. Fight the patriarchy, not me, and read some f***ing Chekhov." Next, she makes it clear that she opposes Moffat's interpretation of Molly and her feelings: "FTR [For the record] I disagree with Steven about the impact of the scene on Molly ... & that's fine. He's allowed to feel something. So am I. So are you" (Frost, "'Sherlock' Star Louise Brealey"). Instead of, as Moffat suggests, "[Molly] probably went and had a drink and shagged someone," Brealey's tweets indicate that Molly would not be "fine," has loved Sherlock for years (even as her character in Seasons Two and Three increasingly stands up to him), and would not act as Moffat states in his interview. She reminds Moffat and fans that everyone can have a different emotional response to that scene—or to that character; differing responses should be expected, and disagreement about interpretations is "fine." What is implied in Brealey's tweets is that Moffat's interpretation does not have to be hers—or fans'. Even one "insider" can disagree with another.

Perhaps what fans can take from Brealey's Twitter discourse is that their personal interpretations, especially if they are empowering and can be supported with evidence from a series, are valid and should not be ridiculed by others. Showrunners' reading of or intent for characters is not indisputable or inviolable, and different interpretations of a character or scene (or a sexual orientation or an identity) should be expected. Even an episode like "The Final Problem," with many possible interpretations espoused by a range of fans and TPTB, should not lead fans to automatically devalue themselves or their reading of a series they have long loved.

Digital fandom, whose subcommunities are especially invested in non-heteronormative readings based on clues within a series, has the power to be empowering and rooted in advocacy, no matter what showrunners or actors believe about a mutually loved television series or its characters. Perhaps *Sherlock* can be perceived over time as most groundbreaking for the ways that fans continue to interpret characters in meaningful ways that are grounded within the series but encourage fans to present their own evidence and gain the support of other fans within the digital community.

Those in the *Sherlock* digital fandom who are FIAWOL must continue to find creative inspiration and positive interaction at least with other fans (if not TPTB) if they are to remain a part of this fandom. That does not necessarily mean that they will move on to another fandom or abandon *Sherlock*, even after the series is canceled. Many fandoms thrive long after new "official" texts such as episodes, films in a franchise, or series of books are no longer forthcoming. Instead, fans for whom FIAWOL continue to create their own texts and merchandise and meet with friends met through fandom or who otherwise share their fannish interests. As long as fans maintain interest in the characters, they can create new plots, original characters, situations, and platforms on which to interact with them.

Because *Sherlock* fans not only have their own fandom based on the BBC's television series but are part of a much larger Sherlock Holmes fandom that has been going on since Conan Doyle was still writing stories, the *Sherlock* fandom is likely to remain vibrant for many years, even if it eventually fades in popularity only to be revisited and revived by new Holmes fans sometime in the future. In this way *Sherlock* fandom might become somewhat like J.R.R. Tolkien's fandom for his *Hobbit* and *Lord of the Rings* books, in particular. The first fans fell in love with the characters and stories shortly after the books were written, but new fans were introduced as adaptations in other media (e.g., radio, television) made the stories more accessible to more people. When Peter Jackson's film adaptations were introduced in the early 2000s, online fandom exploded, especially through updates and discussions with fans in New Zealand, where the films were primarily made. Although no new Tolkien stories seem likely to be discovered, additional adaptations of Tolkien's works probably will be made. Fans of those, as well as the original books, will return to the wealth of online material created and archived by the digital fandom who first embraced Jackson's films. Another way *Sherlock*'s digital fandom may evolve is to emulate the fandom for classic *Star Trek* characters, who survive long after the 1969 cancellation of the original television series. Eventually a series of films starring the cast from the 1960s' series introduced, for example, James T. Kirk and Spock to new audiences and gave new inspiration for fan fiction to the original fans. Beginning in 2009, the rebooted film franchise provided new interpretations of familiar characters for the digital *Star Trek* community to analyze and incorporate into their encyclopedic websites and fan fiction archives. These are only two long-surviving fandoms that have expanded along with digital technology and allowed former and new fans to share their love of characters online. Sherlock Holmes, who has already survived from the late 19th century into the early 21st, likely will be around for decades to come, and the digital fandoms of *Sherlock* or Sherlock Holmes make his continuing popularity possible.

Just like other fandoms' FIAWOL members, *Sherlock*'s will use digital communication to share information, promote gatherings, and populate archives with dozens of new stories each day. They will co-opt clips from favorite scenes to create videos with new narratives. They will make and share products that reflect their knowledge of details about *Sherlock*'s characters, dialogue, and plot. They will role play the characters in RPGs or possibly solve new mysteries provided in ARGs. They will follow the series' actors into new projects and possibly additional fandoms, creating links between past and future fandoms. *Sherlock* fans have grown accustomed to waiting through long hiatuses for new episodes; they will stick around to see what happens next to Sherlock and John, Molly and Mrs. Hudson, "the British government" and New Scotland Yard detectives— and they will respond in highly personal ways online.

Bibliography

Abbington, Amanda. @chimpsinsocks "This just happened." Twitter. 11 May 2016.

"The Abominable Bride." *Sherlock*. Writ. Mark Gatiss. Dir. Douglas Mackinnon. BBC Entertainment, 2016. DVD.

Amphiboly. "A Case of Asexuality." 13 Feb. 2013. Web. 24 Oct. 2015. http://amphiboly. tumblr.com/post/43040807010/a-case-of-asexuality.

Andressa. @whoismcfly Twitter. Several tweets. 11 May 2016. Reprinted in Benedict's Third Testicle. Blog. n.d. Web. 11 May 2016. http://benedicts-third-testicle.tumblr. com/.

Anything Cumberbatch. @anythingbatch. Twitter. 26 Apr. 2016.

_____. Twitter. 31 Aug. 2016.

"AO3 Census: Masterpost." Blog. The Slow Dance of Infinite Stars. 5 Oct. 2013. Web. 25 June 2017. http://centrumlumina.tumblr.com/post/63208278796/ao3-census-master post.

Archive of Our Own. "Terms of Service FAQ." 16 May 2016. Web. 22 May 2016. https:// archiveofourown.org/tos_faq#content_faq.

asdfreoiuzqwert. Comments. Reddit. Jan. 2017. Web. 11 May 2017. https://www.reddit. com/r/Sherlock/comments/5l30gf/john_watson_is_no_longer_updating_his_ blog/#bottom-comments.

Asexual Education. Home. n.d. Web. 30 Mar.2016. http://asexualeducation.tumblr. com/.

_____. "A Lovely Interview About Sherlock Wherein Steven Moffat Says That Asexuality is 'Boring,' That Sherlock is Definitively Not Gay, and That Sherlock Wouldn't Be Living With a Man If Men Were Interesting." Jan. 2012. Web. 30 Mar. 2016. http:// asexualeducation.tumblr.com/post/16193449330/a-lovely-interview-about-sherlock-wherein-steven.

Ausiello, Michael. "Sherlock Season 4: Steven Moffat Teases Looming 'Climax.'" *TVLine.* 6 Apr. 2016. Web. 21 Apr. 2016. http://tvline.com/2016/04/06/sherlock-season-4-spoilers-tragedy-death-steven-moffat/.

Bahadur, Nina. "This is How Trolls Treat Women on the Internet." *Huffpost Women.* 13 May 2015. Web. 22 May 2016. http://www.huffingtonpost.com/2015/05/13/being-a-woman-online-really-sucks_n_7265418.html.

Baker Street Babes. n.d. Web. 11 May 2017. http://bakerstreetbabes.com/.

_____. "About." n.d. Web. 25 June 2017. http://bakerstreetbabes.com/babes/.

The Baker Street Journal. Home. n.d. Web. 24 Apr. 2017. http://www.akerstreetjournal. com/home.html.

Baker-Whitelaw, Gavia. "#Setlock: The Fans Who Stalk the 'Sherlock' Film Set." *The Daily Dot.* 15 Jan. 2015. Web. 17 Jan. 2015. https://www.dailydot.com/parsec/sherlock-2015-special-setlock/.

Bat. Comment. Asexuality.org. "BBC Article Mentioning Sherlock's Sexuality." 20 Jan. 2012. Web. 5 Feb. 2016. http://www.asexuality.org/en/topic/69917-bbc-sherlock-article-mentioning-sherlocks-sexuality/.

BBC One. "Sherlock." n.d. Web. 10 May 2017. http://www.bbc.co.uk/programmes/b018 ttws.

Benedict's Third Testicle. Blog. n.d. Web. 26 May 2017. http://benedicts-third-testicle. tumblr.com/page/2.

Benjamin, Walter. "The Work of Art in the Age of Mechanical Reproduction." *Film Theory and Criticism: Introductory Readings.* Eds. Leo Braudy and Marshall Cohen. New York: Oxford University Press, 731–51. Web.

Beth. @BethBeee. Twitter. 31 Aug. 2016.

Big Chief Studios. "Sherlock." BigChiefStudios.co.uk. n.d. Web. 4 Mar. 2017. https://www. bigchiefstudios.co.uk/collectables/sherlock/sixth-scale-figures/sherlock-holmes-and-dr-john-watson-the-abominable-bride.

"The Blind Banker." *Sherlock.* Writ. Steve Thompson. Dir. Euros Lyn. BBC Entertainment, 2010. DVD.

BoeTechLLC. "Sherlock Cookie Cutter 221B Baker Street Door." Etsy. n.d. Web. 2 Feb. 2017. https://www.etsy.com/listing/160164688/sherlock-pill-bottle-necklace-or?ga_ order=most_relevant&ga_search_type=all&ga_view_type=gallery&ga_search_ query=Sherlock&ref=sr_gallery_16.

BookGirlFan. Comment. "It's All Fine." Archive of Our Own. 13 Aug. 2012. Web. 5 Apr. 2016. http://archiveofourown.org/works/160177.

Booth, Paul. *Playing Fans: Negotiating Fandom and Media in the Digital Age.* Iowa City: University of Iowa Press. 2015. Print.

Brealey, Louise. @louisebrealey. Twitter. 17 Jan. 2017.

Brog, Annabel. "Benedict Cumberbatch Talks Sherlock and Sex." *Elle.* 29 Oct. 2014. Web. 5 Feb. 2016. http://www.elleuk.com/now-trending/benedict-cumberbatch-talks-sherlock-and-sex.

Brooks, Hollie-Anne. "LiveJournal Banned LGBTQ + Topics And The Internet Is Out-raged." We the Unicorns. 11 Apr. 2017. Web. 17 Apr. 2017. https://www.wetheunicorns. com/news/livejournal-lgbt/#Wee4gJrfACSRkLqH.97.

Busse, Kristina. "Fans, Fandom, and Fan Studies." *The Encyclopedia of Communication Theory, Vol. 1.* Ed. Stephen W. Littlejohn. 384–90. Thousand Oaks, CA: Sage, 2009. Print.

Busse, Kristina, and Karen Hellekson, Eds. *Fan Fiction and Fan Communities in the Age of the Internet.* Jefferson, NC: McFarland, 2006. Print.

_____. *The Fan Fiction Studies Reader.* New York: Routledge, 2014. Print.

Byrne-Cristiano, Laura. "'Doctor Who' Showrunner Steven Moffat Deletes Twitter Account." *Hypable.* 9 Sep. 2012. Web. 8 Apr. 2017. http://www.hypable.com/doctor-who-showrunner-steven-moffat-deletes-twitter-account/.

Carr, Nicholas. *The Shallows: What the Internet Is Doing to Our Brains.* New York: W.W. Norton, 2011. Print.

Chin, Bertha. "Sherlockology and Galactica.tv: Fan Sites as Gifts or Exploited Labor?" In "Fandom and/as Labor," edited by Mel Stanfill and Megan Condis, special issue, *Transformative Works and Cultures,* no. 15 (2014). http://dx.doi.org/ 10.3983/twc. 2014.0513.

Choppedcreationcheesecake. Blog. n.d. Web. 11 May 2016. Benedict's Third Testicle. http://benedicts-third-testicle.tumblr.com/.

Chu, Erica. "Radical Identities: Asexuality and Contemporary Articulations of Identity." *Asexualities: Feminist and Queer Perspectives.* Eds. Karli June Cerankowski and Megan Milks. New York: Routledge, 2013. Print.

Conan Doyle, Arthur. "The Red-Headed League." *The Adventures of Sherlock Holmes.* London: BBC Books, 2012. Reprint.

_____. *A Study in Scarlet.* London: BBC Books, 2012. Reprint.

Connie Prince. Blog. 2010. n.d. Web. 10 May 2017. http://www.connieprince.co.uk.
cookieswillcrumble. "Let's Play Murder." Archive of Our Own. 17 May 2014. Web. 4 Jan 2017. http://archiveofourown.org/works/1235479.
Coppa, Francesca. "A Brief History of Media Fandom." Kristina Busse,and Karen Hellekson, Eds. *Fan Fiction and Fan Communities in the Age of the Internet.* Jefferson, NC: McFarland, 2006. Print.
crazyscot. "Farewell LiveJournal." crazyscot.dreamwidth.org. 5 Apr. 2017. Web. 17 Apr. 2017. https://crazyscot.dreamwidth.org/444040.html.
Cuccinello, Hayley C. "Fifty Shades of Green: How Fanfiction Went From Dirty Little Secret to Money Machine." *Forbes.* 10 Feb. 2017. Web. 25 June 2017. https://www.forbes.com/sites/hayleycuccinello/2017/02/10/fifty-shades-of-green-how-fanfiction-went-from-dirty-little-secret-to-money-machine/#62af4e49264c.
Cuddlytogas. "Queer Identities in 'Sherlock': A Study in Embarrassing Failures." 21 Sep. 2013. Web. 24 Oct. 2015. http://cuddlytogas.tumblr.com/post/61803092067/queer-identities-in-sherlock-a-study-in.
Cumberbatchweb. "FAQ." n.d. Web. 10 May 2017. http://www.benedictcumberbatch.co.uk/contact/faq/.
_____. Blog. 2014. Web. 10 May 2017. http://cumberbatchweb.tumblr.com/page/196.
_____. "Sherlock: The Empty Hearse—Cumberbatchweb Review." Jan. 2014. Web. 18 June 2016. http://www.benedictcumberbatch.co.uk/reviews/television-reviews/sherlock-the-empty-hearse-cumberbatchweb-review/.
D'Emilio, John. "Capitalism and Gay Identity." *The Lesbian and Gay Studies Reader.* Eds. Henry Abelove, Michele Aina Barale, and David M. Halperin. New York: Routledge, 1993. 466–76. Print.
Denham, Jess. "Sherlock's Benedict Cumberbatch 'First Sexy Holmes,' Says Mark Gatiss." *The Independent.* 7 Mar. 2014. Web. 24 Feb. 2017. http://www.independent.co.uk/arts-entertainment/tv/news/benedict-cumberbatch-first-sexy-sherlock-holmes-says-mark-gatiss-9175800.html.
Dondero, Jennifer, and Sabrina Pippin. "'It's Traumatic Stress, My Dear Watson': A Clinical Conceptualization of Sherlock." *Who Is Sherlock? Essays on Identity in Modern Holmes Adaptations.* Ed. Lynnette Porter. Jefferson, NC: McFarland, 2016. 70–81. Print.
Dowell, Ben. "Russian Broadcaster at the Centre of Sherlock Leak Believes It May Have Been Hacked." *Radio Times.* 16 Jan. 2017. Web. 2 Mar. 2017. http://www.radiotimes.com/news/2017-01-16/russian-broadcaster-at-the-centre-of-sherlock-leak-believes-it-may-have-been-hacked.
dreamlittleyo. "Inflammable." Archive of Our Own. 30 Jan. 2012. Web. 1 May 2016. http://archiveofourown.org/works/330030.
Duggan, Lisa. *The Twilight of Equality? Neoliberalism, Cultural Politics, and the Attack on Democracy.* Boston: Beacon Press, 2003. Print.
Elderkin, Beth. "Russian-owned LiveJournal Bans Political Talk, Adds Risk of Spying." *io9.* 8 Apr. 2017. Web. 17 Apr. 2017. https://io9.gizmodo.com/russian-owned-livejournal-bans-political-talk-adds-ris-1794143772.
Em is Okay. @emgwortho. Twitter. 10 Jan. 2017.
"The Empty Hearse." *Sherlock: Season Three.* Writ. Steven Moffat. Dir. Jeremy Lovering. BBC Entertainment, 2013. DVD.
Eszter Varga. @VettelGirlUK. Twitter. 31 Aug. 2016.
Eventbrite. "Sherlocked USA: The Official Sherlock Convention 2017. Tickets." n.d. Web. 3 Mar. 2017. https://www.eventbrite.co.uk/e/sherlocked-usa-the-official-sherlock-convention-2017-tickets-27112413960.
Fairclough, Norman. *Critical Discourse Analysis: The Critical Study of Language.* New York: Routledge, 2013. Print.
"Fandom Is a Way of Life." Fanlore.com. n.d. Web. 9 May 2017. https://fanlore.org/wiki/Fandom_Is_A_Way_Of_Life.

Fandom Trumps Hate. "Auction Total." 6 Feb. 2017. Web. 25 June 2017. https://fandom
    trumpshate.tumblr.com/post/156911018924/fth-auction-total.
_____. "FAQ." n.d. Web. 25 June 2017. https://fandomtrumpshate.tumblr.com/FAQ.
Fanrek. "Sherlock Holmes Long Coat Jacket Costume." Fanrek.com. n.d. Web. 4. Mar.
    2017. http://www.fanrek.com/sherlock-holmes-cosplay-long-coat-jacket-costume.
    html?gclid=CN7mirLhvdICFdgKgQodqyAP8g.
The Fellowship of Erdemhart. Blog. 9 Nov. 2015. Web. 22 May 2016. http://the-fellowship-
    of-erdemhart.com/post/132884986971/if-this-goes-too-far-ill-of-course-respect-
    your.
_____. Blog. 24 Apr. 2016. Web. 22 May 2016. http://the-fellowship-of-erdemhart.com/
    page/2.
ffion. @silvershuzuo Twitter. 20 Apr. 2016.
"The Final Problem." Sherlock. Writ. Steven Moffat and Mark Gatiss. Dir. Benjamin Caron.
    BBC Entertainment, 2017. DVD.
"Five Common Myths About Asexuality." The Norwich Radical. 17 Oct. 2016. Web. 25
    June 2017. https://thenorwichradical.com/2016/10/17/five-common-myths-about-
    asexuality/.
flawedamethyst. "It's All Fine." Archive of Our Own. 6 Feb. 2011. Web. 5 Apr. 2016. http://
    archiveofourown.org/works/160177.
Fleming, Amy. "Mark Gatiss and Ian Hallard: 'We Met Online—Back When That Was
    Odd.'" The Guardian. 1 Feb. 2017. Web. 8 Apr. 2017. https://www.theguardian.com/
    stage/2017/feb/01/mark-gatiss-and-ian-hallard-sherlock-we-met-online-back-when-
    that-was-odd.
flynnsarcade. Post. "A Lovely Interview About Sherlock Wherein Steven Moffat Says That
    Asexuality is 'Boring,' That Sherlock is Definitely Not Gay, and That Sherlock
    Wouldn't Be Living With a Man If Men Were Interesting." AsexualityEducation.
    Tumblr.com. Oct. 2012. Web. 5 Feb. 2016. http://asexualeducation.tumblr.com/post/
    16193449330/a-lovely-interview-about-sherlock-wherein-steven.
Foucault, Michel. The Order of Things. New York: Vintage Books, 1970. Print.
Freeth, Becky. "Wat-son Your Screen, Dr? Sherlock Viewers Mock Martin Freeman for
    Pretending to Update Static Picture of His Blog in Epic Blunder... As Opener Gets
    Best Audience of New Year's Day." Daily Mail. 2 Jan. 2017. Web. 11 May 2017. http://
    www.dailymail.co.uk/tvshowbiz/article-4082288/Wat-son-screen-Dr-Sherlock-
    viewers-left-scratching-heads-epic-blunder-series-return-draws-best-audience-
    New-Year-s-Day.htmlee.
Frost, Caroline. "'Sherlock' Star Louise Brealey Disagrees with Steven Moffat about the
    Fate of Her Character." The Huffington Post UK. 18 Jan. 2017. Web. 25 June 2017.
    http://www.huffingtonpost.co.uk/entry/sherlock-molly-louise-brealey_uk_
    587f8206e4b005cc588b6080.
_____. "'Sherlock' Writer Mark Gatiss Tells Complaining Fans: 'Go Read a Children's Book.'"
    The Huffington Post UK. 16 Jan. 2017. Web. 8 Apr. 2017. http://www.huffingtonpost.
    co.uk/entry/sherlock-writer-mark-gatiss-defends-complicated-scruot_uk_576
    cba52e4b0f3b82a380ea7.
Gardner, Eriq. "Legal Fight Brewing over CBS' New Sherlock Holmes Adaptation (Analy-
    sis)." Hollywood Reporter. 25 Jan. 2012. Web. 1 Apr. 2017. http://www.hollywood
    reporter.com/thr-esq/legal-fight-brewing-cbs-new-283966.
Gill, James. "Martin Freeman—'I Don't Love #Setlock. It Makes It Hard to Do Your Job.'"
    Radio Times. 18 Jan. 2015. Web. 20 Jan. 2015. http://www.radiotimes.com/news/ 2015–
    01–18/martin-freeman-i-dont-love-setlock—it-makes-it-hard-to-do-your-job.
"The Great Game." Sherlock. Writ. Mark Gatiss. Dir. Paul McGuigan. BBC Entertainment,
    2010, DVD.
The Great WTF. Comment. Asexuality.org. "BBC Article Mentioning Sherlock's Sexual-
    ity." 20 Jan. 2012. Web. 5 Feb. 2016. http://www.asexuality.org/en/topic/69917-bbc-
    sherlock-article-mentioning-sherlocks-sexuality/.

Haraway, Donna. *Modest_Witness@Second_Millennium.FemaleMan Meets_OncoMouse: Feminism and Technoscience*. New York: Routledge, 1997. Print.

Hartswood Films. n.d. Web. 11 May 2017. http://www.hartswoodfilms.co.uk/.

Hegarty, Tasha. "BBC's Sherlock Asks Fans Not to Spoil the Series Finale for Everyone After It Leaks Online: Talk about a 'Final Problem.'" *Digital Spy*. 14 Jan. 2017. Web. 2 Mar. 2017. http://www.digitalspy.com/tv/sherlock/news/a819024/sherlock-season-4-finale-leaks-online/.

Hibberd, James. "*Sherlock* Showrunner Explains that Intense (and Conclusive?) Finale." *Entertainment Weekly*. 16 Jan. 2017. Web. 25 June 2017. http://ew.com/tv/2017/01/16/sherlock-showrunner-season-4-finale/.

Hicklin, Aaron. "The Gospel According to Benedict." *OUT*. 14 Oct. 2014. Web. 24 Apr. 2017. http://www.out.com/entertainment/movies/2014/10/14/sherlock-star-benedict-cumberbatch-poised-make-alan-turing-hiw-own-imitation-game.

Hills, Matthew. Doctor Who: *The Unfolding Event—Marketing, Merchandising and Mediatizing a Brand Anniversary*. London: Palgrave Macmillan, 2015. Print.

_____. *Fan Cultures*. New York: Routledge, 2002. Print.

_____. "Psychoanalysis and Digital Fandom." *Producing Theory in a Digital World*. Ed. Rebecca Ann Lind. New York: Lang, 2012, 105–22. Print.

_____. "Virtually Out There." *Technospaces*. Ed. Sally Munt. London: Bloomsbury, 2001. 147–60. Print.

"His Last Vow." *Sherlock: Season Three*. Writ. Steven Moffat. Dir. Nick Hurran. BBC Entertainment, 2014. DVD.

Holmes, Jonathan. "Steven Moffat on Setlock: 'We're all genuinely very appreciative that people love our show so much.'" *Radio Times*. 29 Jan. 2015. Web. 1 Feb. 2015. http://www.radiotimes.com/news/2015-01-29/steven-moffat-on-setlock-were-all-genuinely-very-appreciative-that-people-love-our-show-so-much.

"The Hounds of Baskerville." *Sherlock: Season Two*. Writ. Mark Gatiss. Dir. Paul McGuigan. BBC Entertainment, 2012. DVD.

Improbable Studios. "Sherlock: The Game Is On." n.d. Web. 25 June 2017. https://sherlock-thegame.tumblr.com/.

incognitocomics. "FURLOCK—The Exclusive Sherlocked Convention Bear—Sherlock/Cumberbatch." n.d. Web. 4 Mar. 2017. http://www.ebay.co.uk/itm/FURLOCK-Exclusive-Sherlocked-Convention-Bear-Sherlock-Cumberbatch-/291973745331?hash=item43fafdcab3.

Ingrid. @spanglerfish. Twitter. 10 Jan. 2017.

Iwantthatcoat. "Slow Chemistry." Archive of Our Own. 7 Mar. 2016. Web. 25 June 2017. http://archiveofourown.org/works/6135046/chapters/14058898.

JangoFett. Comment. Asexuality.org. "BBC Article Mentioning Sherlock's Sexuality." 20 Jan. 2012. Web. 5 Feb. 2016. http://www.asexuality.org/en/topic/69917-bbc-sherlock-article-mentioning-sherlocks-sexuality/.

Jean. @JeanPattersonxo. Twitter. 19 Apr. 2016.

Jeffries, Stuart. "'There's a Clue Everybody's Missed': Sherlock Writer Steven Moffat Interviewed." *The Guardian*. 20 Jan. 2012. Web. 5 Feb. 2016. http://www.theguardian.com/tv-and-radio/2012/jan/20/steven-moffat-sherlock-doctor-who.

Jenkins, Henry. *Convergence Culture: Where Old and New Media Collide*. New York: New York University Press, 2006. Print.

Jones, Paul. "Sherlock Fans Have Changed the Way We Make the Show, Says Mark Gatiss." *Radio Times*. 25 Nov. 2014. Web. 19 Sep. 2015. http://www.radiotimes.com/news/2014–11–25/sherlock-fans-have-changed-the-way-we-make-the-show-says-mark-gatiss.

_____. "Sherlock Fans Say No to #Setlock." *Radio Times*. 22 Jan. 2015. Web. 24 Jan. 2015. http://www.radiotimes.com/news/2015–01–22/sherlock-fans-say-no-to-setlock.

_____. "Should #Setlock Continue?" *Radio Times*. 18 Jan. 2015. Web. 20 Jan. 2015. http://www.radiotimes.com/news/2015–01–18/should-setlock-continue.

Josie. @claraoswald_12. Twitter. 18 Apr. 2016.

Justyna. @Aleksiejuk. Twitter. 1 Sep. 2016.

Kabra, Reetu. @reetukabra. "I'm Still Sweating." Twitter. 11 May 2016. Reprinted in Benedict's Third Testicle. Blog. n.d. Web. 11 May 2016. http://benedicts-third-testicle.tumblr.com/.

KearaCreations. "Sherlock Pill Bottle Necklace or Keychain." Etsy. n.d. Web. 4 Mar. 2017. https://www.etsy.com/listing/160164688/sherlock-pill-bottle-necklace-or?ga_order=most_relevant&ga_search_type=all&ga_view_type=gallery&ga_search_query=Sherlock&ref=sr_gallery_16.

Keene, Allison. "'Sherlock' Recap: 'The Lying Detective': Merrily Manipulating John Watson. *Collider*. 9 Jan. 2017. http://collider.com/sherlock-recap-the-lying-detective/.

Kemp, Stuart. "BBC Promotes 'Sherlock' Return with Hearse." *The Hollywood Reporter*. 29 Nov. 2015. Web. 1 June 2017. http://www.hollywoodreporter.com/news/bbc-promotes-sherlock-return-hearse-660724.

Kephiso. Comment. "It's All Fine." Archive of Our Own. 13 Aug. 2012. Web. 5 Apr. 2016. http://archiveofourown.org/works/160177.

KinkoWhiteArt. "Sherlock and the Bluebell Rabbit Polymer Clay." Etsy. n.d. Web. 2 Feb. 2017. https://www.etsy.com/listing/484427254/sherlock-and-the-bluebell-rabbit-polymer.

lambrinibudget. Comments. Reddit. Jan. 2017. Web. 11 May 2017. https://www.reddit.com/r/Sherlock/comments/5l30gf/john_watson_is_no_longer_updating_his_blog/#bottom-comments.

Lauren. @LaurenFrida. Twitter. 21 Apr. 2016.

Lavigne, Carlen. "The Noble Bachelor and the Crooked Man." *Sherlock Holmes for the 21st Century: Essays on Adaptation*. Ed. Lynnette Porter. Jefferson, NC: McFarland, 2012. Print, 13–23.

Lesley! Twitter. 31 Aug. 2016.

Linden, Henrik, and Sara Linden. *Fans and Fan Cultures: Tourism, Consumerism and Social Media*. London: Palgrave Macmillan, 2017. Print.

Lisa_Marie. Twitter. 16 Aug. 2016.

"LiveJournal, Now Based in Russia, Bans 'Political Solicitation' in New User Agreement." *Heavy*. 6 Apr. 2017. Web. 17 Apr. 2017. https://heavy.com/news/2017/04/livejournal-russia-censorship-bans-political-solicitation-usr-agreement/.

Lobb, Adrian. "Amanda Abbington: 'Sherlock Is Like Beatlemania.'" *The Big Issue*. 24 Dec. 2015. Web. 1 June 2017. http://www.bigissue.com/interviews/amanda-abbington-interview-sherlock-like-beatlemania/.

_____. "Benedict Cumberbatch: Filming in Front of the 'Superfans' Is Quite Special." *The Big Issue*. 6 Jan. 2017. Web. 9 May 2017. http://www.bigissue.com/interviews/benedict-cumberbatch-interview-filming-front-superfans-special-experience/.

Lodderhose, Diana. "'Sherlock' Finale Jumps in UK Live+7." *Deadline Hollywood*. 24 Jan. 2017. Web. 2 Mar. 2017. http://deadline.com/2017/01/sherlock-finale-ratings-low-bafta-nonsense-kate-middleton-the-sun-1201893060/.

Luke. @lukey_b86. Tweet. 10 Jan. 2017.

"The Lying Detective." *Sherlock*. Writ. Steven Moffat. Dir. Nick Hurran. BBC Entertainment, 2017, DVD.

Mad_Lori. "The Blog of Eugenia Watson." Archive of Our Own. 12 June 2011–14 Jan. 2015. Web. http://archiveofourown.org/works/210788/chapters/315474.

Magnanti, Brooke. "Sherlock, Benedict Cumberbatch, and Fanfic: Don't Mess with These Women." *The Telegraph*. 16 Dec. 2013. Web. 6 Mar. 2017. http://www.telegraph.co.uk/women/womens-life/10521131/Sherlock-Benedict-Cumberbatch-and-fanfic-dont-mess-with-these-women-and-men.html.

"Make Hartswood Films, BBC, Gatiss, and Moffat Answer for the Queerbaiting of Sherlock." Change.org. Jan. 2017. Web. 7 June 2017. https://www.change.org/p/make-hartswood-films-bbc-gatiss-and-moffat-answer-for-the-queerbaiting-of-sherlock.

Martin, Tim. "Behind the Scenes on the Set of Sherlock." *The Telegraph.* 31 Dec. 2015. Web. 18 June 2016. http://www.telegraph.co.uk/culture/tvandradio/12057913/ Behind-the-scenes-on-the-set-of-Sherlock.html.

Massabrook, Nicole. "'Sherlock' Season 4 Spoilers: Benedict Cumberbatch's Character Won't Have a Love Interest; Lack of Romance Explained." *International Business News.* 31 Mar. 2015. Web. 25 June 2017. http://www.ibtimes.com/sherlock-season-4-spoilers-benedict-cumberbatchs-character-wont-have-love-interest-1865146.

McGonigal, Jane. *Reality is Broken: Why Games Make Us Better and How They Can Change the World.* New York: Penguin, 2011. Excerpted. Daryl Paranada, *Marketplace.* 20 Jan. 2011. Web. 25 June 2017. https://www.marketplace.org/2011/01/20/ life/big-book/excerpt-reality-broken.

McLaughlin, Rebecca L. "A Study in Sherlock: Revisiting the Relationship Between Sherlock Holmes and Dr. John Watson." Unpublished thesis. Bridgewater University. May 2013. http://vc.bridgew.edu/cgi/viewcontent.cgi?article= 1015&context=honors_proj.

McLuhan, Marshall, with Eric McLuhan and Frank Zingrone. *Essential McLuhan.* New York: Routledge, 1997. Print.

Merely Contemplating. "OK, I received the final copyright violation warning." 17 July 2016. Web. 1 June 2017. http://milarvela.tumblr.com/post/147544310338/ok-i-received-the-final-copyright-violation.

Minkel, Elizabeth. "Why It Doesn't Matter What Benedict Cumberbatch Thinks of *Sherlock* Fan Fiction." *New Statesman.* 17 Oct. 2014. Web. 25 June 2017. http://www. newstatesman.com/culture/2014/10/why-it-doesn-t-matter-what-benedict-cumberbatch-thinks-sherlock-fan-fiction.

Minn, Hayley. "Did You Spot This Sherlock Mistake? Viewers Notice HUGE Blunder as Dr. John Watson 'Writes Blog Post' in BBC Drama." *Mirror.* 2 Jan. 2017. Web. 11 May 2017. http://www.mirror.co.uk/tv/tv-news/you-spot-sherlock-mistake-viewers-9548958.

MirithGriffin. "XO." Archive of Our Own. 2013-present. Web. 28 June 2017. http://archive ofourown.org/works/470545/chapters/813858.

missyankovic. Post. "A Lovely Interview About Sherlock Wherein Steven Moffat Says That Asexuality is 'Boring,' That Sherlock is Definitively Not Gay, and That Sherlock Wouldn't Be Living With a Man If Men Were Interesting." AsexualityEducation. Tumblr.com. Oct. 2012. Web. 5 Feb. 2016. http://asexualeducation.tumblr.com/post/ 16193449330/a-lovely-interview-about-sherlock-wherein-steven.

Molloy, Mark. "Sherlock Series Finale The Final Problem Leaked Online as Creators Send Fans Spoiler Warning." *The Telegraph.* 15 Jan 2017. Web. 2 Mar. 2017. http://www. telegraph.co.uk/tv/2017/01/15/sherlock-series-finale-final-problem-leaked-online-creators/.

Molly Hooper. Blog. 2010. Web. 10 May 2017. http://www.mollyhooper.co.uk.

mresundance. "Unusual Symmetry." Archive of Our Own. 17 Sep. 2010. Web. 4 Mar. 2016. http://archiveofourown.org/works/117682.

Murray, Janet. *Hamlet on the Holodeck.* New York: Simon & Schuster, 1988. Print.

Natalie K. @nmk1260 Twitter. 11 May 2016. Reprinted in Sophie Hunter Gossip Blog. 11 May 2016. http://sophiehuntergossipblog.tumblr.com.

Nogitsune. Comment. Asexuality.org. "BBC Article Mentioning Sherlock's Sexuality." 20 Jan. 2012. Web. 5 Feb. 2016. http://www.asexuality.org/en/topic/69917-bbc-sherlock-article-mentioning-sherlocks-sexuality/.

Pearson, Roberta. "It's Always 1896: Sherlock Holmes in Cyberspace." *The Fan Fiction Studies Reader.* Eds. Kristina Busse and Karen Hellekson. Iowa City: University of Iowa Press, 2014. Print.

pet. @lilAvengerstark. Tweet. 10 Jan. 2017.

Petersen, Line Nybro. "'The Florals': Female Fans over 50 in the Sherlock Fandom." *Transformative Works and Cultures.* Vol. 23. 2017. Web. 24 Apr. 2017. http://journal. transformativeworks.org/index.php/twc,article/view/956/760.

Porter, Lynnette. "Sherlock Special: The Abominable Bride." *PopMatters*. 11 Jan. 2016.
    Web. 30 May 2016. http://www.popmatters.com/review/sherlock-the-abominable-
    bride/.
Postman, Neil. *Amusing Ourselves to Death: Public Discourse in the Age of Show Business*.
    New York: Penguin, 2005. Print.
Prentice. Comment. Archive of Our Own. "Unusual Symmetry." 18 Sep. 2010. Web. 5
    Apr. 2010. http://archiveofourown.org/works/117682.
prettyvk. "The James Holmes Chronicles." Archive of Our Own. 17 Oct. 2013-present.
    http://archiveofourown.org/series/71221.
Pridelolly 2016. "FAQ." 2016. Web. 25 June 2017. http://pridelolly.tumblr.com/post/
    137130903746/faq-updated-91916.
raonddx. Post. "A Lovely Interview About Sherlock Wherein Steven Moffat Says That
    Asexuality is 'Boring,' That Sherlock is Definitively Not Gay, and That Sherlock
    Wouldn't Be Living With a Man If Men Were Interesting." AsexualityEducation.
    Tumblr.com. Oct. 2012. Web. 5 Feb. 2016. http://asexualeducation.tumblr.com/post/
    16193449330/a-lovely-interview-about-sherlock-wherein-steven.
"The Reichenbach Fall." *Sherlock*. Writ. Stephen Thompson. Dir. Toby Haynes. BBC Enter-
    tainment, 2012. DVD.
Rich, Katey. "Benedict Cumberbatch Knows You Think He Looks Like an Otter." *Vanity
    Fair*. 14 Feb. 2014. Web. 1 Apr. 2017. http://www.vanityfair.com/hollywood/2014/
    02/benedict-cumberbatch-bafta.
Romano, Aja. "Why Fans Are Outraged at Sherlock and Watson Reading Sexy Fanfic."
    The Daily Dot. 16 Dec. 2013. Web. 2 Feb. 2016. http://www.dailydot.com/news/
    sherlock-fanfic-caitlin-moran/.
"A Scandal in Belgravia." *Sherlock: Season Two*. Writ. Steven Moffat. Dir. Paul McGuigan.
    BBC Entertainment, 2012. DVD.
Schab, Katharine. "The Rise of *Buffy* Studies." *The Atlantic*. 1 Oct. 2015. Web. 24 Apr.
    2017. https://www.theatlantic.com/entertainment/archive/2015/10/the-rise-of-buffy-
    studies/407020.
Schulman, Michael. "The Mind-Bending Benedict Cumberbatch." *Vanity Fair*. 4 Oct.
    2016. Web. 11 May 2017. http://www.vanityfair.com/hollywood/2016/10/benedict-
    cumberbatch-cover-story.
The Science of Deduction. 2010, 2012. Web. 10 May 2017. http://www.thescienceof
    deduction.co.uk/.
sienceofdeduction. "Ace + Fandom = Awesome." Dreamwidth. 24 Oct. 2010. Web. 6 Feb.
    2016. http://asexual-fandom.dreamwidth.org/11508.html.
Sheridan, Emily. "First Look at Baby Watson: Martin Freeman Takes on the Dr's Biggest
    Role Yet as He Films Sherlock in London's Borough Market." *Daily Mail*. 26 Apr.
    2016. Web. 12 June 2017. http://www.dailymail.co.uk/tvshowbiz/article-3559686/
    Martin-Freeman-takes-Dr-s-biggest-role-films-Sherlock-London-s-Borough-
    Market.html.
Sherlock. "FURLOCK—The Official Sherlocked Convention Exclusive 12" Teddy Bear."
    n.d. Web. 4 Mar. 2017. https://www.amazon.co.uk/FURLOCK-Official-Sherlocked-
    Convention-Exclusive-x/dp/B01MSXQADK.
"Sherlock: The Final Problem." Viewer poll. *Metro*. 16–17 Jan. 2017. Web. 16–17 Jan.
    2017.
"Sherlock Beats the Queen in Festive TV Ratings." BBC. 2 Jan. 2017. Web. 2 Jan. 2017.
    http://www.bbc.com/news/entertainment-arts-38488141.
The Sherlock Holmes Society of London. "Journal—Winter 2016." 2016. Web. 24 Apr.
    2017. http://www.sherlock-holmes.org.uk/journal-winter-2016/.
Sherlock Holmes-Fan.com. n.d. Web. 10 May 2017. http://www.sherlockholmes-fan.com/.
"Sherlock Like Beatlemania." *Belfast Telegraph*. 23 Apr. 2013. Web. 11 June 2017. http://
    www.belfasttelegraph.co.uk/entertainment/news/freeman-sherlock-like-beatlemania-
    29226501.html.

SherlockBBC LiveJournal community moderators. "Migration underway." 13 Apr. 2017. Web. 17 Apr. 2017. https://sherlockbbc.livejournal.com/6863772.html.

Sherlocked the Event. @SherlockedEvent. Twitter. 30 Aug. 2016.

Sherlocked USA. Convention. 25–28 May 2017. Los Angeles Airport Marriott Hotel. Los Angeles, CA.

sherlockhasthetardis. Comment. Asexuality.org. "BBC Article Mentioning Sherlock's Sexuality." 20 Jan. 2012. Web. 5 Feb. 2016. http://www.asexuality.org/en/topic/69917-bbc-sherlock-article-mentioning-sherlocks-sexuality/.

Sherlocked USA. Web. 24 Feb. 2017. http://www.sherlockedusa.com/tickets.

_____. "Meet and Greets." 1 May 2017. Web. 9 May 2017. http://www.sherlockedusa.com/activities/99-meet-greets.

Sherlockology. "The Abominable Bride: A Set Visit Report." 2 Jan. 2016. Web. 1 June 2016. http://www.sherlockology.com/news/2016/1/2/abominable-bride-set-visit-020116.

_____. "Sherlockology on Set: A Day on Location in Cardiff." 10 Jan. 2014. Web. 1 June 2016. http://www.sherlockology.com/news/2014/1/10/sherlockology-on-set-a-day-on-location-100114.

_____. "Sherlock S3E1The Empty Hearse—Advance Spoiler-free Review." 15 Dec. 2013. Web. 1 June 2016. http://www.sherlockology.com/news/2013/12/15/empty-hearse-review-151213.

_____. "Sue Vertue, Hartswood Films." n.d. Web. 15 Apr. 2016. http://www.sherlockology.com/.

_____. "Terms and Conditions." n.d. Web. 22 May 2016. http://www.sherlockology.com/help/terms-conditions.

"The Sign of Three." *Sherlock.* Writ. Stephen Thompson, Steven Moffat, Mark Gatiss. Dir. Colm McCarthy. BBC Entertainment, 2014. DVD.

Sinisterporpoise. Comment. Asexuality.org. "BBC Article Mentioning Sherlock's Sexuality." 20 Jan. 2012. Web. 5 Feb. 2016. http://www.asexuality.org/en/topic/69917-bbc-sherlock-article-mentioning-sherlocks-sexuality/.

Sirens. 2014–2015. Created by Bob Fisher and Denis Leary. Perf. Michael Mosley, Kevin Daniels, Kevin Bigley. USA Network.

"The Six Thatchers." *Sherlock.* Writ. Mark Gatiss. Dir. Rachel Talalay. BBC Entertainment, 2017, DVD.

Smith, Nigel M. "'Sherlock' Star Benedict Cumberbatch on the Sleuth's Sexuality and How His Own Stock Has Increased." *Indie Wire.* 4 May 2012. Web. 10 Oct. 2015. http://www.indiewire.com/article/sherlock-benedict-cumberbatch-talks-the-sleuths-sexuality-and-how-his-own-stock-has-increased.

Sommers, Kat. "Mark Gatiss Says 'Sherlock' Fans Have Missed 'Blindingly Obvious' Clues." BBCAmerica. Anglophrenia. Sep. 2016. Web. 2 Jan. 2017. http://www.bbcamerica.com/anglophenia/2016/09/mark-gatiss-says-sherlock-fans-have-missed-blindingly-obvious-clues.

Sonja. @maggymcbee. Tweet. 10 Jan. 2017.

SophieHunterGossipBlog. Blog. 18 Sep. 2015. Web. 22 May 2016. http://sophiehuntergossipblog.tumblr.com/post/129351075660/tbh-what-happened-to-astral-was-always-coming.

_____. Blog. 30 May 2017. Web. 30 May 2017. http://sophiehuntergossipblog.tumblr.com/post/161262094095/dixit-wanda-at-the-us-sherlocked-con-she-used-it#notes.

_____. "On Doxxing and Trolls." n.d. Web. 22 May 2016. http://sophiehuntergossipblog.tumblr.com/troll.

The Sophie Hunter Hype Report. "New Interview with Amanda." 28 Dec. 2015. Web. 12 June 2017. https://sophiehunterhypereport.wordpress.com/2015/12/28/new-interview-with-amanda-she-comments-about-the-2/.

Steinem, Gloria. Speech. University of Central Florida. Orlando. 19 Oct. 2012.

Stevens, Non. @non_intofilm Twitter. 20 Apr. 2016.

"A Study in Pink." *Sherlock: The Complete First Season*. Writ. Steven Moffat. Dir. Paul McGuigan. BBC Entertainment, 2010. DVD.

Telophase. "Well, they finally did it." Dreamwidth. 4 Apr. 2017. Web. 17 Apr. 2017. https:// telophase.dreamwidth.org/2763732.html.

Thomas, Sian. "#SherlockLive: Integrating TV and Social Media." Bronco. Blog. 12 Jan. 2017. Web. 8 Apr. 2017. https://www.bronco.co.uk.or-ideas/sherlocklive-integrating-tv-and-social-media/.

Three Patch Podcast. "Episode 52: 221B Pride." 1 Aug. 2016. Web. 25 June 2017. http:// three-patch.com/2016/08/01/episode-52/.

———. "Episode 64A: Fans Over 40—The Extended Cut." 7 June 2017. Web. 25 June 2017. http://three-patch.com/2017/06/07/episode-64a/.

———. "Episode 65: Sherlocked USA." 17 June 2017. Web. 25 June 2017. http://three-patch.com/2017/06/17/episode-65/.

———. "The Three Patch Podcast." n.d. Web. 25 June 2017. http://three-patch.com/ podcasts/regular-episodes/.

Transformative Works and Cultures (TWC). "Peer Review Process." n.d. Web. 24 Apr. 2017. https://journal.transformativeworks.org/index.php/twc/about/editorialPolicites# custom-0.

Turkle, Sherry. *Life on the Screen: Identity in the Age of the Internet*. New York: Simon & Schuster, 1995. Print.

Twitter. "The Twitter Rules." Help Center. n.d. Web. 18 Apr. 2017. https://support.twitter. com/articles/18311#.

———. "Twitter Terms of Service." n.d. Web. 18 Apr. 2017. https://twitter.com/tos?lang= en.

Unovis. "Continuing." 10 Apr. 2017. Web. 18 Apr. 2017. https://221b-recs.livejournal.com.

———. "Proposal to move and input?" 8 Apr. 2017. Web. 18 Apr. 2017. https://221b-recs. livejournal.com.

Valens, Ana. "Users Are Fleeing LiveJournal over Russian Owners' Possible Anti-LGBTQ Terms." *Daily Dot*. 6 Apr. 2017. Web. 17 Apr. 2017. https://www.dailydot.com/irl/ livejournal-users-anti-lgbtq/.

Van Djiik, Teun. "Discourse in Society." n.d. Web. 13 Apr. 2017. http://www.discourses. org/.

veronamay. Comment. Archive of Our Own. "Inflammable." 31 Jan. 2012. Web. 5 Apr. 2016. http://archiveofourown.org/works/330030.

Vertue, Sue. @suevertue. Tweet. 9 Sep. 2012.

Warrigan. "No Love Interest for Sherlock in Season 4." AVEN. Post. 31 Mar. 2015. http:// www.asexuality.org/en/topic/116326-no-love-interest-in-sherlock-season-4/.

The Whedon Studies Association. *Slayage: The Journal of Whedon Studies*. n.d. Web. 24 Apr. 2017. http://www.whedonstudies.tv/slayage-the-journal-of-whedon-studies. html.

wordstrings. "An Open Letter About Fic Writers to Fic Readers." Archive of Our Own. 25 Aug. 2014. Web. 4 Jan. 2017. http://archiveofourown.org/works/2195070.

Index

McFarland

Title: *Sherlock* and Digital Fandom
Loc:
Author: Wojton

Publication date: March 2018

Page Count:	200pp.
Binding:	softcover
Price:	$39.95
pISBN:	978-1-4766-7020-1
eISBN:	978-1-4766-3286-5
LC:	

Publisher: McFarland • www.mcfarlandpub.com • 800-253-2187

This book is sent to you for review. We ask that our website (www.mcfarlandpub.com) and our order line (800-253-2187) accompany the review and that the publisher be listed as "McFarland" (one word). Send one copy of the review to marketing manager Beth Cox at beox@mcfarlandpub.com. We prefer reviews as PDF files (or links to online reviews), but alternately, publications and tearsheets can be mailed to Beth Cox, McFarland, Box 611, Jefferson NC 28640.

Note about ebook availability: McFarland titles are available from all major ebook providers, including consumer/retail suppliers (e.g., Google Play, Amazon Kindle) and library suppliers (e.g., Overdrive, ebrary). For a complete list of ebook providers, see www.mcfarlandpub.com/customers/ebooks.